Myths about Suicide

MYTHS ABOUT SUICIDE

Thomas Joiner

HARVARD UNIVERSITY PRESS
Cambridge, Massachusetts / London, England

First Harvard University Press paperback edition, 2011

Library of Congress Cataloging-in-Publication Data

Joiner, Thomas E.
  Myths about suicide / Thomas Joiner.
     p. cm.
  Includes bibliographical references and index.
  ISBN 978-0-674-04822-5 (cloth : alk. paper)
  ISBN 978-0-674-06198-9 (pbk.)
  1. Suicide.   2. Suicide victims—Psychology.   I. Title.
  HV6545.J648 2010
  362.28—dc22   2009039732

TO

the memory of my dad and maternal granddad,
to my friends,
to the memory of John Kalafat, and,
with every fiber and without stint,
to my family, as ever

Contents

Myths about Suicide

Introduction

Our Most Basic Terror and
Our Most Tragic Thoughts

A cross human history and across cultures, what has been the most stigmatized of human behaviors? What behavior is condemned by Islam and Christianity, for example? It is not the keeping of human slaves, which occurred through the last thirty centuries at least, usually with approval of many segments of society. Slavery was hardly viewed with condemnation by the Bible, for instance (if you doubt this, check Leviticus 25:44–46, or if you prefer the New Testament, Ephesians 6:5). And it is not murder, as this has been defended on a mass scale as necessary and good by many political regimes, often with the support of their respective populations and with easy comfort available from religious texts.

For example, it is recommended in Deuteronomy that heresy should be met with immediate murder, including, explicitly, when the heretic is one's own daughter or son.

If not human slavery or murder, even of one's own child, what then? A plausible answer to this question is suicide. The topic has created revulsion and disgust across cultures and time. The Koran (4:29) dictates, "Do not destroy yourselves," and suicide is *haram*—very strictly forbidden—in the hadith (collected sayings by and anecdotes about the prophet Mohammed). Since the fourth century, Christian scholars have been unanimous in their condemnation of suicide, which was termed "the sin against the Holy Ghost" (why specifically against that aspect of the Trinity is confusing). Indeed, according to George Minois's *History of Suicide,* some theologians from the fourth century onward have argued that Judas Iscariot was more damned for his suicide than for his betrayal of Jesus (p. 235)—a betrayal, incidentally, that Jesus himself arranged, at least according to one interpretation of the recently discovered gospel of Judas.

No doubt influenced by these early Christian attitudes, Dante wrote in the *Inferno* that the seventh circle of hell contained those who died by suicide. "If e'er the frenzied soul the body quit, from which by its own will it separates, the Minos sends it to the seventh pit" (Canto VIII). Even below the burning heretics and the murderers stewing in a river of hot blood (excepting, one supposes, the murderers of heretics), the souls of those who die by suicide grow in the shape of warped, poisonous thorns. On Judgment Day, those not condemned to hell will have their bodies and souls reunited in paradise, but the bodies of those who die by suicide will hang from the thorns for eternity.

But surely attitudes have progressed since Dante's time. Perhaps so in some quarters, but people still say and think shocking things about suicide decedents. Those who have recently lost a loved one to suicide are stunned by many things following their loss, including the profound change in their address books—once trusted friends fall away after ignoring a loved one's suicide or after saying hurtful and appallingly glib things like "It was God's will." Of the many survivor anecdotes that have touched and moved me over the years, a memorable one came from a powerful Southern man who had been "comforted" by hearing that his son's death by suicide was God's will. In reaction, he thundered in his drawl: "It was NOT God's will that my precious son shot himself in the head." Good for him that he said that; I wish I had said more such things (though I said some, no doubt) in reaction to the inanities I heard after my dad's death by suicide. In Shakespeare's *Hamlet,* Ophelia has died, and a priest would deny her full funeral rites because she died by suicide. Her brother responds, "I tell thee, churlish priest, a minist'ring angel shall my sister be, when thou liest howling." Most people bereaved by suicide can identify with this sentiment.

A May 2007 case in Oklahoma involved the family of a young woman who had died from a gunshot wound to the head. It was not clear if the wound was self-inflicted or not, but the family felt determined to show that it was not, and to have an insurance company pay death benefits. A judge decided that the insurance company's lawyer did not adequately demonstrate the manner of death as suicide, and ordered them to pay the family (which they would have had to do anyway, as long as the death by suicide occurred more than two years after the policy was initiated. That is the standard policy, at any rate). The family's lawyer was quoted as saying, "It wasn't about the money . . . This is about clearing a daughter's name of the stigma of having committed suicide."

Really? It's more about clearing a stigma than about finding the woman's actual killer?

Psychiatrists and psychologists—highly trained, doctoral-level mental health professionals—sometimes whisper about or panic about or skirt around the issue of suicide, an aversion that has always puzzled me, and one that strikes me as similar to a surgeon being afraid of blood. I know about this too: I'm a clinical psychologist who specializes in the understanding and treatment of suicidal behavior. Why this profound stigma? For any stigma, the usual ingredients are fear and ignorance. If suicide is special in the degree to which it is stigmatized—and I and others believe it may be—then it is simply because the fear and ignorance are so great. Stigma about suicide should be reduced, of course, and it is a point of this book to do so, but I think it should be reduced via a decrease in ignorance, not in fear. I would prefer to leave the fear of death by suicide more or less intact. Fear can be quite healthy, and its absence can be deranged. Some of the most consistently fearless people are the most dangerous and disturbed.

Fear of injury and death, and of self-injury and self-inflicted death in particular, is natural and normal. Fear is self-preservation's substrate. In his biography of Jack London, Alex Kershaw described the author thus: "he was aware that mankind's terror has always been its most basic emotion . . . it has far deeper roots than love, tracing back to the days before history, when man was just another wild, frightened savage" (p. 125).

The self-preservation instinct is hard-wired and strong, and, as Voltaire understood centuries ago, relevant when it comes to understanding suicidal behavior. Voltaire wrote of the death by suicide of the Roman orator Cato, "It seems rather absurd to say that Cato slew himself through weakness. None but a strong man can surmount the most powerful instinct of nature." Centuries earlier still, the Jewish historian Flavius Josephus understood this as well; he wrote that suicide "is contrary to the instincts shared by all living things." This view is found as well in Camus' *The Myth of Sisyphus*, in which he states, "The body's judgment is as good as the mind's, and the body shrinks from annihilation." The simple but compelling idea that occurred to Voltaire, Josephus, and Camus is that one must first grapple with one of nature's strongest forces—self-preservation—before one dies by suicide.

Based in part on this insight, I developed a new theory of suicidal behavior (in the 2005 book *Why People Die by Suicide*). In my view people die by suicide because they have both the ability and the desire to do so. This may seem glib or superficial, and if things were left here, it would be. What is the ability to die by suicide and in whom and how does it develop? What is the desire for suicide, what are its component parts, and in whom and how do they develop?

Self-preservation is a powerful enough instinct that few can overcome it by force of will. The few who can have developed a fearlessness of pain and death, which they acquire through a process called "habituation." Formally, habituation is defined as "a response decrement due to repeated stimulation." Less formally, it can be defined as "getting used to something." In his *Memoirs from the House of the Dead,* Dostoevsky wrote, "Man is a creature who can get used to anything, and I believe that is the best way of defining him."

Getting used to pain, injury, and death—becoming fearless about it—is, according to my theory, a prerequisite for serious suicidal behavior. People get used to such things by having repeatedly experienced them, often through previous self-injury, but other painful experiences serve too. A corollary to this view is that the self-preservation drive—the fear of pain, injury, and death—protects people from death by suicide (which is why this fear should remain more or less intact). This corollary is supported time and again by cases of people who report that they genuinely desired to die by suicide, but that their bodies would not allow it (e.g., people have cut at their veins for hours, only to eventually surrender to their bodies' ability to clot the wounds).

Who desires suicide? I believe that when people hold two specific psychological states in their minds, simultaneously and long enough, they develop the desire for death. These two states are the perception that one is a burden and the sense that one does not belong, which in this book and elsewhere I call *perceived burdensomeness* and a *sense of low belongingness.* Perceived burdensomeness is the view that one's existence burdens family, friends, and society. This view produces the idea, "my death will be worth more than my life to family, friends, or society." This same mental calculation motivates those who die in their homes by self-inflicted gunshot wounds as well as those who leave their homes to blow up themselves and others as an act of religious martyrdom. It also motivates insects that self-sacrifice under certain conditions (e.g., when they are infected with a parasite that will destroy an entire colony)—conditions under which their death will be worth more than their life to their genes (which reside in other insects spared the infection). It further characterizes a scenario that NASA has been contemplating regarding a flight to Mars. When should care be withheld from a critically ill astronaut who is using up precious resources like oxygen and water and thereby endangering the rest of the crew on the very long trip between Earth and Mars? In May 2007, the *New York Times* quoted a bioethicist on this question, who said, "There may come a time in which a significant risk of death has to be weighed against mission success. The idea that we will always choose a person's well-being over mission success, it sounds good, but it doesn't really turn out to be necessarily the way decisions always will be made." That is, an astronaut's death may be worth more than his or her life to the mission. That the same calculation appears to apply to insects as to astronauts on their way to Mars—what pre-eminent psychologist Paul Meehl would have termed "a damn strange coincidence"—lends some credence to this perspective, I think.

This point of view can be misconstrued, however, and it is very important to me that it not be. Emphasis should be placed on the term *perceived* in "perceived burdensomeness." The message is that this is what suicidal people perceive, not what suicidal people actually are. The perception of burdensomeness, though mistaken, can prove lethal. The distinction between actual and perceived burdensomeness does require emphasis. To see this, consider that in December 2004, a member of the British parliament in the House of Lords advocated that elderly people not only have the right but the obligation to kill themselves rather than become "a nuisance."

In addition to perceived burdensomeness, the other important psychological state in my model of suicidal behavior is the perception that one does not belong—the feeling that one is alienated from others and not an integral part of a family, circle of friends, or other valued group. Two striking examples of the connection between belonging and suicidal behavior have resulted from studies of two very different populations. A study in Norway involved approximately a million women who were followed for fifteen years. Over 1,000 of the women died by suicide during those years. A key finding of the study was that women with children had lower suicide rates than those with no children. The more children, the more dramatic the effect: Women with six or more children had one-fifth the risk of suicide as compared to other women (Hoyer & Lund, 1993).

Let us pause to ponder this last sentence. Women whose stress levels must be extreme—they had at least six children! —had one-fifth the risk. Not one-half or one-third, but one-fifth. How can women with high stress levels nevertheless have had markedly reduced suicide rates? My answer is that they were protected by the sense of belonging inherent in having a lot of children.

A similar logic applies to identical twins, who have, on average, slightly higher rates of mental disorders than the rest of the population. Mental disorders constitute a clear risk factor for suicidal behavior. (The reason why twins have slightly higher rates of mental disorders is not entirely clear, but it may have something to do with the neurobiological consequences of sharing a womb.) Yet twins have lower rates of suicide than others. Why would a group with a clear risk factor for suicide nevertheless experience low suicide rates? A sense of belonging, inherent in twinship, offers a protective benefit.

My theory asserts that when over a sustained period people believe that they do not belong and that they burden others, they lose their desire for life. Put somewhat differently, the theory argues that contributing and connecting are necessary for the will to live, and that their joint thwarting is sufficient to produce the desire to die. This view is consistent with an array of conceptual frameworks, including Sigmund Freud's, which, among other things, emphasized instinctual aspects of drives toward love and work. This view is also consistent with approaches ranging from Henry Murray's work in the 1930s on various psychological needs to twenty-first-century social psychology's work on loneliness, as, for example, summarized in *Loneliness,* John Cacioppo's 2008 book.

There exists a staggeringly diverse collection of facts about suicide, as well as the perversions of truth that have sprung up around this collection. Using my theory as a guide and unifying thread, I hope to expose myths, shatter misunderstandings, and encourage real understanding of suicide, though leaving a healthy fear of it intact. Of course, my theory is not the only theory of suicidal behavior, but I have chosen it as a guiding framework for this book because its combination of specificity and comprehensiveness allows it to shed light on a wide array of suicide-related phenomena, and because it is empirically supported (Van Orden et al., 2008) and conceptually compatible with other leading frameworks (e.g., Shneidman, 1996).

Three chapters follow: one on the suicidal mind, one on suicidal behavior, and one on causes, consequences, and subpopulations. In each of these chapters, eight or nine myths or misunderstood topics are described and then debunked, dispelled, or simply explained, as the case may require. The ones that I view as myths are printed within quotation marks (e.g., "Suicide's an easy escape, one that cowards use"); misunderstood topics are stated without quotation marks and more dispassionately (e.g., suicide and genetics).

These myths and misunderstandings will serve as ways to teach and explore a diverse collection of facts about suicide, facts that I think deepen understanding of suicide, death, and the will to live—and thus of human nature itself. Taking on myths and misunderstandings has some potential to backfire, it should be acknowledged, by inadvertently reifying the very notions one wants to dispel. But "truth will out," and I trust that this process will allow us to compassionately understand suicide for what it is: A profound and fearsome human tragedy. It is a tragedy because it has tractable causes that can be understood and thus counteracted (but currently are not, at least not enough); it is fearsome because it requires a forsaking of our basic nature as self-preserving creatures, because it kills a million people a year worldwide, and because no one should have to die alone in a mess in a hotel bathroom, in the back of a van, or on a park bench, thinking incorrectly that the world will be better off. Like any dangerous and lethal thing that causes human suffering, suicide needs to be understood so as to manage and allay its fearsomeness—survivors deserve this understanding (not to mention compassion). So do those who have died by suicide; we honor them by understanding and combating their cause of death. Dispelling myths and misunderstandings about suicide seems to me a good place to start.

1 / The Suicidal Mind

Wdhat was going through her mind? This is a question that plagues survivors, whether they are family, friends, or health professionals. Although we cannot reconstruct the exact thoughts and feelings of a person who has died by suicide, many have tried to do so, and in the process, many misperceptions have become commonplace. In this chapter I will go to some lengths to show what the suicidal mind is *not;* it is not, for example, primarily characterized by cowardice or anger. Second, although I agree with past theorists that profound misery is of course involved in serious suicidal behavior, I want to be more specific about the sources and nature of that misery. As some of the myths and misunderstandings I turn to next will show, suicidal people's pain is caused by feeling alienated and cut off from others, and believing that their deaths—as we will see shortly, sometimes horrible deaths—will benefit others. A deeper and truer understanding of the suicidal mind, I hope, will not only refine intellectual views about suicidality, but also inspire sympathy and compassion for those experiencing real agony.

"Suicide's an Easy Escape, One that Cowards Use"

If it's so easy, why then is it so difficult to do? Why are so few attempts actually fatal (the accepted ratio being one death for every twenty attempts)?

In March 2007, newswires carried the story that, years before, actress Halle Berry attempted suicide over a failed relationship by carbon monoxide poisoning in her car. She could not carry through with the attempt, and later commented, "I promised myself I would never be a coward again." An irony of Berry's comments is that she resolved never to be a coward again, meaning she would never attempt suicide again, overlooking the fact that she cowered from the act of attempting suicide itself.

Many do . . . and it only stands to reason in light of nature's self-preservation imperative. Consider, for example, comments taken from a clinical case report of a woman who attempted suicide by cutting her arms. She stated, "I know now that slitting my wrists was not as poetic nor as easy as I imagined. Due to blood clotting and fainting, it is actually difficult to die from such wounds. The evening dragged on with me busy reopening the stubborn veins that insisted upon clotting up. I was patient and persistent, and cut away at myself for over an hour. The battle with my body to die was unexpected, and after waging a good fight, I passed out." Or consider the death of Meriwether Lewis, half of the famous pair of explorers, Lewis and Clark. In his biography of Lewis, *Undaunted Courage* (note the title), Stephen Ambrose documents that during the night before his death by suicide, Lewis was up pacing—people could hear him as he walked back and forth on the wooden floorboards. This, incidentally, is an important detail. Agitation (a behavioral indicator of which is pacing) is an acute risk factor for suicidal behavior, a fact to which I will return in several places throughout the book. After pacing all night, Lewis shot himself twice, with neither wound proving lethal at the time. Servants and others rushed in and found him "busily cutting himself from head to foot" with a razor. Lewis looked up and said, "I am no coward, but I am strong, it is so hard to die." Lewis, an American hero, died from his injuries a few hours later.

These anecdotes, as different as they are, seem to me to contradict the idea that suicide is an easy escape, the recourse and province of cowards. People as different as Voltaire ("none but a strong man can overcome the most basic instinct of nature") and the musician Marilyn Manson seemed to understand this contradiction. The latter, in explaining his own suicidal crisis, was quoted in May 2007 as saying, "I was clearly at the point where I was ready to give up, and it wasn't that I didn't have the motivation to [die by suicide], it was almost as if I couldn't bring myself to make a conclusion . . . Did I want to kill myself? Yes. Did I come close to doing that? More than I'd like to think. The only thing I can say about it is, I feel like maybe I wasn't strong enough to make that choice."

Robert Louis Stevenson realized this fact, too, and used it in his fiction. In his novella *The Suicide Club*, the premise is that there is a secret yet popular London club, the function of which is essentially assisted suicide. The club arranges for the death of its members, making their deaths seem accidental—members, incidentally, who are stalwarts of the community, not cowards. The luck of the draw determines who will die each night. The popularity of the club, according to the story, is that it provides a service that members cannot perform for themselves, because suicide is too fearsome a prospect.

Of course Stevenson was writing fiction, but his premise that suicide is very difficult to do is borne out by numerous nonfiction examples. In the May 2007 issue of *Atlantic Monthly*, an article on homosexuality in Saudi Arabia describes the ordeal of a young man who came out to his Saudi parents after spending time in the United States. The article says the man's father "threatened to kill himself, then decided that he couldn't (because suicide is *haram* [forbidden]), then contemplated killing [his son] instead." In this anecdote, killing another, indeed one's son, is viewed as easier—or at least less forbidden—than killing oneself.

Florida felon John Blackwelder also viewed killing someone else as easier than killing himself. He was serving a life sentence without the possibility of parole for a series of convictions for sex crimes. Blackwelder killed his cellmate, Raymond Wigley, pleaded guilty to first-degree murder, and waived all appeals because, according to the admittedly suspect source of Blackwelder himself, he wanted to die by suicide but could not bring himself to do so. That is, killing someone else (and committing a series of sex crimes) was not beyond him, but suicide was. On May 26, 2004, Blackwelder was executed by the state of Florida for the murder of Raymond Wigley.

The life of Aileen Wuornos, a Daytona Beach prostitute who became a serial killer, illustrates a similar process. As depicted in the film *Monster,* based on her life, Wuornos, like Blackwelder, proved capable of killing others but claimed she could not kill herself, though she wanted to. She is quoted in the movie as saying, "People always look down their noses at hookers. Never give you a chance, because they think you took the easy way out, when no one could imagine the willpower it took to do what we do." According to Wuornos (again, a suspect source), her willpower was so strong as to be unimaginable to most—strong enough to bear the violence and humiliation of prostitution, and strong enough to kill others—but not strong enough to kill herself.

There is at least one kernel of truth in the remarks of Wuornos and Blackwelder, and it is that killing is hard to do. This appears to be particularly true when it comes to killing a member of one's own species, a fact than can be observed across the animal kingdom. As Dave Grossman points out in his book *On Killing,* within-species fights are often charmingly nonlethal. For instance, rattlesnakes do not use their venom on each other; they wrestle instead. Piranhas do not viciously bite each other, but they have a kind of swordfight with their tails. When humans fight, even with guns, a related phenomenon can occur; soldiers in battle often miss each other at rates that far exceed chance. It's not that their aim is bad or that their weapons malfunction; they intentionally avoid inflicting injury or death on others. For example, Grossman quotes an eyewitness at the U.S. Civil War battle of Vicksburg in 1863, who said, "It seems strange that a company of men can fire volley after volley at a like number of men at not over a distance of fifteen steps and not cause a single casualty. Yet such was the facts in this case."

Jon Krakauer's 2003 nonfiction book *Under the Banner of Heaven* describes two brothers initially intent on killing their sister-in-law. One's aversion to killing kicks in, but the other's does not. As Krakauer chronicles, the two men believed they had received a direct revelation from God to perpetrate the killing. During the brutal assault, one man asked the other to get something to tie around the woman's neck. He did so, and then, in the words of the killer, "another fascinating thing took place: as he attempted to put the cord around her neck, some unseen force pushed him away from her. He turned and looked at me and says, 'Did you see that?!' I said, 'Yes, I did. Apparently this is not for you to do. Give me the cord.' I wrapped it around her neck twice and tied it very tightly" (pp. 188–189). He then killed his sister-in-law and her baby.

The implication within this appalling tale is that the "unseen force" is God. This strikes me as implausible, to put it mildly. The force was the same one that rattlesnakes, piranhas, and soldiers feel: the ancient and ingrained reluctance to kill one's own. Both brothers intended murder. That one brother was reluctant—the one in fact who received the original "revelation"—and that the other brother proceeded to commit the murders anyway shows both that the prohibition to kill is strong but that it can be overcome.

Even punishing one's own is hard to do. Bronson Alcott, a nineteenth-century writer and educator associated with Emerson and Thoreau, made his students punish him as a punishment to them. It seemed to work—his students were averse to punishing him. If punishing one's own is hard, it stands to reason that killing one's own is more so. A principle of nature is that killing is hard to do, a dictate that is specific to one's own species. The natural prohibition against killing one's own kind surely extends to killing one's own self.

Terrorist leaders know that killing is hard to do, which is why they assign the most technically difficult—and the most lethal—suicide attacks to the hardiest of their recruits. A 2007 study by the National Bureau of Economic Research showed that the most complex operations killing the most people were carried out by individuals who were on average five years older than other bombers and had or were pursuing advanced degrees.

The phenomenon of "hesitation wounds" in those who die by self-inflicted knife wound (often to a central organ like the heart) also illustrates the fearsome quality of killing, in this case taking one's own life. This fear evidently affects even those who go on to overcome it. Hesitation wounds are essentially minor, nonlethal "practice" cuts that people make in the area of their body that they intend to cut lethally. As medical examiners will attest, those who die by suicide by puncturing their hearts will often have minor knife cuts on their chests—

hesitation wounds—whereas those who are murdered with a knife do not (but often do have defensive wounds on their hands and arms from trying to ward off the attack). This fact is considered in differentiating cause of death in cases where suicide and homicide are both possibilities. The very name "hesitation wounds" contradicts the idea that suicide is easy in any respect.

The myth that "suicide is easy" was implicated in a case in the news in June 2008. A hedge-fund scam artist, convicted of defrauding investors of $400 million and sentenced to twenty years, disappeared on the day he was supposed to report to prison. His car was found on a bridge, and the phrase "suicide is painless" (the name of the theme song from M*A*S*H) was written in the dust on the hood of his car. When this was reported, I had grave doubts about whether this man actually died by jumping from the bridge (or by any other method)—in addition to the fact that he is a convicted fraud, someone intent on suicide knows, through his or her planning and reflection, that suicide is fearsome and daunting. This is why so many shy away from it, and why it is very unlikely that someone resolved to die by suicide would write a phrase like "suicide is painless." A fraud might, though. Subsequent reports indicated a very high likelihood that the man faked his death, and in fact the man turned himself in to authorities in early July 2008 (claiming, not particularly convincingly, that he really had attempted to die by suicide, but by overdose).

There are, it should be noted, individuals who have no hesitation at all when it comes to causing their own deaths. An individual like this will have previously become inured to the fear and pain involved in self-injury and death through an array of painful, fear-inducing experiences. In his 1996 book *Into the Wild*, Jon Krakauer described several examples of people who have faced the harshness of the Alaskan wilderness. One was a man named Gene Rosellini, who lived in the forest using only technology he could make with his hands— no electricity, no central heat, not even an ax or a hatchet. If he needed to cut a log in two, he would do so with a sharp rock, even if it took him days. He lived there for years, even through the severe winters, surviving on berries, roots, and whatever game he could catch or spear. In addition to all of this, he exercised voraciously, at one point running an average of eighteen miles per day, occasionally with a bag of rocks on his back. He eventually decided on a new life goal, specifically walking around the world, but that goal was prevented by his death by suicide at age 49 by self-inflicted knife wound.

Rosellini was a hardened man, hardly the type who conforms to the "suicide is for cowards" myth. His choice of self-inflicted knife wound is, I think, important in this regard. This method of suicide is fairly rare, and it is not because sharp objects are rare; rather, it is because it is more fearsome. Those who have died by suicide need to have become fearless about injury and death, else they, like the vast majority, would have backed away from it. Those like Rosellini who engage in particularly fearsome (and thus rare) methods, I would suggest, are especially fearless characters.

Rosellini could be viewed as (among other things) a kind of virtuoso of endurance, given what he put himself through. Among actual sports, the one that many see as the most grueling of all is long-distance cycling, such as is seen in the Tour de France. Not only do riders routinely experience crashes, but training for such races can be especially painful. Interestingly enough, as can be gleaned from Daniel Coyle's 2005 book *Lance Armstrong's War*, which also discusses cycling in general, there appears to be an association between having won the Tour de France and death by suicide. At a minimum, three of the less than sixty winners have died by suicide, and a fourth winner's death, ruled accidental, had many signatures of being a suicide instead. Three or four of approximately sixty may not sound like a high rate, but it is far higher than the population rate in the United States, for example, where ten out of every 100,000 people die by suicide. That makes the Tour de France rate several hundred times higher. The high rate of suicide among a group of people that few would call cowards and that most would view as among the toughest in sports casts considerable doubt on the notion that "suicide is for cowards."

Are Holocaust victims and survivors cowards? Evidence suggests that the suicide rate in the camps themselves was astronomical, described as "the highest in human history" by one article (Barak, 2007). Rates of suicide attempts and deaths are elevated among survivors as well. This connection between Holocaust experience and suicidal behavior does not support the "cowardice" view, but it is quite consistent with the view that past experience with injury, pain, and the like creates a familiarity and fearlessness, which, if combined with desire for death, can prove fatal.

The life and death of the poet Hart Crane offers another

clear example of an individual who, through years of experience, developed a kind of fearlessness about injury, pain, and death. From approximately age 16 until his death at age 32, Crane attempted suicide at least six times. He also led a life full of physical pain and provocation (e.g., drunken, violent outbursts for which he spent time in jail in three separate countries; frequent anonymous gay sex, which given his temperament and his drinking, likely turned violent from time to time). At least two of Crane's suicide attempts involved him being physically restrained moments before jumping off a tall structure; Crane thus had had the opportunity to get used to the idea of jumping to his death. He died at age 32 by jumping off a cruise ship into the Atlantic Ocean. Through years of frequent provocative and painful experiences, specifically including trying to jump from high places in Crane's case, people like him have little hesitation in dying by suicide. In fact, witnesses described Crane as "vaulting" over the rail of the ship with no hesitation whatsoever. A documentary film about the Golden Gate Bridge, described below, shows people jumping to their deaths—some with visible and protracted hesitation, others with none at all.

My view is that those with no hesitation are the most fearless of all, people who have become fearless through either lengthy experience or mental preparation regarding their eventual means of death. Those who hesitate but who nevertheless proceed are somewhat less fearless, but only as compared to the "no hesitation" group, not as compared to everyone else. After all, they too have overcome the potent force of self-preservation. Another, more fearful group includes people whose hesitation is enough to save them.

Tina Zahn, who wrote the book *Why I Jumped,* is in this latter group. She intended to jump to her death, but was saved, and the evidence indicates that part of what saved her was her fear. Zahn was in the midst of a recurrent, very severe (at times near-catatonic) postpartum depression, during which relatives were caring for her. She bolted away from the relatives and fled in her car; the relatives called the police. The police located her car as she raced toward a bridge. They followed her and clocked her at 120 mph. To this point, she displayed considerable resolve in her desire to die—she broke away from relatives and tried to speed away from authorities.

Two accounts of what happened when she arrived at the bridge are available—one is from Zahn's book, the other is from the police video. The two sources agree on some major details: Zahn stopped the car at the bridge's high point, exited the car to the railing, and jumped, but was caught at the last instant and dragged back by a very brave police officer. The video reveals some other details that are not emphasized in Zahn's book; indeed, it is possible that she is not fully aware of them. As she exited the car—after having arrived at very high speeds—she walked toward the railing, and walked rather slowly at that—no sprinting and vaulting like Hart Crane. Had she sprinted and vaulted, she would have died, as the officer would not have had time to catch her. In fact, despite her walking somewhat slowly, he still would not have had time to catch her, had she not hesitated at the railing for two or three seconds.

What is going on here? Was Zahn threatening suicide without the intention to die? Is her account in the book of a genuine desire to die a lie? I don't think so. All the evidence suggests that she was desperately depressed and suicidal, with the serious intention to die by suicide. But even all of this is not sufficient for death; what is also needed is an ability to look death in the eye and not shudder. Zahn shuddered as she approached the bridge's railing. She may not have been aware of her hesitation because the body can automatically take over in such circumstances—and this gave the officer time to save her. If suicide were easy, Zahn would be dead now.

Eric Steel's documentary film *The Bridge* depicts an incident with some similar qualities. Steel and his crew filmed the Golden Gate Bridge every day for a year, using zoom lenses hundreds of yards from the bridge. In doing this, they captured on film several people jumping to their deaths; they also saved many people, as they immediately phoned the California Highway Patrol about anyone who concerned them. One such person was a young woman whom a photographer noticed as she was preparing to jump. The photographer reached over the railing, and, initially with one hand, lifted the woman back over the railing to safety. The photographer did a brave thing, but he did not have superhuman strength; the woman's fear kicked in, and through her gestures of protest it can be seen that she is helping the photographer in her own rescue.

Most everyone shudders when they try to stare down

death. But there are groups who are practiced at vanquishing life instincts. A 2007 report in the *British Medical Journal* studied sword swallowers, performers who can, among other feats, do something called "the drop." This involves placing a sword in one's mouth, and letting the sword plummet into one's stomach. The report documents that these performers are remarkably healthy, but their behavior shows that people can, through practice, do unnatural things—things that nature surely did not intend.

My students and I have studied another such group, one with serious health problems—women who suffer from anorexia nervosa (an eating disorder characterized by self-starvation). Mortality is extremely high in anorexic women; they are over fifty times more vulnerable to early death than similar women who do not have the disease. Why are they at such high risk for early death? It is an underappreciated fact that, should an anorexic patient die prematurely, the cause of death is more likely to be suicide than complications arising from compromised nutritional status.

There are at least two possible accounts of the high association between anorexia and suicide. In one view—what we have termed the "fragility hypothesis"—anorexic women die by suicide at high rates because they are unable to survive attempts of relatively low lethality due to the physical fragility caused by self-starvation. Anorexic women also may be "socially fragile"—social isolation is common among anorexic people—and social isolation can make it less likely that one will be rescued following a suicide attempt.

In another view, informed by my theory of suicidal behavior, anorexic women die by suicide at high rates because their histories of self-starvation habituate them to pain and inure them to fear of death, and they therefore make highly lethal attempts, intending to die. That is, staring down a major life instinct—hunger—has prepared them to stare down life in general.

We pitted these two accounts against each other in a study of 239 women with anorexia, followed over approximately fifteen years. During the follow-up period, the leading cause of death was suicide, consistent with the previously documented fact that early mortality in anorexia is largely due to suicide. Nine of the 239 women in the sample died by suicide. That may not sound like a large proportion, but it is staggeringly high—in a sample of 239 nonanorexic women followed for fifteen years, the expected number of suicides would be zero.

In exploring the methods by which these women died, it was clear that they tended toward extreme violence. To get a sense of this, consider the least violent of the methods used by the nine women who died by suicide: ingestion of 12 oz. of toilet bowl cleaner, along with an unknown amount of a powerful sedative and alcohol (blood alcohol content = 0.16%). The woman bled to death because the hydrochloric acid in the toilet bowl cleaner hemorrhaged her stomach. This disturbing case corroborated the view that anorexic women die not from fragility, but from a kind of unnatural steeliness, a quality derived, at least in part, from their past attempts to grapple with the self-preservation drive in the form of hunger. Had someone desired an "easy way out," drinking hydrochloric acid seems an unlikely choice.

The view that suicide is very difficult to carry out is borne out not only by the fact that the vast majority of people shy away from it—and this includes actively suicidal people—and not only by cases of those like Hart Crane and some anorexic women who have steeled themselves against death, but also by stories of the extreme lengths that people sometimes go to bring about their own death. In September 2007 in Michigan, to take another example, a man bought the parts for a self-constructed guillotine, built it in the woods, and used it to die by suicide. A police officer who investigated the scene said, "I can't even tell you how long it must have taken him to construct. This man obviously was very determined to end his life."

In March 2007 in Atlanta, two men decided to die together by cutting off their arms with a circular saw. One man cut off both the other's arms, and then one of his own. What makes this gruesome story all the more incredible—and consistent with the extreme difficulty of death by suicide—is that both men survived because their landlord found their suicide note and called police, who arrived in time to save them. A May 2007 incident affirms that not everyone survives such ordeals—a man and his mother were found dead in Los Angeles, both with extreme injuries to their neck from a circular saw, which the man had used to fatally injure both of them.

Numerous examples exist of people who try to die by one method, survive, and then immediately die by another method. It is telling, incidentally, that these examples almost always involve a highly lethal activity followed by yet another highly lethal activity; the resolve to die in these cases is hard to conceive of and flatly contradicts the view that "suicide is an easy way out." In March 2008 in Iowa, a man killed his family and then attempted to kill himself in the garage by carbon monoxide poisoning. Probably due to ventilation in the garage, he survived. He then attempted to drown himself in a local river, but could not. Finally, he drove his car on the interstate at a very high rate of speed into an abutment, which he did not survive. Several cases have been documented in which an individual self-inflicts a gunshot wound to the head, survives, and then shoots a second, lethal shot—or, as in the case of Meriwether Lewis mentioned earlier, survives multiple gunshots, then dies by other means. In April 2007 in Alaska, a woman drove her car off a high bluff. Amazingly, she survived. As the newspaper report stated, "Police believe the woman then got out of the car and walked several yards across the ice, before throwing herself into the inlet," where she drowned. A more harrowing case was reported in the *American Journal of Forensic Medicine & Pathology* in 2005. A man had tried to die by suicide by cutting himself severely. After surviving this, in the words of the article's authors, "The man tied a rope between a fence and his neck and, while seated on the driver's seat, accelerated the vehicle, which resulted in complete decapitation."

This is the stuff of severe mental illness—not to mention of horror—but this is not the stuff of ease and cowardice. One might protest, along with Camus in *The Myth of Sisyphus,* that suicide is a confession that life's problems are too much—that the "easy way out" view refers not to the fact that death by suicide is easy, but rather that turning away from life's problems in this way is easy. Easier than what? Facing them, drinking them away, retiring to one's bed, fleeing to Mexico? No, death by suicide requires staring the product of millions of years of evolution in the face and not blinking; it is tragic, fearsome, agonizing, and awful, but it is not easy.

"Suicide Is an Act of Anger, Aggression, or Revenge"

In a first-person account, "David Kent" writes that during his time on an inpatient psychiatry ward, he noticed that the aides seemed more interested in playing volleyball with each other than in paying attention to him. This upset "Kent"—an aide was supposed to be watching him; he was, after all, on suicide watch status. "Kent" stated, "His game was more important than my life." To retaliate in anger, "Kent" began to look around the grounds for a garden hose to use to hang himself. Not finding any, he gave up, but then "stumbled on a piece of worn and weathered rope lying in the grass." "Kent" writes, "Joy! Fear! And the beginnings of a consuming anger that could emerge now that a mode of expressing it had been found. I would show them! I sat . . . in plain sight . . . and tied a hangman's knot in the rope . . . It was all decided now. No other alternative presented itself nor did I seek one. The only way I could punish them and avenge myself and disturb their holy routine and show them I meant business and escape any punishment they might wish to visit on me and mock and hate and spit on them all—the *only way*—was to hang myself."

"Kent" threw the noose over a tree limb and used the rope to abrade his neck so that it was reddened a little. What spurred his impulsive wish to die, it should be emphasized, amounted to revenge ("I would show them!"). This seems to support the view that suicidal behavior may be mostly about revenge.

But "Kent" did not die, and by his own report, did not intend or make a genuine suicide attempt. This was because he was acting—"Kent" was the cultural anthropologist David K. Reynolds, who had arranged to be admitted to inpatient psychiatry so as to study it, unbeknownst to staff (this is all described in the 1976 book *Suicide: Inside and Out* by Reynolds and Norman L. Farberow). These kinds of studies have been done before and since, the most well-known instance probably being David Rosenhan's "On Being Sane in Insane Places."

The reporting of "Kent's" experience is, I believe, problematic and even pernicious, because it is written as if it were genuine when it is no such thing (indeed Reynolds claimed, implausibly, to have experienced serious depression in his enacting of "Kent"). In the writing, shopworn ideas about suicide influence the script that is made up for "Kent"—the spurned individual vows revenge and "shows others" through suicidal behavior, impulsive suicidal behavior no less (another myth confronted elsewhere in this book). A mistaken view of suicidal behavior is adopted, enacted, and then the fact that it was enacted is taken as evidence for the truth of the view in the first place. This is an unfortunate way to test knowledge claims, and though it arises in many areas of scholarship, it seems to attach itself particularly to claims about suicidal behavior.

Like many myths and misunderstandings, the view that suicide is an act of aggression or hostility toward others contains a grain of truth (together with much chaff). First the grain of truth: Marked anger and vengefulness can represent a risk factor for suicidal behavior. In fact, it is included in the American Association of Suicidology's mnemonic for suicide warning signs—IS PATH WARM?

"I" is for ideation (as in suicidal ideation);
"S" is for substance abuse;
"P" is for purposelessness;
"A" is for anxiety and agitation (including being unable to sleep);
"T" is for "trapped" (as in feeling trapped);
"H" is for hopelessness;
"W" is for withdrawal;
"A" is for anger;
"R" is for recklessness; and
"M" is for mood fluctuations.

So "A"—well, the second "A"—is for anger, and the guidelines supporting the mnemonic expand the phrase to "rage, uncontrolled anger, and seeking revenge." This is indeed a documented risk factor for suicidal behavior, but it operates like most such risk factors do—the vast majority of those who have the risk do not display the outcome, and many of those who have the outcome do not possess the risk factor.

There are a lot of angry people, and very few of them die by suicide; and, of all the people who die by suicide, the majority are not angry.

Why, one might reasonably ask, is it a risk factor, then? Assume, for purposes of illustration, that rage and revenge-seeking characterize 30 percent of those who die by suicide, whereas they characterize 20 percent of others. Given a large enough sample, this represents a significant difference, and thus a risk factor is born.

Also, there are plausible neurobiological reasons to view aggression as a risk factor for suicidal behavior. One of the most well studied involves 5-hydroxyindoleacetic acid (5-HIAA), which is the major metabolite of serotonin (an important neurochemical involved in the regulation of things like sleep and appetite); that is, when the body breaks down serotonin, one of the main things it breaks it down into is 5-HIAA. Studies have found that low levels of 5-HIAA in the spinal fluid characterize people who have engaged in violent acts like arson and murder, and more to the present point, people who have engaged in suicidal behavior. Studies have also shown that low levels of 5-HIAA in suicide attempters are predictive of subsequent attempts, a finding that hints at but is not fully demonstrative of a causal role for aggression-related biomarkers in suicidal behavior.

Here is why aggression is implicated in suicidal behavior. People who have been through regular experiences of pain and provocation—and this would include episodes of aggression—habituate to the idea of injury in general, including self-injury in particular. It is not, then, that aggressive people die by suicide; rather, it is those who have developed the capability for aggression who are at risk for suicidal behavior, and only when they have the additional risks of feeling they do not belong and that they burden others. The distinction between aggression per se and the potential for aggression may seem obscure, but it is not—consider NASCAR drivers, NFL football players, some military and police personnel, and even physicians. Few are violent in the sense of committing illegal assaults, but all have a kind of fearlessness about injury—and thus an increased capacity to sustain and tolerate it—due to their professional experience. Physicians are of special interest in this regard, because they have many protections against death by suicide (e.g., access to good health care), and yet they die by suicide at high rates. This may be at least partly due to the fact that they see pain and injury regularly, are thereby inured to it, and thus have the ready capacity to enact their own deaths should they desire to do so. I would make this prediction about any profession that involves a lot of pain and injury: The fearlessness needed to enact suicide is there in these individuals and will result in higher suicide rates unless the risk is offset by lower desire for suicide.

The desire for suicide involves feeling alienated as well as that one is a burden on loved ones. The "suicide is revenge" view makes the mistake of focusing on a secondary motive for suicide and elevating it to a primary position. The idea "I'm going to get revenge" is primary when it comes to harming others. This idea does not lead to suicide, however, unless it is layered over the more fundamental ideas of "I do not belong" and perhaps especially "my death will be worth more than my life to my loved ones." In suicide, the primary calculation involves burdensomeness and alienation; in some small proportion of suicides, a secondary overlay can involve thoughts like "and this will show all of them, to boot." But it is crucial to recall that this overlay does not usually occur in suicide, and when it does occur, it nonetheless remains secondary to the bedrock motives of burdensomeness and alienation.

So there is a grain of truth to the myth that suicide is about revenge on others, but this grain of truth has been perverted into the view that suicide is primarily about revenge. It is not, despite the misleading pronouncements of people like Freud—for instance, from his *Totem and Taboo,* "We find that impulses to suicide in a neurotic turn out regularly to be self-punishments for wishes for someone else's death"—or Harry Stack Sullivan—for instance, from his *Conceptions of Modern Psychiatry,* "[Suicide] is merely a question, then, of when a derogatory and hostile attitude, ordinarily directed toward the outer world, is directed with full force toward the self." These men and others have promulgated the view, trite in my opinion, that suicide amounts to aggression turned inward.

These kinds of pronouncements reverberate still, and their cultural permeation is impressive. Charles Robert Jenkins was a U.S. soldier based in the Demilitarized Zone (DMZ) between South Korea and North Korea in the 1960s. One night, drunk, scared, confused, and cold, he deserted, and walked across the DMZ, which led to his forty-year imprisonment in North Korea. In his 2008 memoir, *The Reluctant Communist,* Jenkins reported that his experiences spurred deep hate in him, and he attributed his suicide attempt while imprisoned to "hate turned inward." Jenkins grew up in impoverished circumstances in the rural U.S. South, did not finish high school, and spent forty years in the wasteland that is North Korea, and still, the idea that suicide is aggression turned inward has gotten through to him.

As another example, consider this statement from the 1989 book *American Suicide*, which describes the treatment of the bodies of those who died by suicide up through the 1800s: "The practice of burying suicides under crossroads under a pile of stones or with stakes through their hearts comes from ancient fears, *no doubt* based on the unarticulated understanding that suicide is often an act of anger aimed at those left behind" [italics added; I would add too that this practice occurred unless the decedent was a priest, which strikes me as a little hypocritical].

No doubt? To hold "aggression turned inward" as a general principle requires an obvious lack of actual contact with those who go on to die by suicide, as well as with their families. This certainly describes Freud, and to a lesser degree, Sullivan. It also requires a lack of rigor to view "aggression turned inward" as explanatory without satisfactorily addressing why so many people turn aggression outward instead, and why relatively few people with depression turn their aggression inward enough for it to become lethal. Finally, and crucially, it fails to explain why so many people who die by suicide take steps to make their deaths easier on loved ones.

Dante stated, *"Omne superfluum Deo et Naturae displiceat"* ("Everything superfluous is displeasing to God and Nature"). Although I think he was mistaken about the souls of those who die by suicide contending with thorns and such for eternity, I think Dante is right about parsimony. "Aggression turned inward" is displeasing because, among other reasons, there are simpler and more compelling explanations available.

Consider any crowd of people, such as those who have gathered for a lecture, a sermon, or a sports event. Some proportion of them, by chance alone, will be angry and vengeful sorts. To use this fact to describe the entire crowd is an obvious error in reasoning. As we have seen, the crowd of people who die by suicide are somewhat more likely than others to have anger issues—and so of course many of them express this in death. The key point, however, and one that gets lost all too easily in uninformed discourses about suicide, is that most do not. In any given activity, whether it is writing a letter to a newspaper editor or disciplining one's children, the angry personalities will express their anger. Suicide is no different—angry personalities sometimes express their anger in their choice of place and method of suicide.

In fact, this was the premise for one of Arthur Conan Doyle's Sherlock Holmes stories, "The Problem of Thor Bridge." In the story, a woman has died from a gunshot wound to the head; her body is at the foot of a bridge, and no firearm is found at the scene . . . but one is found in the closet of the woman's main romantic rival. The rival is arrested for murder, but is later freed after Holmes deduces that the dead woman framed the hated rival by placing a duplicate gun in the rival's closet and using another, identical gun to shoot herself—a gun to which a stone was tied by a string, with the stone suspended above the water. The woman shot herself, releasing the gun from her hand, which was pulled into the water by the weight of the stone.

In this case, reality mirrors fiction—this same method of suicide was reported in a case study in the *American Journal of Forensic Medicine & Pathology* in 1998. There are people who arrange their deaths by suicide so as to implicate others in their deaths—aggressive indeed. One wonders if this has ever succeeded—is anyone on death row, or already executed, for someone's suicide?

Suicides staged as homicides are, to the best of our knowledge, exceedingly rare. A more common though still rare scenario is a situation in which the death is not staged as a homicide but is arranged to express anger or maximize negative impact on those left behind. Lee Whittlesey's *Death in Yellowstone* tells of a park employee who was fired from her job. She was later found dead from a self-inflicted gunshot wound in front of the house of the person she blamed for the end of her job. I was told, as another example, of a situation in which a young man was distraught over the dissolution of a relationship with his girlfriend. He went to where she lived, entered the picket fence that surrounded the snow-filled front yard, and shot himself in the head. Blood-drenched snow was a painful and indelible image for the girl and her family, who believed, understandably, that this was an act of aggression and revenge.

Of course, cases like this also stand out in newspapers and other media. One case like this will generate considerable media attention; the deaths of another eighty-five individuals, on average, who also died by suicide in the United States on that same day generate little attention. This leaves the public with the idea that these kinds of angry and vengeful suicides are representative, when they are not.

Even those whose choice of suicide method may seem vengeful or mean-spirited may have harbored more benign motives. Consider, for instance, those who have died by self-inflicted gunshot wounds while driving in their cars. Studies in the *American Journal of Forensic Medicine & Pathology* document at least four such cases, often on interstate highways. It is plausible to view the behavior of intentionally dying in a moving vehicle at relatively high speed as an aggressive act, given the risk to those in other vehicles. However, in these cases, no other vehicles were involved. These death scenes are often viewed, at least initially, as single-vehicle fatal accidents, and one wonders whether the decedents had imagined that their relatives would find their deaths by accident easier to cope with than their deaths by suicide.

As another example of the difficulty in assigning motives to those who have died by suicide, consider the death of a student at Grinnell College in Iowa. The young man disappeared in September, 2006, and authorities discovered from his computer that he had been researching ways to die by suicide. But they could not locate his body. Six months later, they found him at the bottom of a country club swimming pool that had been covered for the winter. Approximately two weeks after the pool had been covered for the winter, the man had slipped under the pool cover and drowned himself.

Given that he had been researching ways to die, and given

the forethought that his method of death entails, one wonders whether he considered the fact that his body would not be discovered any time soon, and perhaps viewed this as a way to forestall and allay relatives' grief. He was almost certainly mistaken in the view that this would help his family members cope, but it nevertheless could have been on his mind. It is hard to view this young man's choice of method as involving anger and revenge against others.

Death by suicide invariably involves planning, but it also involves emotional crisis, which interferes with logic and planning. The result is often a train of thought and behavior that includes serious lapses in logic and judgment, and these lapses can produce pernicious consequences that the suicidal person does not intend. The young man who died in the Iowa swimming pool may have intended to die *and* to ease the shock of his death by not having his body discovered for months. He was in a suicidal crisis, and so he could not see that this would not help his relatives at all.

Just as there are people who arrange their deaths in ways they mistakenly believe will ease the shock, there are individuals whose death scenes clearly are not meant to be shocking, but are. The writer David Foster Wallace died in 2008 by hanging at his home. His wife, the only other person who lived at the residence, discovered him sometime later. Was this a malicious, vengeful thing that Wallace did to his wife? All of the evidence indicates otherwise. Wallace's happiest years in a life full of emotional struggle were due to his marriage. Wallace's suicide, including its method and setting, had nothing to do with his wife; it had to do, rather, with Wallace's intense major depressive disorder, which had gotten out of control after a change in his medication regimen. One might retort, "If Wallace had been in a different state of mind, he might have been more considerate of his wife." But of course this misses the essential point—if Wallace had been in a different state of mind, he would not have died in the first place.

There are other cases that are clearer still. In his 1971 *The Savage God*—an influential literary exploration of suicide— A. Alvarez described the death by suicide of a distinguished scholar as follows: "One afternoon he put all his papers in order, paid every bill to the last cent, wrote farewell letters to all his friends, saying he was sorry, put out food and milk for his cat, packed an overnight case and carefully locked his apartment. Down in the street, he mailed the letters . . . and then took a taxi downtown. He checked into a scruffy hotel and took a room on an upper floor" (p. 154). He jumped to his death, and did so, incidentally, in the same sprinting and vaulting way as Hart Crane. In this case, the scholar ran across the room and hurled himself through the glass of the unopened window. His actions toward himself were of course aggressive, but his actions toward others had a considerate, not an aggressive, character.

Alvarez described another case that does not fit the view that suicide is aggressive (p. 84). In the 1700s in England, where as elsewhere garish spectacle was the norm for public entertainment, a man offered to die by suicide in public in exchange for money from each spectator for his poverty-stricken family. This anecdote clearly illustrates how some hold the mistaken idea that their deaths will help, not hurt their loved ones, contradicting the notion that suicide is inherently aggressive.

It is common for those who die by suicide to take steps to lessen the impact of their death scenes on loved ones. People will often notify 911 of a death without mentioning that they are referring to their own imminent death. They do this as a way to immediately involve emergency personnel who will serve as a buffer between the death scene and the family. Others leave instructions in notes that are meant to help the survivors, both with regard to the death scene and to more long-term matters like finances and raising children. Some choose remote or anonymous locations of death (e.g., a forest), perhaps with the idea of buffering family from suicide's immediate aftermath.

I view my dad's death by suicide in this way. He died by self-inflicted knife wound to the heart early one summer morning, well before sunrise, in the back of his van, which he had parked in the lot of an office park around a mile from his home. Two mornings later, people who worked at the office park understood something was wrong and called police, who discovered my dad's body. His death was agonizing to my family and me, but his choice of method did not strike us as vengeful. To say it was sad that he died alone and in pain in the dark in a parking lot is to massively understate things; to say that his choice of method was aggressive is to massively misunderstand things.

When angry, one is more likely to attribute angry motives to others. For instance, angry people are more likely than others to perceive hostility in pictures of faces, regardless of whether the faces are angry, neutral, or even happy (Knyazev et al., 2008). I think a main contributor to the myth that suicide is fundamentally about anger is the anger of survivors. Survivors of a loved one's suicide are often very angry themselves (and of course experience other emotions too, especially devastating sadness). Questions like, "How could he have done this to us?" are common and understandable. I certainly wrestled with the question myself in the years following my dad's death. Angry survivors sometimes attribute anger to the lost loved one's act, when really the act was motivated by a perception of deep disconnection from others and perhaps especially by the view that one's death will be a net benefit to others, including loved ones. Suicide is not primarily about anger or revenge; it is sadder than that, in that those who die by suicide have concluded that they are bereft and that their deaths will be a service to others.

"Suicide Is Selfish, a Way to Show Excessive Self-Love"

In 1805, Presbyterian minister Samuel Miller wrote that suicide "is generally prompted by the most sordid and unworthy selfishness. It is a crime which sacrifices everything on the altar of individual feeling" (cited in Kushner's 1989 *American Suicide*, p. 31). As mentioned in the section on the myth that "suicide is easy," actress Halle Berry has arrived—independently, I presume—at the same conclusion. In March 2007, media reports quoted her in reference to her suicide attempt, years before, by carbon monoxide poisoning. She said, "I was sitting in my car, and I knew the gas was coming, when I had an image of my mother finding me. She sacrificed so much for her children, and to end my life would be an incredibly selfish thing to do."

Needless to say, I would urge those interested in the truth about suicidal behavior not to prioritize the comments of Hollywood stars or even Presbyterian ministers, whatever their other merits may be. Nevertheless, there is an aspect to Berry's comments that hints at something important. Berry did not die by suicide; indeed, she did not attempt to do so because she aborted her attempt. Why did she do this? According to her, and to others who have backed away from suicide attempts, the realization that she still had ties she could not ignore intervened; in Berry's case, an image of her mother. She did not die because her connection to her mother prevented her—an illustration of the principle that a fulfilled need to belong can be lifesaving.

Suicide felt selfish to Berry specifically because her connections to others remained intact. But it is a mistake to generalize from those who backed away from suicide attempts to those who stare down the potent force of self-preservation. I think it is almost self-evident that these two groups of people have different states of mind, and yet many people—scholars included—have conflated the two. That is, they take the intact social connections and attendant feelings of selfishness of some suicide attempters to be representative of those who die by suicide. This is a mistake because those who die by suicide have experienced rupture in their social connections, and thus ideas like "my mother would be distressed if I were gone" do not occur to them, not because they are selfish, but because they are alone in a way that few can fathom. Rather, ideas like "my mother will be better off when I am gone" are primary. These are the antithesis of selfishness.

One can understand somewhat the idea that suicide is selfish, in the sense that those left behind are often convinced that those who die by suicide did not consider the impact of their deaths. This is a terrible error. Those who die by suicide certainly do consider the impact of their deaths on others, but they see it differently—as a positive instead of a negative. They are wrong, but it is their view nevertheless.

There is scant evidence that those who die by suicide are more selfish than others. On the other hand, there is abundant evidence that, far from being selfish, suicide decedents (incorrectly) believe their deaths will be a blessing to others.

If the idea that suicide is selfish is mistaken but plausible, the idea that suicide involves excessive self-love is an absurd flight of fancy, unmoored from reality. In this case, the unmooring influence is psychoanalysis. The psychoanalytic corpus on suicide is, in places, obfuscatory and contradictory; in his 1971 book *The Savage God,* Alvarez wrote, "Psychoanalytic theory offers no simple explanation of the mechanics of suicide. On the contrary, the closer the theory gets to the facts of any case, the more complex it becomes and the less the act is explained" (p. 132). Explaining less with more is not promising for a scientific theory, as many philosophers of science have made clear. In any event, the gist of at least one thread of psychoanalytic thought is that suicide represents a murderous act not against the self per se, but against images of others that have been internalized within the self. For instance, the psychoanalyst Karl Menninger, in *Man against Himself* (pp. 31–32), describes an adolescent boy who, a few hours after a disagreement with his father, hanged himself in the barn. Menninger asserted, "It must have been his father whom he really wished to kill." I have met fathers whose sons hanged themselves after a disagreement with them; Menninger's assertion leaves me in doubt if he had. In this view, suicide is a killing of the "not-me" part of self, in an effort to spare the true self and let it live and thrive. Killing "another" to benefit oneself does seem selfish.

The trouble, of course, is that this interpretation is implausible. We have already seen that most suicides do not have an aggressive character in terms of their method and location choice, and that a primary—possibly the primary—motivation in death by suicide is the mental calculation that the individual's death will be worth more than his or her life to others. The psychoanalytic view has also spawned some other peculiar notions: for instance, the idea that masturbation and suicide have a deep connection. Had psychoanalysts wished to elucidate "excessive self-love," masturbation, instead of suicide, seems the wiser target.

There is a psychological state that is important in suicidal behavior and that resembles selfishness in some ways, but differs in others—namely, cognitive constriction or cognitive deconstruction. According to theorists like my colleague Roy Baumeister, individuals who are experiencing intense negative emotion may react by retreating into a numb state of "cognitive deconstruction." In this state, attentional focus is narrowed to lower-level awareness of concrete sensations and movements, and of very immediate, here-and-now goals and tasks. Abstract thought and forethought are impaired in a state of cognitive deconstruction, an important consequence of which is reduced inhibitions. Impaired cognition and disrupted impulse control are, according to this viewpoint, a mixture that may facilitate suicidal behavior (Baumeister, 1990).

Elsewhere in this book, I described a man who wrote "suicide is painless" in the dust on the hood of his car, left it on a bridge, and then disappeared. This was a faked suicide, which was evident even before the ruse was uncovered: A phrase like "suicide is painless" is too abstract (and rings false for other reasons too) for the cognitively constricted mind of the person intent on suicide.

A tragic incident involving a genuine suicide attempt, as well as the death of an innocent motorist, in Atlanta in October 2006 may illustrate the phenomenon of cognitive deconstruction, as well as its distinction from selfishness. A 16-year-old girl was involved in a car crash that killed a woman in another car. At the time of the crash, the girl was text-messaging her intention to die by suicide to another girl, in response to the latter's refusal to have sex with her. The district attorney was quoted as saying the girl was texting "her imminent threat: 'Nine, eight, seven, six, I'm going to do it.'" She then crossed the road's center line and struck an oncoming car, killing the woman driving it and injuring the woman's 6-year-old daughter. The girl herself survived the incident and was charged with felony murder, among other things.

A highly similar incident occurred in Minnesota in March, 2008: A 16-year-old boy, who had left a suicide note at home, drove head-on into the car of a woman who was approaching from the other direction. In this case, unlike the Atlanta case, the boy died, and the woman was injured but survived.

In a state of cognitive deconstruction, the focus is so narrowed on the here and now that even the most obvious consequences of an action do not register. It is possible that the girl in Atlanta was focused only on her suicide, so much so that the oncoming car was processed not as containing people who would be killed or hurt by the accident, but rather as a means of death, full-stop. That is, the oncoming car was perceived as the means to the end of suicide and not further cognitively processed. Her focus on her goal of suicide may have had paradoxical effects; the more she accelerated toward the oncoming car as it braked, the more momentum transferred to the other car, making it more likely that she would kill or injure those in the other car but not herself.

This girl was self-focused to say the least but may not have been selfish in the full sense of the word. Given the result of her actions, that may seem preposterous to say, but I think it may not be. By way of comparison, consider people who are in intense physical pain—they are definitely self-focused, but even if they do things that seem rash and hurt others, selfishness is not usually the attribution. Rather, the attribution is usually something like desperation induced by the pain.

Yet it is still possible that this girl was a very selfish type after all. It should be recalled that those who die by suicide include a diverse array of personalities. But there is another reason still to question whether selfishness is involved in suicidal behavior, and it has to do with a syndrome called antisocial personality disorder. As described in the *Diagnostic and Statistical Manual of Mental Disorders (DSM)*, the most widely accepted diagnostic manual used by mental health professionals, the disorder is characterized by a long-standing pattern of aggressive behavior and reckless, impulsive, and out-of-control disregard for others and for rules and norms. In his classic 1941 book *The Mask of Sanity,* Hervey Cleckley argues for the existence of a different subtype of antisocial personality. Whereas individuals described in the *DSM* as antisocial are under-controlled and reckless, those described by Cleckley are characterized by controlled and controlling, callous, sometimes charming behavior. These individuals also show marked emotional detachment (i.e., low anxiety, fake or shallow emotions, immunity to guilt and shame, and incapacity for love, intimacy, and loyalty). The *DSM*'s antisocials are out of control but not necessarily unfeeling; the "Cleckley psychopath" is very much in control and utterly unfeeling . . . except, that is, when it comes to himself. One cannot be a Cleckley psychopath and not be selfish—it is part of the core of the syndrome, although one can be classified as antisocial by the *DSM* and not be selfish. So one group is selfish to the core; the other less so. Which group is more prone to suicidal behavior?

My colleagues and I studied 313 inmates and found that *DSM* antisocial characteristics were clearly associated with suicidal behavior, whereas "Cleckley psychopath" features were not, and in fact were negatively associated with suicidal behavior, although to a nonsignificant degree (Verona et al., 2001). That is, the most selfish group was relatively immune to suicidal behavior, whereas the less selfish group was relatively more vulnerable—a pattern of findings that directly contradicts the "suicide is selfish" perspective.

It would be an exaggeration to claim that Cleckley psychopaths never die by suicide, although such deaths are rare. In June 2007 in the Miami area, a suicide and a murder occurred that may have involved one such individual. Helder "Sonny" Peixoto, who had been in several legal and interpersonal disputes throughout a career involving police and security work, was described by many as charming and always in the middle of fashionable parties in the Miami area. He had been dating a Miami model, who was beginning to ponder ending the relationship. This caused Peixoto to become even more possessive and controlling than he had been. It is not clear how the situation escalated to the point of violence, but Peixoto killed his girlfriend with a hammer and left her in his apartment. He then engaged a real estate agent to show him a vacant eleven-story condominium and jumped to his death from the balcony—"calmly," in the words of the real estate agent.

Several aspects of this case are consistent with that of the Cleckley psychopath. A history of numerous disputes, a need for interpersonal control (e.g., possessiveness of the girlfriend), and charm are all common among such individuals, as are egregious crimes like murder. Moreover, Peixoto's last moments involved interpersonal exploitation, this time of the real estate agent, whom Peixoto manipulated to be part of the method of his death as well as audience to his death (which may have appealed to the narcissism that is part of this syndrome). Finally, Cleckley psychopaths are relatively fearless characters, and Peixoto was described as facing an eleven-story fall without fear. Cleckley psychopaths are too selfish to die by suicide commonly, but when they do, they do so in very selfish ways, contributing to the "suicide is selfish" myth.

Also, and tellingly, I think, suicides contrived to have an audience are quite rare. In *New York* magazine in 2008, Phil Zabriskie reported on the fact that, of all those who die by suicide in New York City, approximately 10 percent are from out of town. Why travel to the city for the purpose of suicide? Some of those interviewed for the piece mentioned themes associated with selfishness—wanting an audience and the like—and indeed there are a lot of people in New York. And yet none of the examples in the piece seemed to fit this view. For instance, a young man jumped from a high floor of the inner atrium of a busy hotel in Times Square . . . but with virtually no audience, because it was 4 A.M. My own take on this phenomenon of "suicide tourism" in places like New York City is the opposite of views that favor grandstanding and a need for an audience. I think it is more likely that people are doing this to make sure that loved ones are *not* the audience; it is done to spare them at least a little bit of the inevitable anguish. This is not what selfishness and narcissism are about.

My colleagues and I recently solved a mystery involving both antisocial and narcissistic features. The mystery involved the fact that some people desire to die by suicide but do not intend it, whereas others endorse intent to die by suicide but do not desire it. The former group—those who desire but do not intend—are not difficult to understand; indeed, my theory of suicidal behavior predicts such individuals, because even though numerous people have ideas about suicide, few intend to act on those ideas because of the fearsome obstacles to the act instilled by nature.

By contrast, individuals who intend to die by suicide but do not desire to do so are puzzling. We first wanted to affirm that these people actually exist. In a data set of 330 individuals who were suicidal at the time of assessment, we searched for those who endorsed an index of suicidal intent at high levels, but endorsed an index of suicidal desire at low levels. Sure enough, ten individuals displayed this profile, around 2.5 percent of the total sample of suicidal individuals.

Having affirmed that these individuals exist, we next wanted to characterize them on an array of personality and clinical variables. We compared this group to other individuals on the array of variables, and the mystery was solved—the group who intended suicide but did not desire it obtained high scores on measures of narcissism and antisocial personality features. These individuals were likely "Cleckley psychopaths" who actually did intend suicidal behavior without desire . . . in order to run some sort of con on others, much as the "suicide is painless" hedge-fund fraud did. This is precisely the pattern of results that Cleckley would have predicted—"Cleckley psychopaths" never engage in suicidal behavior unless it is intended to manipulate or deceive others (e.g., to deflect attention from their crimes; to get out of responsibility).

Primarily as a thought experiment, a pretty persuasive argument has been made that the biblical figure of Samson (Judges, chapters 13–16) met criteria for *DSM* antisocial personality disorder (ASPD). Samson appeared to meet six of the seven criteria for ASPD, including, for example, failure to conform to social norms with respect to lawful behavior (Samson's arrest was sought for acts like burning the Philistines' fields); impulsivity (burning fields); and irritability/aggressiveness (Samson was involved in numerous fights). Samson also engaged in numerous conduct-disordered behaviors, such as fire setting, cruelty to animals, and weapon use. However, he did not come across as a selfish figure. Samson buckled the pillars of the building in which the Philistines were holding him, bringing the building down and causing many deaths, including his own. He seemed prone to negative emotion and impulsive outbursts (Judges 14:19 describes him as "burning with anger," for example), and these were implicated in many of his possibly antisocial acts, including his self-caused death. By contrast, there is little evidence of Samson's "emotional detachment." *DSM* may have diagnosed Samson with antisocial personality disorder, but Cleckley would not have viewed him as a psychopath, again consistent with the view that *DSM* antisocials are not necessarily selfish and thus are vulnerable to suicidal behavior, as opposed to Cleckley psychopaths, whose selfishness inures them to suicidal behavior. The stories of Samson and Cleckley psychopaths, like other evidence described above, contradict the view that suicide is selfish.

"Suicide Is a Form of Self-Mastery"

A 2008 article in the London *Times* opens, "Who is responsible for a suicide? The crude answer is: the person who takes their own life. It's the ultimate act of autonomy." This quotation echoes a sentiment that one hears with some frequency in clinical practice in managing suicidal patients. When suicide risk is elevated, it is wise for clinicians to inquire as to potential means of death and to engage in commonsense actions to restrict access to those means. For instance, if someone is thinking of death by self-inflicted gunshot wound, having the person bring the gun and ammunition to someone for safe-keeping is worth serious consideration. In these conversations, it is common for patients to voice some reluctance, not necessarily because they want to retain the means of death (though this can occur), but rather because they feel a sense of control in having a last-resort escape plan in suicide.

Many clinicians have witnessed this phenomenon, and I believe it is a key source for the myth that death by suicide is primarily about mastery or control. It is crucial to distinguish between, on the one hand, wanting an array of options, including the last-resort option of suicide, and, on the other hand, deciding to die by suicide. In the former state of mind, there are multiple options, and this alone distinguishes it from the state of mind of the truly suicidal individual, for whom there is only one option (or more accurately, for whom the option of death is increasingly towering over other options). The person who wants to keep suicide as a last-resort option is clearly implying that there are other "resorts" that can be tried out first. In saying they want control over the option to die, they are affirming that there are prior options, at least one of which involves living.

The myth that suicide is primarily about self-mastery is an instance of a larger, general category of suicide myth that involves mistakenly assigning primacy to a motive that is either secondary or epiphenomenal (and often doing so with a distinctly moralizing tone). That is, although it is certainly true that some people—including suicidal people—ascribe to suicidal behavior a "take my life in my own hands" function, imagining it to be the primary reason for suicidal behavior, it is also true that these people might be mistaken. This kind of mistake, it should be noted, is the same kind that occurs when people confidently attribute to suicidal behavior motives such as selfishness and revenge.

And, like the misunderstandings regarding selfishness and revenge, the myth about self-mastery contains some grains of truth. The mistake is not the assumption that self-mastery (or revenge or selfishness) is or can be involved somehow; rather, the mistake is about what is fundamental. To take a totally different example, attributing the behavior and consequences of hurricanes to the contour of the affected shore is not wrong per se; often, shore contour is important. But it is not always important, and other, more fundamental things always are, such as wind speed and tides.

Self-mastery is of obvious importance in the course of our lives. In the time it took me to write that last sentence, I received two separate spam e-mails on impotence, and by the time I finish the paragraph, I expect to receive others on this topic, or on obesity, and so on. All of these e-mails either explicitly or implicitly prey on people's frustrated needs for self-mastery in one or another life domain. Anyone up late at night can observe the televised version of this same phenomenon, and it is not hard to imagine that this can be a depressing experience. Though relatively little research has been done on the topic, one study of a weight-loss infomercial found that thin women appeared on the infomercial three times as often as other women, and the ad portrayed heavyweight people as particularly unhappy and unattractive (Blaine & McElroy, 2002).

It is also not hard to imagine a depressed person up at night (because insomnia is a symptom of depression) when these ads are most visible, harboring vague suicidal ideas while absentmindedly watching a "take control of your life" infomercial. As the commercial and its host talk about "control" this or "take back" that, the message melds with the individual's ongoing suicidal ideas. Though I doubt very much that my dad watched infomercials, his note, perhaps a suicide note, perhaps not, which consisted entirely of the question, "Could this be the answer?" rings of this motive: "Yes, here at last, might be a way, albeit a very desperate one, to regain some control."

This description is not intended to lay depression or deaths by suicide at the doorsteps of the late-night self-improvement or teleadvertising industries. It is meant, rather, to illustrate that issues of self-mastery are prevalent and pervasive in our society, and that certain segments of the population—certainly including suicidal people—are vulnerable to messages, almost always false, that promise to fix things through a quick and easy increase in self-mastery. Although causing one's own death may seem to the suicidal person a means of total or ultimate control, this is a lethal fallacy, because dead people have no control. Just as suicidal people mistakenly imagine that their deaths will be worth more than their lives, and this mistake proves fatal, so may suicidal people make the lethal mistake of thinking that suicide represents self-control.

There are people who fantasize about suicide, and paradoxically, these fantasies can be soothing because they usually involve either fantasizing about others' reactions to one's suicide or imagining how death would be a relief from life's travails. In both cases, an aspect of the fantasy is to exert control, either over others' views or toward life's difficulties. The writer A. Alvarez stated, "There are [people] . . . for whom the mere idea of suicide is enough; they can continue to function efficiently and even happily provided they know they have their own, specially chosen means of escape always ready . . ." (p. 154). In her riveting 2008 memoir of bipolar disorder, *Manic*, Terri Cheney opened the book by stating, "People . . . don't understand that when you're seriously depressed, suicidal ideation can be the only thing that keeps you alive. Just knowing there's an out—even if it's bloody, even if it's permanent—makes the pain bearable for one more day" (p. 5).

This strategy appears to be effective for some people, but

only for a while. Over longer periods, fantasizing about death leaves people more depressed and thus at higher risk for suicide, as Eddie Selby, Mike Anestis, and I recently showed in a study on violent daydreaming. A strategy geared toward increased feelings of self-control (fantasizing about the effects of one's suicide) "works" momentarily, but ultimately backfires by undermining feelings of genuine self-control in the long run.

A crucial difference between those who think that suicide represents ultimate control and those who think they are a burden on others is that evidence suggests all those who die by suicide believe they are a burden on others, whereas not all of that group believe that suicide represents self-mastery. This alone provides a clear clue as to the relative importance of self-mastery—it is hard to see how it would be primary if not all suicidal people endorse it.

In other cultures and other eras, the issues of self-mastery and suicide are treated differently. Cross-culturally, some of the highest rates of suicide are in Asia, where self-mastery is secondary to interdependence, as social psychological research has repeatedly shown (e.g., Kitayama, Markus, & Kurokawa, 2000). If self-mastery were fundamental, then one might expect that cultures that are very focused on such values—like the United States and Australia—would have high rates of suicide. Within this group, one might expect high rates of suicide motivated by frustrated self-mastery. Yet neither expectation is fulfilled—the United States and Australia have suicide rates that are in the average to slightly above average range compared to the rest of the world, and many of the countries with higher rates of suicide have cultures in which social connectedness and interdependence are most valued. It also seems doubtful that self-mastery has been the primary motive for suicidal behavior in the past, though this would be an interesting research question to pursue.

Make no mistake, self-mastery is a primary motive for many other behaviors. In his 2006 book *Stumbling on Happiness,* psychologist Dan Gilbert states that "people find it gratifying to exercise control—not just for the futures it buys them, but for the exercise itself. Being effective—changing things, influencing things, making things happen—is one of the fundamental needs with which our human brains seem naturally endowed, and much of our behavior from infancy onward is simply an expression of this penchant for control" (p. 20). In this context, Gilbert cites a well-known study in which elderly nursing home residents were given a houseplant; half were told that the care of the plant was up to them, and half were told that the plant would be cared for by staff. This simple difference was associated with a difference in mortality rates: Six months later, 15 percent of those caring for their own plants had died, as compared to 30 percent of those whose plants were cared for by staff. The simple exercise of mastery or control appeared to make a life-or-death difference.

There are certainly deaths by suicide that appear to invoke mastery as a primary motive. For instance, the famous South Korean actress Jeong Da-bin died by hanging at age 27 in a Seoul apartment. She posted some thoughts on her Web site in the days and weeks preceding her death, including the day before her death on February 10, 2007. As reported in the May 2007 *New York Times,* under the title "The End," Jeong posted, "For no reason at all, I am going crazy with anger. Then, as if lightening [sic] had struck, all becomes quiet. Then the Lord comes to me. The Lord says I will be O.K. YES, I WILL BE O.K." The actress found a solution and was empowered by it, which left her with the feeling that all would be well.

Self-mastery seems to be a primary motive in much of human behavior—why not in suicidal behavior? There are a couple of key arguments against a primary role for self-mastery in suicidal behavior.

The first is that huge numbers of people struggle with issues related to self-mastery and self-control, fueling a thriving late-night infomercial industry on exercise, weight loss, and finances. Yet serious suicidal behavior (i.e., deaths by suicide and near-fatal attempts) are, relatively speaking, rare. If all those struggling with self-mastery issues engaged in serious suicidal behavior, there would be even more of a worldwide problem with it than there already is.

One might protest that an important risk factor for a condition can be more common than the condition and yet be crucial. For example, smoking is an obvious risk factor for lung cancer, and yet more people smoke than get lung cancer. True, but this brings us to the second point, which is that the details of deaths by suicide show mastery as a motive only very rarely (whereas deaths by lung cancer implicate smoking quite regularly).

In *The Savage God,* A. Alvarez states, "I think there may be some people who kill themselves . . . in order to achieve a calm and control they never find in life. Antonin Artaud, who spent most of his life in lunatic asylums, once wrote: 'If I commit suicide, it will not be to destroy myself, but to put myself back together again . . . By suicide, I reintroduce my design in nature, I shall for the first time give things the shape of my will'" (p. 153).

From Artaud's perspective, suicide is not meant to "introduce design" in the first place—an account that would be consistent with mastery as primary. Rather, it is meant to "reintroduce" it, which implies that something has occurred in the first place to disorganize one's design in nature. What occurs first, I believe, are repeated experiences leading to the belief that one is a burden on others and alienated from them. Mastery through suicide is a secondary, reactive phenomenon.

Alvarez also quotes the Italian writer Cesare Pavese: "it is conceivable to kill oneself so as to count for something in one's own life. Here's the difficulty about suicide: It is an act of ambition that can be committed only when one has passed beyond ambition." The difficulty, really, lies in misunderstandings like Pavese's—suicide, far from being an act mainly of ambition, is an act of profound loneliness and inconsequentiality. The reason it seems ambitious is that it is so fearsome and daunting. It is ironic that some recognize the "ambitious" quality of suicidal behavior but do not recognize the acquired fearlessness of injury, pain, and death necessary to carry through such an act.

These same kinds of misunderstandings affect mental health professionals too. Karl Menninger wrote, "To kill oneself instead of being slain by fate, is to retain for oneself the illusion of being omnipotent, since one is even by and in the act of suicide, master of life and death. Such omnipotence fantasies . . . are to be regarded as infantile relics. They presuppose or assume the certainty of a future life, a reincarnation." The briefest conversation with someone who has been to the brink of suicide and survived by chance alone—for example the rare person who survives the jump from the Golden Gate Bridge—will immediately dispel these ideas about omnipotence, reincarnation, and the like.

Consider, for example, the death by suicide of Jeong Dabin, mentioned above. It is true that she posted a message on her Web site that implied mastery as a possible motive, and indeed, in the *New York Times'* coverage of her death, this is the only Web posting of hers that is mentioned. But she left others. For instance, under the heading "Finished," she wrote, "I'm complicated and I feel like I'm going to die . . . I have lost my identity." Even when mastery themes are invoked, as they were by Jeong, they are usually accompanied by other themes too, like feeling insignificant, miserable, misunderstood, or trapped. It is even more common for motives of giving up, submission, or hopelessness to be prominent in the absence of mastery, and these motives, I believe, are fundamentally underlain by the perceptions that one is both a burden to and alienated from others. Even in those instances in which people intimate that suicide is one last grasp at control, control is not the primary motive. To claim that it is overlooks the reasons why the person has so desperately lost control in the first place.

"Most People Who Die by Suicide Don't Make Future Plans"

As noted earlier, in his book *The Myth of Sisyphus*, Camus observed, "The body's judgment is as good as the mind's, and the body shrinks from annihilation." Although it is true that the "body shrinks from annihilation," it is also true that some individuals engage in behaviors that train the body to not shrink from it so much. Indeed, people develop the capacity to inflict unthinkable physical ordeals on themselves.

However, even those who are very resolute in the matter of their own deaths experience fear in the moment. The most common example of this phenomenon involves those who jump from high places and survive. Recall the example of Tina Zahn, who, in her memoir *Why I Jumped*, described her desperate depression and the urgent desire to die by jumping off of a high bridge. She did eventually jump, but the urgency of her desire to die waned in the moments beforehand, which caused her to hesitate and gave a law enforcement officer the crucial few seconds he needed in order to catch her just as she jumped. Zahn's fearlessness flagged in the seconds before she jumped, which saved her life.

There are others whose resolve decreases after they jump. Of those who jump from the Golden Gate Bridge, approximately 3 percent survive. The comments of two survivors, included in Tad Friend's 2003 *New Yorker* article on suicide at the bridge, illustrate this phenomenon. One survivor stated, "I instantly realized that everything in my life that I'd thought was unfixable was totally fixable—except for having just jumped." Another said, "My first thought was 'What the hell did I just do? I don't want to die.'"

A man who jumped into the water leading up to Niagara Falls in 2003 was one of very few to survive going over the falls. He said that he changed his mind the instant he hit the water. "At that point," he said, "I wished I had not done it. But I guess I knew it was way too late for that." The psychiatrist Harry Stack Sullivan described his interactions with several people who had ingested the very lethal substance bichloride of mercury. Sullivan wrote, "One is horribly ill. If one survives the first days of hellish agony, there comes a period of relative convalescence—during which all of the patients I have seen were most repentant and strongly desirous of living." The tragedy for these patients is that they almost never live to see their new desire for life realized; another phase of several days of agony later resumes, usually ending in death.

In a study on suicide in anorexic patients conducted by my colleagues, students, and me, one of the cases involved ingestion of a household cleaning product containing around 35 percent hydrochloric acid. The person drank twelve ounces of this product and then felt regret, at least as evidenced by her calling 911 soon thereafter. Efforts to save her were not successful; she died at the hospital four hours later from internal bleeding caused by the hydrochloric acid's injury to her stomach.

A crucial implication of these cases is that the fear of death is universal and virtually unshakeable. It is so powerful that it persists even in people who have suppressed it enough to drink horrible poisons like bichloride of mercury or hydrochloric acid, to jump off the Golden Gate Bridge, or to go over Niagara Falls. Therefore, it is a safe assumption that virtually everyone who desires death also simultaneously desires life. The suicidal mind is characterized by ambivalence, with competing forces tugging at the suicidal individual from the sides of both life and death. The fact that this applies even to the very resolutely suicidal makes the point all the more clear.

If, in the very moment preceding a fatal act—indeed, the very moments during the fatal act—a person feels substantial ambivalence, then it stands to reason that such ambivalence would be observed as well in the days and weeks leading up to the potentially fatal act. In this light, it is not only unsurprising that people often make plans for jobs, trips, and relationships in the days and weeks before their deaths by suicide, it would be surprising if they didn't. Of course they do, because the "life" side of the struggle that they will eventually lose and that will eventually kill them is still active and still compelling them to plan for life, just as everyone else does.

This is a very simple truth that could save the family and friends of those who die by suicide a lot of uncertainty and anguish. Understanding a death for what it is and for what caused it and coming to some terms of acceptance is not easy; but it is easier than never coming to terms with a death because of lingering and in some cases festering doubts and ideas about the person's cause of death.

Uneasiness about this topic abounds in those who doubt their loved one died by suicide, but it also occurs in those who have no doubt at all. In 2007 in Australia, two girls died together by hanging themselves in a remote area. Though they had talked to others—peers—of their impending deaths, they did not talk to their parents, a pattern that evidently is common in young people; studies have found that few parents are aware when their child is having suicidal ideas. For the parents of the Australian girls, the deaths came out of the blue, leaving them stunned and deeply agonized. One of the parents said that her daughter often talked of future plans: "She wasn't just someone who thought there was nothing ahead of her, she talked about what she wanted in the future, she had dreams." The girl's plans and dreams were real; it is just that their source, the will to live, eventually lost out in a struggle with the desire for death; and it is likely that this struggle continued until very near the time of the girls' deaths.

A murder-suicide that occurred in 2007 in Atlanta also illustrates the fact that people simultaneously intend death and intend life (and this applies to murder-suicide just as it does to suicide). A man killed his wife and then killed himself. Associates of the couple were puzzled about the incident, because the couple had plans to sell their house and move to Florida, where the man had plans for a job, and where he could more easily combine his work with his main hobby of deep-sea fishing. The couple had bought a car in Florida and had just been there to test drive it. It is precisely this kind of planning—thinking ahead to a time when one can better combine work and leisure, buying and test driving a car in the future location—that perplexes those who are left behind in the wake of a suicide. The key is to understand that two simultaneous processes are occurring—one geared toward life, the other tending toward death.

The death of the Italian writer Primo Levi further illustrates the consequences of such understanding, or in this case, misunderstanding. Levi was a young man during the Holocaust, and he survived the concentration camps. His later writings are viewed as poignant and potent affirmations of life in the face of unspeakable cruelty and brutality. Levi died by suicide decades after his Holocaust experiences by jumping from the tall staircase in his apartment building. Notably, Levi's grandfather also died by suicide, also by jumping from a high place. The totality of evidence points quite clearly to suicide as the method of death, but to this day, some harbor doubts, and the reasons for their doubts are instructive. The doubts take two forms: First, that the details of Levi's death do not suggest suicide; and second, that the kind of person who wrote in the affirming way Levi did could not, in the end, decide to die by suicide. Both of these doubts are in error, the kind of error that keeps misunderstanding alive.

First, regarding the details of Levi's death, the evidence adduced against suicide will be familiar by now: He left no note, yet he did participate in activities and leave behind documents that indicated engagement in day-to-day and long-term plans. For example, on the day of his death, he engaged in his usual activities, like receiving an injection from a nurse who would visit him daily. As this section and another in this book make clear, features like these are, if anything, more characteristic than less of death by suicide. Those who die by suicide usually do not leave a note; they usually do show evidence of planning for their future lives.

The idea that Levi the writer could not be the "type" for suicide includes numerous faulty assumptions. First, there really is no "type" per se—the fact that someone wrote about affirming topics at one phase in life is no guarantee that in another phase of life (or even in that same phase) the person won't die by suicide. Second, and relatedly, there is an implication that beautiful writing (or more broadly, beautiful art) cannot be accomplished by those who later die by suicide. Even a cursory review of the history of poetry and literature settles this issue very quickly. Third, there is no requirement that a writer's true personality shine through in his or her writing. Levi's own biography shows that his melancholic temperament and frequent bouts of depression did not find their way into his writing.

Shneidman's (2004) book *Autopsy of a Suicidal Mind* describes in detail the death by suicide of a man named "Arthur." The night before his death, Arthur intentionally overdosed on lithium, but he threw it all up and survived (showing, incidentally, how the body fights). The next day, he went to meet a close friend, and went to lunch with his dad, having resolved to attempt suicide again that night, when he did in fact die. In the words of Arthur's brother, "on the very day he killed himself, he had lunch with my father. He asked my father for money. He said 'Dad, I just had to pay all my taxes and I don't have much money left, can I have $500 to help me through the month?' And my dad said he was going to go home and write him a check and send it in the mail. That wasn't a trick on Arthur's part. There is no way in the world that he was trying to trick my father, but I think part of him wanted to go on" (p. 81).

I think the brother has this exactly right. There was a fight going on in Arthur's mind (and his body had chosen sides, as evidenced by its refusal to die the night before). The fight was between death, which eventually won out in Arthur's case that same day, and life, which motivated a sincere request for financial help from his father. In January of 2008, the president of a prestigious private high school in Atlanta checked into a downtown high-rise hotel. He left a suicide note in the hotel room and then jumped to his death. Hours before, on the very day of his death, he had given a rousing speech to people connected with the school as part of the kick-off of a new semester and new year. Within the school president's mind, as in Shneidman's "Arthur," life and death forces were battling it out, and this battle can continue up to very near the time of death, leaving people confused about why someone would do something life-affirming one moment and then die the next. The only way out of this confusion is to recognize the deep ambivalence that characterizes even the most suicidal person.

The death of actress Lana Clarkson puts a unique spin on this topic. There is little question of how she died (gunshot wound to the face), where she died (the mansion of music producer Phil Spector), or who was present when she died (Spector was there). The question is whether the wound was self-inflicted or perpetrated by Spector. Among much other evidence, Clarkson's mother testified on the stand that Clarkson shopped for and purchased shoes the day before her death. Why, the prosecution asked, would she buy shoes on the day before she planned to kill herself? The prosecution believed that no one would do such a thing, and Clarkson must have died by homicide, not suicide. Buying shoes, however, has no probative value—people who die by suicide buy shoes and do other such things on the day before their deaths, as do people who die by homicide. (This, of course, is not a general defense of Spector, who was convicted of second-degree murder in 2009).

Those who die by suicide have two simultaneous mental processes unfolding. One is mundane (and yet in a way incredible) and is happening in virtually everyone (including those whose deaths by suicide are impending): "Should I change jobs? What will I do this weekend? Should I get a new car? Should I ask so-and-so on a date, or to marry me?" The other is far from mundane, and is difficult for most people to even conceive of: "Why don't I just die? It would be a relief. There's an aspect to death that is comforting, even beautiful, people would be better off, why don't I just get it over with?" Though it is difficult and uncomfortable to conceive of this last process, that does not change the fact that it is a true process that characterizes the minds of suicidal people. It is even more difficult to come to terms with the fact that people can harbor this very unusual state of mind at exactly the same time that they are thinking of weekend plans, or mowing the lawn, or going to the grocery store. Again, difficulty in conception does not necessarily bear on the truth of that conception. It is hard to believe that people do this, but they do, and the fact that they do explains why those who are dead by suicide today had plans for the future yesterday.

"People Often Die by Suicide 'on a Whim'"

Yes, indeed, that's true . . . but only in works of fiction. Tellingly, the only documented cases that I can find that were clearly "die on a whim" suicides are from fictional sources. In his 2006 book *Cliffs of Despair,* Tom Hunt quotes the eminent sociologist Durkheim on this point: "the suicidal tendency appears and is effective in truly automatic fashion, not preceded by an intellectual antecedent. The sight of a knife, a walk by the edge of a precipice, engender the suicidal idea instantaneously and its execution follows so swiftly that patients often have no idea of what has taken place" (p. 66). This passage reminds Hunt of a suicide he has read about . . . in fiction. "This reminds me of Anna Karenina's impetuous lunge under the wheels of a train." The French poet and polymath Paul Valéry wrote, "The victim lets himself act and his death escapes from him like a rash remark . . . he kills himself because it is too easy to kill himself."

This is simply not how it works in the real world, else there would be millions more suicides per year as people glance at knives and trains and the like. This is a pervasive and entrenched misunderstanding about suicide, and I wonder if its source may be that early scholars and writers, like Durkheim and Valéry, took at least some of their cues from the likes of

Shakespeare and Tolstoy, forgetting that these men, while undeniably great, wrote *fiction.*

A death that occurred in June 2008—and the reporting of it—illustrates well how ingrained is the idea that it is common for someone to die in spur-of-the-moment fashion. A man in his late twenties went on a skydiving trip with a few other people in New York State. As is often the case on such trips, he went just to ride along in the plane and to take pictures; he did not intend to skydive, had no training in it, and had no parachute or other gear for it. At an altitude of 10,000 feet, after three people with parachutes jumped, so did the man, whose impact caused damage to a house below.

Initial reports of an incident like this are often sketchy and therefore can imply many misleading things. This incident was no exception. First, it was intimated that the man was part of a group of friends who were skydiving enthusiasts. The reality, by contrast, is that the man was socially isolated and talked his way on to the plane; he was not friends with the three skydivers. Second, initial news of the incident suggested that the three parachuted skydivers jumped in turn, and then the man, who was up and about in the plane, suddenly jumped too. In reality, as the last of the three chuted jumpers exited the plane, the man was still buckled in his seat. The pilot then began to close the door, and as he did so, the man quickly undid his restraints, struggled with the nearly closed door and the wind, and before the stunned pilot could react with much force, the man had jumped out of the plane. (Had the pilot been able to attempt more of an intervention and had a struggle ensued, the man may have been saved, or else both men would have been pulled out of the plane, and the pilotless plane would have crashed, perhaps injuring or killing those on the ground.)

The most misleading aspect of initial reports of the incident, however, was the implication that the man simply jumped on impulse. Further investigation of this tragedy demonstrated that this was quite untrue (as I would argue it always is . . . except, again, in fiction). According to subsequent newspaper reports, "For months, [the man] had unnerved some of his co-workers in the seafood department at [a grocery store] in Schenectady. He asked the same question frequently, the assistant manager remembered. He said, 'If you had to die, would you rather jump off a building or jump out of a plane without a parachute?'" Moreover, the man had been to the airstrip the week before, asking to go on one of the flights to take aerial photographs for a class assignment. He had arrived too late, however, and the pilot told him to come back the next week—which he did, for the fatal flight. Still further indication that the man had planned this out and thought it through in considerable detail was that, as he fell to his death, he appeared calm and did not flail, according to the pilot.

Somewhat in contrast to most myths and misunderstandings about suicidal behavior, this one on "death on a whim" rides the wave of a large amount of reasonable theorizing and empirical work . . . but it's still a myth. For example, in his book *The Myth of Sisyphus,* Camus wrote, "Rarely is suicide committed (yet the hypothesis is not excluded) through reflection" and "An act like suicide is prepared within the silence of the heart, as is a great work of art. The man himself is ignorant of it. One evening he pulls the trigger or jumps." These statements are mistaken in the assertion that people are unaware of their developing plans for suicide—on the contrary, people who end up dead by suicide are the most deliberate in their plans. Not only are the statements wrong, they compound the error by romanticizing suicide, implying that it is akin to an artistic act that brews in a person's heart until its sudden artistic expression. Those who have been to suicide death scenes will not view this perspective charitably.

The empirical literature on the role of impulsivity replicates these same errors, repeatedly documenting a real but misunderstood connection between impulsive personality features and suicidal behavior, and thereby reifying the view that suicide on a whim is not only a real phenomenon, but a common one.

It is neither. An English coroner, who was interviewed about the death by suicide of a 15-year-old boy who hanged himself with a belt in his bedroom, gets a little closer to the truth. He stated, "The actual act is not pre-meditated although the mental preparation, with hindsight, can be seen to be there." The problem with this statement is that the actual act is quite often premeditated, but the insight of the coroner's statement is important too: Mental preparation for the eventual act of suicide is an essential characteristic of the phenomenon.

A study from Australia is typical in this domain of study, in that it collects valuable and interesting data but then tends to misinterpret them. The researchers interviewed people in the emergency room, as soon as possible after they were admitted after surviving a suicide attempt. The study found that 51 percent of the participants who attempted suicide reported contemplating the act for ten minutes or less; an additional 16 percent reported thinking about it for less than thirty minutes. The lead researcher stated, "the research dispels the myth that suicide attempts are always a pre-meditated, long-planned act."

But it does nothing of the sort. Leaving aside the 33 percent or so who thought about their impending attempt for more than thirty minutes, let's focus on the 67 percent who did not. What the study demonstrated was that, for these 67 percent, the time frame in which they reported thinking about suicide approaching their attempt lasted, at most, thirty minutes. People's self-reports about such things can be unreliable, but regardless, what the study leaves unaddressed—and this is crucial—are the hours and days and weeks and months and—in some cases—years during which the participants may have thought about suicidal acts.

An analogous thing happens regarding many things for which people make advance plans. Take wills, for instance. There are people who make a will decades before their deaths, and then they don't think about the will again—it is taken care of. People make plans for vacations, and then don't necessarily think about the vacation until they're hurriedly packing and leaving to go. In both of these examples, impulsivity really was not a major factor. Plans can be made well in advance, and then, as it were, taken off the shelf at a later date.

Similarly, people who die by suicide have thought of the possible methods and locations and so forth well in advance, often years in advance. A recent case I am familiar with illustrates this tragic reality. A man of approximately fifty years of age is struggling with chronic depression. During the worst of his depression, he has ideas about suicide, either involving medication overdose or self-inflicted gunshot wound. In psychotherapy, he articulates these ideas fairly clearly, but also is certain that he has no plans to actually carry through with plans for suicide. He is ambivalent about psychotherapy, and drops out against the therapist's advice. Approximately three years later, he re-engages psychotherapy, still depressed, but now seemingly less suicidal than before. He dies several days later by self-inflicted gunshot wound.

On the surface, this could be counted as an "impulsive" suicide. The person states no clear plans for suicide, yet relatively shortly thereafter, dies. It is even possible that the person pondered his impending death for less than thirty minutes beforehand, which would thus qualify him as an "impulsive" suicide in the study mentioned above. But the man had thought of death by self-inflicted gunshot wound many times over the years; his plan was "on the shelf" and it takes virtually no time to take a plan like this back off the shelf. The man died after a process that took years; to view this as impulsive is to neglect all but the act itself, when the act was just a part of something that had been going on for a long time.

Of course, another issue with the Australian study mentioned above is that the focus was on suicide attempts, not on deaths by suicide. The same "on the shelf/off the shelf" process can apply to both, but it is very likely that clearly lethal behavior gives people much more pause than less lethal behavior. There are instances of this in the film *The Bridge,* the documentary that captured several people's deaths by suicide at the Golden Gate Bridge. Several of those who died showed understandable hesitation—the lethal nature of what they were contemplating gave them pause. In at least one case, the hesitation led to being rescued (filmmakers called authorities about people who worried them); tragically, in many other cases, the urge toward death prevailed and overcame the fear and hesitation.

And in still other cases, there was little hesitation at all. Were these, therefore, impulsive suicides? Not at all. These were people who purposefully made their way to the bridge (after previous visits, in all likelihood, as in the case of the poet Weldon Kees). Even those who had not previously visited had very likely envisioned the scene, and had thereby mentally steeled themselves to the fearsome prospect.

One of the myths covered elsewhere in this book—the one on why people might make plans for a job interview in a few days or dinner with a friend and then die by suicide—might exacerbate this myth on impulsive suicide. "Impulsive suicide" does fit the facts of such cases in a way—the person made the plans for the dinner or the interview genuinely, but then the impulse to suicide came up suddenly and intervened. As discussed in that section, however, a much more plausible explanation is that people contemplating suicide are deeply ambivalent, and so simultaneously make plans for life and death. In the vast majority of cases, life wins, in part because the will for it is so strong (evolution has seen to that). But in a few tragic cases, the plan for suicide wins out over the plans to keep living and to keep having job interviews, dinners, and the like.

The suicide of President William J. Clinton's childhood friend and White House adviser, Vince Foster, was of this sort. Despite wildly irresponsible speculations to the contrary, Foster died by self-inflicted gunshot wound. The day before his death, he had agreed to go out with his wife the next night, and had agreed to a business meeting the day after that. Yet on the day of his death or perhaps before, Foster secretly took a gun out to his car in an oven mitt. On the day of his death, he drove out to a secluded area of a park and shot himself. To imagine that Foster's death was impulsive is to ignore all of the facts in what was by far the most investigated suicide in the history of the world. (Multiple congressional inquiries were conducted into his death, as well as multiple additional forensic investigations.) It is also to ignore the character of Vince Foster; he was a thoughtful and deliberate person. No one who knew him would have described him as impulsive.

Still another issue that plagues studies like the one from Australia mentioned above involves the role of alcohol and drugs. In the Australian study, 29 percent of those who harmed themselves had been drinking at the time. Of this subgroup, almost all of them (93 percent) reported that they had planned their attempts for less than ten minutes. A common interpretation of such reports is that alcohol fuels impulsive behavior. An alternative interpretation, and one that I think is more plausible in light of the totality of evidence on suicidal behavior, involves two facts: 1) as already noted, people can take well-developed and well-considered plans from months or years ago "off the shelf," and doing so takes very little time; and 2) regarding the specific role of alcohol, those who have been drinking are not necessarily accurate reporters of what they were thinking at the time; alcohol is likely to cloud memories related to how long one pondered an attempt before acting on it.

The study from Australia produced valuable data, and it is quite representative of larger problems in the field, problems that the study itself of course did not cause—but there is one remaining complaint I have about it. The study found that about one-fifth of the participants continued to feel suicidal twelve hours after their suicide attempt; this was interpreted to mean that suicidal impulses are short lived. But this is the wrong interpretation. Most people who attempt suicide— including those who ponder the act for many months or years—do not feel suicidal after the attempt. Indeed, to my knowledge, all those who have survived a jump from the Golden Gate Bridge ceased feeling suicidal even as they plummeted toward the water. It is not that their impulse came and went; rather, their will to live was shocked back to the forefront by the primal fear of death they experienced as they fell.

According to a 2006 news report, the coordinator of mental and brain disorders for the World Health Organization commented accurately on a similar phenomenon, but then wrongly interpreted it. He stated, "We have very good studies interviewing people between the act of ingesting pesticides and their deaths. More than 95 percent are desperate when they learn they are going to die." This is quite right—the desperation arises from the fear of death. He then went on to state that "nearly everyone" who died by suicide acted on impulse. This is quite wrong, and the fact that prominent people within the World Health Organization have this wrong is a clear indication of the power and pervasiveness of myths and misunderstandings about suicide, and the urgent need to dispel them.

It is impressive just how pervasive this myth is. As reported in the *Kennebec* [Maine] *Journal* in 2004, a psychiatrist said many smart and compassionate things about the nature of suicide, including that not having a suicide barrier on a bridge in Augusta, Maine represented a public health menace. He then added, inaccurately in my view, that jumping from a bridge is often an impulsive act undertaken without planning. The briefest glance into the lives of those who have died by jumping from the bridge would demolish this view, as would interviews with those who walk on the bridge—including extremely impulsive people—with no intention or even the foggiest conception of wanting to jump. It is not impulsivity or some kind of whim that differentiates those who jump from the bridge from the hordes of people who cross and do not jump. Rather, it is that the tragic few who jump do so in a culmination of a process of thinking about suicide for months and years, a process fueled by mental illnesses, especially mood disorders, schizophrenia, and borderline personality disorder.

Here is how it actually works, with no involvement of whims and the like. In early 2005, well-known "gonzo journalist" Hunter S. Thompson died by self-inflicted gunshot wound in his Colorado home. Thompson's son stated afterward that the family had known for at least ten years that this would be Thompson's cause of death. The son told the *Rocky Mountain News,* "I've known for many, many years that this is how Hunter would go. It was just a question of when. This was a big surprise and I didn't expect it to be now, but the means was exactly as we expected."

The death by suicide of television news reporter Christine Chubbuck also illustrates how suicide is not in essence impulsive, though the final act can have impulsive qualities, leading people to misattribute impulsivity to the entire suicidal process. Chubbuck died by self-inflicted gunshot wound on the air, as she was reporting the news. Chubbuck had been open with her family about feeling depressed and suicidal; she attempted suicide by overdose four years before her death and frequently discussed the incident.

A few weeks before her death, she sought the permission of her station to research a story on suicide. In conducting interviews for the piece, a police officer told her that a particularly lethal means of suicide was a shot to the back of the head (rather than the temple) using a particular caliber gun with specific kinds of bullets. A week before her death, she told a colleague that she had bought a gun, and she joked with him about killing herself on the air.

On the day of her death, Chubbuck insisted that she needed to read a newscast to open the talk show program she hosted, which was not her usual opening. Part of the news copy contained her report of her impending suicide. A recurring feature of the show was for Chubbuck to do puppet shows, and she had a bag of puppets for this purpose. On the day of her death or possibly even before that, she had placed a gun in the puppet bag.

During the show, Chubbuck covered a few news items, and then turned to a shooting that had happened the day before in the local area. The station had footage of the restaurant shooting, but the tape jammed. Chubbuck shrugged and stated, "In keeping with Channel 40's policy of bringing you the latest in blood and guts, and in living color, you are going to see another first, an attempted suicide," at which point she took out the gun and shot herself behind the right ear.

To view Chubbuck's death as impulsive flies in the face of all the facts. She had been suicidal for years, had spoken openly of it, had attempted suicide before, had bought a gun and "joked" that she might shoot herself on air, had stowed the gun in her bag, and had prepared newscopy about her own suicide. And yet, there was a somewhat impulsive element: Chubbuck could not have known that the tape would jam at that point, and so her choice of timing occurred then and there. This is a classic scenario that confuses so many, professionals included. Her plan had been months in the making; her plan to enact it was decided during the news program, the only one in which she changed the usual procedure of the show; the only thing that had not been decided was the exact moment, and that decision did appear to be made on the spur of the moment. The mistake many have made regarding scenarios like this is of the cart and horse character: To view a death like Chubbuck's as impulsive is to assign primacy to that spur-of-the-moment decision as to when to pull out the gun, instead of focusing on all the plans that led up to that moment.

My doctoral students and I conducted a study on this issue (Witte et al., published in a 2008 issue of the *Journal of Affective Disorders*). We used data sets collected from 1993–2003 by the Centers for Disease Control and Prevention (CDC) on health-related behaviors among high school students (grades 9–12). Questionnaires from students over 700 schools across the United States were obtained; a total of 87,626 were completed between 1993 and 2003.

We focused on distinct groups of adolescents, with "groups" defined by their answers to two questions regarding suicidal behavior. The first question was, "During the past 12 months, did you make a plan about how you would attempt suicide?" The second was, "During the past 12 months, how many times did you actually attempt suicide?" Happily, most adolescents neither attempted suicide in the past twelve months nor endorsed making a plan for doing so, and these kids were excluded from our study. We then focused on two groups, both of whom reported suicide attempts: 1) those who reported no plan for a suicide attempt but nonetheless did attempt suicide—"impulsive attempters" ($n = 1,172$); and 2) those who reported both making a plan for a suicide attempt and attempting suicide ($n = 4,807$). We asked which of these two groups is the most generally impulsive?

We found that individuals who had planned and enacted their suicide attempt were significantly more likely to have engaged in other impulsive and risky behaviors than those who had attempted suicide without prior planning. The planful group was more generally impulsive than the impulsive group! As a result, the study undermined the "spur of the moment" view of suicide by showing that those who had the most impulsive personalities were also the most planful when it came to suicidal behavior.

If the "spur of the moment" view of suicidal behavior held water, the group who attempted impulsively should be at least as impulsive as the group that planned and attempted. If, on the other hand, the role of impulsivity in suicidal behavior exists because impulsive people are exposed to repeated painful and provocative experiences (which in turn can steel resolve for serious self-injury), the planful group should show the most impulsivity, which is what happened.

Some other points worth noting: Less than a quarter of all attempters in the sample attempted "impulsively," indicating that impulsive suicide attempts are not the norm, at least not among adolescents, a group who are widely viewed as impulsive. If "spur of the moment" phenomena were prominent, one would expect that a higher proportion of suicide attempts would be made without prior planning. But this certainly was not the case, and this in a sample that was extremely large and representative of U.S. adolescents.

Some of our analyses were limited only to those whose suicide attempts required medical care. All the same results held with this subgroup. Earlier I criticized the study from Australia for relying on self-report and pointed out that the study was related to suicide attempts, not deaths by suicide. In fairness, some of these same limitations apply to our study on U.S. teens.

Except in the fiction of authors like Shakespeare and

Tolstoy, people do not die by suicide on impulse. On the contrary, the extremely fearsome and often painful prospect of bringing about one's own death requires previous experiences and psychological processes that take months—at least—to accumulate. Those who end up dead by suicide have thought the act through many times, often in detail—only this allows them to carry out something so drastic and so final. Even this is often not enough. The vast majority of people who ideate about suicide do not attempt, and even fewer die by suicide. Now, it is true that certain deaths by suicide contain impulsive details, as we saw, for example, regarding the death of Christine Chubbuck. These impulsive details have confused many, and this confusion I believe is pernicious. It is pernicious because the idea that suicidal acts come out of the blue undermines attempts to study, assess, treat, and prevent them. If suicidal behavior is part of a process that can be understood and tracked, there is hope of intervening. If, on the other hand, suicide mysteriously materializes out of the mists, what's the use? Suicide is tractable, and we owe it to the memories of those who have died already and to those who are at risk in the future to make it more so.

"You Can Tell Who Will Die by Suicide from Their Appearance"

Two of the myths I have disputed—that suicide occurs on a whim, and that people have no future life plans on the day of their death by suicide—taken together, imply clearly that people who are about to die by suicide may look very much like they always have, very much like you or me. Given what happens to the bodies of suicide decedents—sometimes very disturbing and graphic—many people reason backward and assume that someone whose end point is so tragic must have appeared thus in the minutes and hours leading up to the death. But this is not at all necessarily so.

In fact, many of the examples described throughout this book are of people who appeared as they usually did to others before their deaths. The high school president who gave a rousing speech to those connected to the school, then jumped to his death hours later, gave no sign of his impending death. Former president Clinton's friend and aide Vince Foster saw many people on the day of his death by suicide, including his wife and people with whom he worked closely; none noted a change in his usual appearance. Newscaster Christine Chubbuck, whose death occurred on the air, did not give clear clues about her suicidal plans, certainly not with her physical appearance. A local politician in Pennsylvania who was under some suspicion for wrongdoing called a press conference to address the issues, pulled a gun during the press conference, and died by self-inflicted gunshot wound in front of the assembled press. His appearance gave no hint as to what was about to happen. In her compelling memoir about bipolar disorder, *Manic,* Terri Cheney wrote regarding her plan for suicide, "I'd already carefully laid out what I was going to wear as my farewell attire: A long black cashmere dress—not to be macabre, but because cashmere would never wrinkle and black would hide any unexpected blood or vomit" (p. 8). Indeed, like Cheney, there are many people who dress particularly well for their deaths by suicide.

Many people who dress well for their suicides tended to

dress well for most things during their lives—the principle being that there are ongoing behavioral tendencies that pervade much of what people do. As noted in another section, people who had anger problems throughout their lives may, when planning their deaths by suicide, express anger in their deaths. This does not mean that suicide is about anger; it only means that people with anger issues may express anger in many things they do, including death by suicide. Similarly, those who dress well in life may dress well in planning their suicides.

Following the same logic, those who did not care for their appearance throughout some or most of their lives may appear unkempt or haggard in the hours or days preceding their deaths by suicide. Suicide is a common form of death among those who are addicted to heroin, for instance. Many heroin addicts had looked unkempt for years preceding their deaths by suicide, simply as a function of their lifestyle.

It is important to reiterate that warning signs for suicide do clearly exist. The clearest ones of all are when people say or otherwise indicate that they are about to die by suicide. Though not quite as clear, if a person who usually dresses well and appears well groomed suddenly does not, this of course suggests something is amiss. Yet appearing well dressed and well groomed does not clearly indicate that someone is safe from suicide. As the deaths of the private school president and Christine Chubbuck show, a person's physical appearance can be the same (even better than usual in some instances), and the person can still die by suicide seconds, minutes, or hours later.

"You'd Have to Be Out of Your Mind to Die by Suicide"

When people say this, what they usually mean is that suicide is so foreign to their minds that, in order to do it, they'd have to be psychotic, demented, intoxicated, or delirious. Indeed, in the next section on how death can merge into themes like belonging in the minds of suicide terrorists and others, I will point out that this merging requires a kind of break in the mind. Most who have not experienced this break find it extremely difficult to conceive of suicide, and so understandably attribute all kinds of motives and qualities to the suicidal mind to make it more understandable. One way of doing this is to imagine "they're simply crazy." Yet that is definitely not the case. This break in the mind is very specific; it has to do with breaking from the universal fear and revulsion that people have about death, coming instead to embrace and invite it, in a way, lovingly. Is this the same thing as being psychotic, demented, intoxicated, or delirious?

In a word, no. Anecdotes abound in which a person was seen or spoken with at one point in time; seemed coherent, calm, in tune with reality, and sober; and then was dead by suicide minutes or hours later. The high-school president who gave a lucid and rousing talk to students, faculty, and others on the future of the school, both for the short- and long-term, is a good example. This kind of performance from him was typical; no one noticed anything unusual or erratic about his appearance or behavior. On the contrary, he was composed and articulate, just as he usually was, and then approximately four hours later, he jumped to his death from the upper floors of a downtown hotel.

It is conceivable that the principal's mental status deteriorated markedly in the hours after the speech, just before his death. This strikes me as possible, but extremely unlikely. For one thing, those who are prone to dramatic deteriorations in mental status tend to show those tendencies early in life and relatively often. This did not appear to be the case with the principal. For another thing, there are numerous documented cases in which people have been in communication with family or authorities in the seconds and minutes leading up to their deaths by suicide. In the vast majority of these cases, those about to die were not incoherent or psychotic.

Filmmakers of the documentary *The Bridge* remarked that one of the most surprising things about the entire experience was that they could not tell who was who. Passersby on the bridge who seemed obviously distraught, unusual, or erratic would concern the filmmakers, leading them to call authorities. When authorities arrived, virtually none of these individuals seemed at risk. By contrast, those whose deaths were filmed shocked the filmmakers, because seconds before, they appeared to be just one of the bridge's many day-to-day pedestrians. Were it the case that those about to die by suicide are always psychotic or otherwise "out of their minds," the filmmakers would have been better at discerning those at risk.

Physician John Gray, editor of the *American Journal of Insanity* from 1854 to 1886, held this same view. In the journal, he stated that "in the large proportion of cases, if not the majority, [suicide] is committed by sane people." Much turns here on the definition of "sane"; it seems clear that what Gray meant was that most who die by suicide are not delusional or otherwise psychotic.

People who die by suicide do, I believe, undergo a kind of mental break involving their views of death—they come to see death as a comfort to others and to themselves—but this mental break is not the same thing as psychosis, intoxication, dementia, or delirium. Am I arguing then that people who die by suicide do not have mental disorders? Emphatically no. The best evidence to date indicates that around 95 percent of those who die by suicide have a diagnosable mental disorder at the time of their death. Personally, I believe that is probably an underestimate, and that the figure is closer to 100 percent—I believe that, in the vast majority of cases, the 5 percent without clear mental disorders at the time of their death are experiencing subclinical variants of mental disorders.

The claim, then, is that virtually all suicide decedents were experiencing mental disorders at the time of their deaths, but that relatively few were psychotic, demented, intoxicated, or delirious at the time of their deaths (some are, it should be emphasized; a point to which I will return). This may appear to be a contradiction, but it is not.

Mental disorders are surprisingly common, but most people who have a mental disorder are neither psychotic, demented, intoxicated, nor delirious. I got an early glimpse of this as a graduate student, when we were testing out one of the first generations of computerized psychiatric interviewing. We had several hundred undergraduates undergo the computerized interview, and the computer used preset algorithms to diagnose the students. Overall, the computer gave diagnoses to approximately 45 percent of the students . . . students who were selected at random from large subject pools. Our knee-jerk reaction was "that's too high, something is wrong with our algorithms." But that wasn't the problem at all. The fact is that when all mental disorders are surveyed, including those related to substance abuse and dependence and specific phobias, the percentages add up. The students legitimately met criteria for conditions like alcohol abuse and the various anxiety disorders, yet virtually none of the students who met criteria for these disorders was psychotic, intoxicated, demented, or delirious. Subsequent surveys of the U.S. general population have returned similar findings.

At any given time, around 5 percent of the U.S. population is experiencing major depressive disorder. The disorder involves sadness, insomnia, loss of energy, and the like, and it causes serious distress and affects people's lives negatively. But in the majority of cases, it does not involve psychosis, dementia, intoxication, or delirium.

Perhaps an even more interesting example is substance use disorders. In the most serious version of these conditions, substance dependence disorders, people are clearly addicted to a substance, they have developed tolerance for the substance, they have prominent withdrawal from the substance in its absence, and the condition negatively affects their lives in clear ways (e.g., they don't work because they are drug-seeking instead). Even among the subset of people with substance dependence disorders, most do not spend the majority of their time intoxicated. Even when using the substance in question, many are not particularly incoherent, because they have been using long enough that their bodies have adapted to the substance. This is not to say, of course, that alcohol and drugs cannot make people incoherent.

Many people have witnessed or experienced firsthand the cognitively incapacitating effects of severe alcohol intake, and the results can of course seem "crazy" indeed. Those without these firsthand experiences have no doubt seen them depicted in various media. Is it this kind of "craziness" that leads someone to something as hard to understand as suicide, many may wonder?

To reframe the question, what is the blood alcohol level of the average person who has died by suicide? And what is the blood alcohol level of matched controls (i.e., the average person who has not died by suicide but otherwise resembles suicide decedents regarding factors like age, race, psychiatric condition, and so on)? In answer to the first question, a review that appeared in the June 2006 issue of the *American Journal of Forensic Medicine & Pathology* is informative. The review looked at over 200 deaths by intentional overdose that occurred in Kentucky over a ten-year span. The majority, 67 percent, had no alcohol in their systems. A study from Australia on suicide attempts mentioned earlier indicated that 29 percent of attempters had been drinking at the time of their attempt. It appears that the majority of people are not even drinking at the time of their attempt or death by suicide, much less intoxicated.

Tom Hunt's book *Cliffs of Despair* relates an interesting anecdote about the involvement of alcohol in death by suicide.

Hunt reviewed the coroner's file of a man who had jumped to his death by suicide off the cliffs of Beachy Head in England. In his suicide note, the man stated that although he had recently celebrated seven years of sobriety, the coroner will undoubtedly discover alcohol in his system. "He wants to make clear, though, that it wasn't the booze that drove him to suicide. 'It was clinical depression, existential angst, cosmic alienation or whatever'" (p. 165). Indeed, this man had arranged for his funeral years earlier, aware that he might eventually die by suicide. This man's blood alcohol level was above zero as he died by suicide, but to imagine that alcohol caused his death seems far-fetched. Indeed, the man's death shows another potential role for alcohol in suicide—to brace people against its fearsome and daunting qualities.

Another principle illustrated by the man's death is that "above zero" alcohol level by no means ensures intoxication. From the Kentucky study noted above, about a third of suicide decedents had some alcohol in their blood at the time of death. Of these, most had blood alcohol levels below .08, the legal limit for driving under the influence in the United States. The man who died at Beachy Head almost certainly fit this description, and my dad certainly did. My dad's blood alcohol level in his autopsy report was .02. My guess is that he had had three or four drinks a few hours before his death, perhaps in an unsuccessful attempt to take the edge off of his sleepless depression. Or perhaps he had a drink, maybe two, in the hour or so before his death, as he was contemplating what he ultimately would do. In either scenario, the "raving intoxicated madman" scenario of suicide did not fit my dad, as it does not fit most who die by suicide. In fact, even for those whose blood alcohol is above the limit of .08, not all of them are raving or even particularly intoxicated. By law, they should not be driving, but most are not "out of their minds." For many of those who drink regularly, their behavior at a blood alcohol of .10 is not much different from their behavior when their level is zero; for some of them, they can seem calmer and more lucid at a level of .10.

Still another explanation for the association between alcohol and suicidal behavior is that they are related to each other mostly because they both relate to a third variable. Consider a 1991 study that appeared in the *American Journal of Public Health*. The study was on Navajo adolescents, and found that consumption of hard liquor was associated with past suicide attempts in a linear way. That is, those who never consumed hard liquor had relatively low rates of past suicide attempts; those who drank hard liquor at least monthly had higher rates; and those who drank hard liquor at least weekly, the highest rates of all. If the story stopped there, it would not be particularly interesting, nor would it be especially relevant to the third variable issue mentioned above.

But the story continues in two interesting ways. First, the same pattern of results on alcohol intake and suicide attempts did *not* pertain when beer or wine were examined instead of hard liquor. Or, to put it a little more accurately if complexly, the same pattern only held among beer and wine drinkers who also drank hard liquor. There was no association between beer and wine drinking and past suicide attempts once hard liquor consumption was controlled for. Why would this association be specific to hard liquor versus beer and wine? Is hard liquor more facilitative than beer or wine, or is it that hard liquor drinking is an indicator—a signal—of a broader, underlying risk for suicidal behavior?

I think it is the latter, and this gets to the second compelling finding from this same study. As already noted, a strong predictor of past suicidal behavior was the participant's own use of alcohol, specifically hard liquor. But there was another alcohol-related index that outperformed even the participant's own report of hard-liquor drinking—namely, the participant's mother's use of hard liquor. The effect of the participant's father's hard-liquor drinking was detectable too, but was weaker than both the participant's report of his own liquor drinking and the mother's report of her liquor drinking.

This is a fascinating finding. Liquor drinking is predictive of past suicidality—interesting enough but not too surprising. But that your mother's drinking is predictive, not of her past suicidality, but of yours, and that it is more predictive of your suicidality even than your own liquor drinking—now that is interesting *and* surprising. That your father's drinking predicts your suicidality but less powerfully than your own or your mother's drinking adds another layer to these results.

What explains this intriguing set of findings? It seems not to be well explained by the idea that alcohol intake is a facilitative factor in suicide in the moment. If it were, why would liquor drive the effect and not wine or beer? Perhaps one could argue that it is simply that liquor is more intoxicating in the moment . . . but then how to explain that one's mother's liquor drinking is more predictive than one's own? Whether this effect is genetic or related to family conflict (extreme alienation from family and community was also a robust predictor), it does not clearly support a proximal facilitative role for alcohol use; it is more consistent with the view that alcohol use is a signal of a deeper substrate of chronic risk—a risk that is passed on from parents to children. And why would a mother's drinking and not a father's drinking be predictive? Probably because it represents a clearer signal. That is, if one's father drinks excessively, that can be a problem, but relative to other men, a lot of whom have the problem, the underlying condition is probably not severe. But if one's mother drinks excessively, that almost certainly will be a problem, because not a lot of women do that; for her to do so means that she has a severe underlying condition, and that severity is getting signaled to you either genetically or through family environment.

Overall, the role of alcohol use in suicidal behavior seems to be much more complex than it is usually portrayed. The situation is similar to that involving impulsivity and suicidal behavior. There is a documented empirical association, but such an association can mean many things. It can conceivably mean that impulsivity leads people to die by suicide on the spur of the moment, and though this idea seems to have caught on, it is almost surely wrong. Impulsive people can have rough lives—accidents, arrests, fights—precisely because they are impulsive. People who regularly go through such experiences toughen up. Should they develop ideas about suicide, and some do because of difficulties like accidents, arrests, and fights, then, more so than others, they have the wherewithal to enact those thoughts.

The logic is very similar regarding alcohol use—indeed, there is an empirical association between impulsivity and alcohol use. If one is prone to use alcohol excessively, difficulties like fights, arrests, and accidents are more common, as are other demoralizing incidents like relationship loss and job failure. It is this web of demoralizing events and development of a tough shell that links alcohol use to suicidal behavior, rather than alcohol making people suicidal in the moment.

Having said that, it is the case that impulsive people can get very emotional and thus act rashly, including acting in suicidal ways. In the section on impulsivity and suicide, I argued that even in this scenario, impulsive people are not dying by suicide on the spur of the moment; rather, they are impulsively resorting to a plan that they have in reserve. The plan "on the shelf" has the more prominent causal role in death in these cases, though impulsivity played some role too.

Alcohol use can function similarly. I have already noted that some people, perhaps including my dad, use it as a way to brace themselves for the very fearsome thing that they are contemplating. Another role for alcohol in suicidal behavior involves what my FSU colleague Al Lang and others have termed "alcohol myopia." This psychological state involves an alcohol-induced "tunnel vision" that focuses on only relatively salient and immediate cues and stimuli. For most people who are intoxicated, their myopia does *not* predispose them to anything having to do with suicidal behavior because they don't have any suicidal plans. This is true even for people who are prone to negative emotions when drinking. But for a subset of people who have pondered suicidal behavior over months or years, alcohol intoxication can narrow their field of view, such that a crisis focuses them on suicide. In this scenario, alcohol intake is playing a role, but not a primary causal one. Rather, intoxication is a contextual factor, a setting condition. Acute alcohol intake can focus people on only one or a few plans of action; for people who are vulnerable to suicidal behavior to start with, a plan of action can involve death by suicide.

Although there is little doubt that some suicide decedents are intoxicated at the time of their death, this obscures two important facts: 1) most are not; and 2) most of those who are occasionally or even regularly intoxicated do not attempt, much less die, by suicide. This same general line of reasoning applies to other states in which people's mental status is impaired. That is, some people who die by suicide are psychotic (out of touch with reality, having hallucinations, delusions, and cognitive confusion) at the time of their death, but most are not, and most psychotic episodes do not include suicide attempts. Those with other impaired mental statuses, including various forms of dementia (that is, severe cognitive decline that includes memory loss) and delirium (a state of serious mental confusion), behave similarly.

In fact, those few individuals who do cause their own deaths while psychotic, demented, or delirious represent a challenge to frameworks that attempt a nomenclature for suicidal thoughts and behaviors. One such framework was put forth by Silverman and colleagues in 2007 in the journal *Suicide & Life-Threatening Behavior*. One of the categories in this nomenclature is "Undetermined Suicidal Behaviors," which are self-inflicted potentially injurious behaviors where intent is unknown. This term is applied when the intent to die is unknowable due to the fact that an individual is psychotic, demented, or delusional. These behaviors are classified differently than clear suicide attempts and death by suicide. An example of an "undetermined suicidal behavior" under the Silverman et al. guidelines would be an individual who has bipolar disorder and is delusional in the midst of a mixed episode—such episodes are characterized by a mixture of manic and depressive symptoms as well as anger and irritability. Friends report that he has been rambling about themes of religious self-sacrifice, Jesus coming down from "the air to the earth to save us all," and so on. He is later found dead after falling to his death from the roof of his apartment building. In this example, intent is impossible to decipher. It is possible that the man intended suicide, but it is also possible that he intended something very different by jumping—specifically, to save others as a messiah. The latter idea is psychotic, but whether or not it is clearly suicidal is a bit of a conceptual conundrum.

As another intriguing example, I am aware of a legal case in which an older person has died by suicide. The person had accumulated wealth, and had changed his will months before his death to leave most of the money to an agency of his choosing, rather than to family members. A lawsuit resulted, claiming that the later suicide proved that the man was not competent to make decisions of that sort when he changed the will. One sympathizes with the family—they have lost a loved one; to add to their distress, my sense is that such lawsuits are not particularly successful because it is simply not the case that those about to die by suicide suffer mental impairment in the same way as those declared incompetent for legal proceedings.

The mental state of those who are on the precipice of suicide is different from that of others to be sure, but it is the nature of that difference that is in question. Many think the difference can be explained with reference to various impairments in cognitive status such as intoxication or psychosis. Although it has intuitive appeal, it does not fit the facts. The majority of suicide decedents did not display impairments like psychosis, dementia, or delirium before their deaths. What they *did* display is difficult for most to understand. Just as many cannot fathom losing touch with reality, most cannot imagine a state of mind in which death seems an inviting comfort. Even though it may be hard for most to imagine, this, not intoxication or psychosis, is what suicide decedents experience.

Suicide Terrorists and Others Subvert the Need to Belong

Should suicide terrorism be analyzed along with what one might term more conventional suicide-related deaths? Few if any suicide theorists have confronted this issue head-on; those who have commented state fairly emphatically and from the outset that these kinds of phenomena are beyond their scope. Yet the phenomenon of suicide terrorism can be viewed as one of the key geopolitical challenges of our time, and a phenomenon like suicide terrorism obviously does have suicidal elements. Therefore, it seems to me incumbent on the theorist either to explain why it is "out of bounds" or else to take it on directly. I prefer the latter course, though the terrain presents many additional ambiguities. I think that examining it systematically and identifying which elements of suicide terrorism overlap with conventional death by suicide—and which do not—is worth the trouble.

The theory I developed in *Why People Die by Suicide* claims that serious suicidal behavior only exists under conditions of convergence between three psychological and interpersonal processes (themselves underlain by an array of processes ranging from the molecular to the cultural). The three processes can be termed *learned fearlessness, perceived burdensomeness,* and *failed belongingness.* With regard to suicide terrorism (as well as the sort of heroism that leads people to fall on grenades), the first two factors are clearly relevant. Suicide terrorists *do* learn fearlessness of the daunting and horrible act they are planning; indeed, they are specifically trained to unlearn the natural fear that should and for most people does accompany such behavior. And suicide terrorists *do* engage in a calculation that involves perceived burdensomeness. The calculation is "my death will be worth more than my life to others." In *The Myth of Sisyphus,* Camus said, "what is called a reason for living is also an excellent reason for dying." Suicide terrorists believe this, and it is a fundamental motivation for their behavior; those who die by suicide also believe this, and this also is a fundamental motivation for their behavior, as I and others have demonstrated repeatedly in empirical studies.

In *Why People Die by Suicide*, I touched on these issues regarding learned fearlessness and perceived burdensomeness. But what of the third factor, failed belonging? It seems not to fit in as well. Suicide terrorists do not feel lonely and isolated before their deaths. Instead, as documented in works like Christian Reuter's book *My Life Is a Weapon*, suicide terrorists derive a profound sense of community from their impending plan, and this is a primary motivation for their being willing to follow through.

I believe that the belonging that suicide terrorists feel is not merely about the promise of an ideal afterlife and not only about their living on in the memories of family and friends as admired martyrs (though this is no doubt a factor). Suicide terrorists are able to do what they do because of four elements: learned fearlessness; a "death worth more than life" mindset; turning in the mind that romanticizes death to such a degree that they literally become "in love" with death; and a related process in which the need to belong, usually compelling positive, prosocial, affiliative actions, gets subverted, so that death satisfies the need to belong. I theorize that all four of these elements are characteristic of the suicidal mind *in general*, including suicide terrorists but also including people who die by suicide more conventionally.

In the June 2003 issue of *Atlantic Monthly*, Bruce Hoffman contributed an article entitled "The Logic of Suicide Terrorism." In it, he wrote, "suicide terrorists are often said to have gone to their deaths smiling. An Israeli policeman told me, 'A suicide bomber goes on a bus and finds himself face-to-face with victims and he smiles and he activates the bomb—but we learned that only by asking people afterwards who survived.'" Hoffman continued, "This is what is known in the Shia Islamic tradition as the bassamat al-farah, or 'smile of joy'—prompted by one's impending martyrdom. It is just as prevalent among Sunni terrorists. (Indeed, the last will and testament of Mohammed Atta, the ringleader of the September 11 hijackers, and his 'primer' for martyrs, 'The Sky Smiles, My Young Son,' clearly evidence a belief in the joy of death.)"

There is a clear sense of connection in death for these terrorists. Not only do they possess a "smile of joy" before killing themselves and others, but they believe that the very sky itself smiles back. For contrast, consider the kinds of activities that usually invoke words like "the sky smiles on you" or "the world smiles back at you"—setting a world record at the Olympics, making an intellectual contribution that saves lives, devoting oneself to helping the especially poor, sick, or disenfranchised. For people of a certain mindset, add "blowing up yourself and others" to that list. This is what I mean by subversion of the belongingness motive. It is almost as if a prosocial and positive motive is sent through a kind of distorting prism; it emerges from the other side, still itself in some ways (it is still about belonging), but changed and distorted (the violent death of innocent people now accomplishes belonging).

Consider also some of the rituals that have developed

around suicide terrorists in the Mideast. After a suicide ter-rorist's death, the family and community often have a celebra-tion, and, were one to observe from a distance without prior knowledge of the context, one would surely conclude that the celebration was a wedding party. In fact, in a fundamental sense, it is. The groom is the dead terrorist, who, though not there physically, is remembered with photos and shrine-like memorials. The bride is death itself, with symbols of death lit-erally combined with various bridal symbols. It is my view that suicide terrorists derive a sense of belonging from their giving themselves over to death, and this marital ritual repre-sents evidence for this view.

For most people, death and belonging don't go together, and the assertion that they might causes a kind of instinctual revulsion. This revulsion is natural and ingrained, but that does not mean it can't be overcome, and not just tolerated but enjoyed. We have initial revulsions to many substances; for example, many people can tell you about their first ac-quaintance with nicotine. For a substantial subset, the experi-ence included nausea to the point of vomiting. Of those who had these initial negative reactions, some are smokers years later, and they will have no trouble telling you about its plea-sures. Similar stories can be told about most psychoactive substances, including alcohol and caffeine. Stories like this can also be told about food for which one has to cultivate a taste. People can even cultivate sexual appetites that, to most people, seem unappealing. Through exposure, habituation, and practice, the cigarette smoke or the foie gras that seemed disgusting to the early teenager has become a cultivated taste for the adult. Similarly, for a very small segment of the population, the fear, loathing, and disgust associated with death can turn, not into mere tolerance, but into an appetite.

Reactions of some of the participants in the Rwandan genocide point to this same process, a merging of belonging and death themes. As noted elsewhere in this book, nature has seen to it that killing one's own—whether oneself or others—is hard to do. This is why rattlesnakes wrestle instead of bite each other and why soldiers shooting at one another in the Civil War and many other wars sometimes miss each other at very close range; and it is why many people who think about and even desire suicide do not enact it. Killing is usually too hard to do.

But circumstances can change this. They clearly did in the Rwandan tragedy. In the 1990s, ethnic divisions between Rwandan Hutus and Tutsis escalated and resulted in a several-month bloodbath in which Hutus killed several hundred thousand Tutsis, mostly face to face using machetes. In Jean Hatzfield's 2003 book *A Time for Machetes,* many instances are touched on in which Hutus, initially reluctant to inflict violence on their fellow countrymen, develop a taste for killing. There also developed a kind of fellowship in killing. A Hutu who had killed several of his Tutsi countrymen said, "In the tumult of the killings, stepping aside is not viable for a person, since that person would then find only his neighbours' backs to talk to about ordinary concerns. Being alone is too risky for us. So the person jumps up at the signal and takes part, even if the price is the bloody work" (pp. 226–227). To not belong, to be ostracized and "find only neighbors' backs," would risk death. Better to kill to belong, at least according to this individual.

Hutus killed to belong; suicide terrorists die to belong. In Japan, it is not rare for the need to belong to influence even conventional deaths by suicide. Numerous incidents have been documented in which people seek out companions over the Internet—not for a date, not for friendship, not to share hobbies and interests—but rather, to die together. The modal method is carbon monoxide poisoning, usually arranged by lighting charcoal in an enclosed space. In commenting on this phenomenon, the *New York Times* (May 2007) quoted Seoul's director of the Metropolitan Mental Health Center, who stated, "People are social animals. Some apparently want a companion even when committing suicide."

Why would people want a companion in suicide? The power of the belongingness motive and its potential to be subverted into accomplishing death offer one answer. Another involves the fact that death by suicide is fearsome and daunting. To face something fearsome (e.g., basic training in the military), most people would prefer to have help, to not have to go it alone. Most people who die by suicide are alone in death and were in life, intolerably so. That some who die by suicide want companionship in the act suggests to me: 1) belongingness is like fire in a drought-stricken forest—it is hard to eliminate and will spring up persistently and in surprising places; 2) the motive can be subverted and distorted in some instances, and I believe this characterizes not only the minds of suicide terrorists but also the minds of others who are suicidal; and 3) even though most people who die by suicide do so alone and in bereft circumstances, one wonders if they have belongingness wishes in their last moments. Do they see images of loved ones and maybe even come to regret their deaths for a second or two, too late to save themselves? Those who have survived near-fatal suicide attempts usually report that the answer to this question is probably "yes."

This viewpoint explains why some people want companionship even in death by suicide; a similar process may be relevant to why many people seem to want beauty even in death by suicide. There are numerous deaths by suicide every year in U.S. National Parks; in recent years, Arizona's Grand Canyon has been the most frequent spot. An article in the *Kansas City Star* (June 2008) quoted a spokesman for Yellowstone National Park, where five suicides had occurred since 1997, who stated, "Parks hold a special place in people's hearts. There are some individuals who feel it's important to have that kind of connection in those final moments." In his book *Death in Yellowstone,* Lee Whittlesey made a similar point: "Perhaps they chose Yellowstone in which to suicide because it was an idyllic or famous place to die. Or perhaps for some reason they wanted their deaths inextricably linked to nature" (p. 172). In her 2008 memoir, *Manic,* Terri Cheney wrote, "I had long since decided that Christmas Eve would be my last day on this earth. I chose Christmas Eve precisely because it had meaning and beauty—nowhere more so than in Santa Fe, with its enchanting festival of the *farolitos.* Every Christmas Eve, carolers come from all over the world to stroll the lantern-lit streets until dawn. All doors are open to them, and the air is pungent with the smell of warm cider and pinon. I wanted to die at such a moment, when the world was at its best, when I could offer up my heart to God and say, thank you, truly, for all of it" (pp. 8–9).

A surprising proportion of people who die by suicide in New York City are from out of town. One explanation—argued against elsewhere in this book—is that these are people who did not come to the city to die by suicide, but who, once there, did so impulsively. In my view, logic and evidence contradict the existence of truly rash, act-on-unplanned-impulses suicides. A more plausible view is that some people planfully go into the city on the occasion of a serious and momentous prospect, their own death by suicide. They do so for multiple reasons, some psychological and some pragmatic. Among the psychological reasons is that they see it as a fitting setting for an act that is final, fearsome, and daunting. The size and status of the city seems to them proportionate to an act that is momentous, not, I rush to add, in a romantic or glorious way—indeed often in a way that is tragic and grisly—but momentous nonetheless.

Although the analogy may seem jarring, some people may choose the spot of their death by suicide in a way that resembles the choice of a honeymoon location. For a honeymoon, people choose locations that are memorable, that seem fitting to an important occasion like marriage. Death is an important occasion too, and for some people, choices like New York City, the Eiffel Tower in Paris, or the Beachy Head cliffs in England may seem to fit the occasion.

This process seems to me a likely explanation for the fact that many people choose to die by suicide by jumping from

San Francisco's Golden Gate Bridge, whereas virtually no one chooses to jump from the Bay Bridge, also in San Francisco, also accessible, also lethally high. A main difference between the two bridges is aesthetic—the Golden Gate is very scenic and beautiful; the Bay Bridge, less so.

A couple of general caveats should be acknowledged. First, it is probable that people choose locations for death by suicide based on other reasons too. For instance, "hotspots" for death by suicide like the Golden Gate Bridge likely become hotspots not only because of factors related to aesthetics, but also because people have learned over the years that jumping from the bridge is indeed a lethal act. For an individual who has resolved death by suicide, lethality often is a consideration. Another consideration has to do with what might be termed "vicarious habituation." Death by suicide is a fearsome prospect, and to enact it, people have to grapple with their natural fear of it. To know that many others have already done a scary thing may encourage those who are fearful of it.

Other considerations involve pragmatics. As noted in the section on suicide and revenge, which emphasized that most suicides are not particularly vengeful, people may choose locations of death that will not directly involve their family and friends. To die in a downtown area of a major city, in a very remote location, or by jumping from a bridge ensures that discovery will be by authorities like police or EMTs. Family and friends are thus spared at least one aspect of suicide's traumatic aftermath. Relatedly, authorities in New York City or at the Golden Gate Bridge have repeatedly faced deaths by suicide, and so know what to do when it occurs. The person contemplating suicide may feel they will thus be less affected than authorities in less prominent places. That people consider factors like this may seem oddly calculating. But that is how suicidal behavior is—it is planful and often involves foresight certainly about the death itself but also about aspects of its aftermath.

The second general caveat is that of course not all people who die by suicide do so in scenic, momentous locations. Most do not. Most view their deaths as the result of alienation from and burdensomeness to others, and thus do not tend toward locations with elements of grandeur or beauty. In the section on suicide and revenge, I pointed out that some suicides are angry simply because some people are angry. In any large group of people, a subset will have angry temperaments, and that subset will tend to carry things through in an angry fashion, and this is so whether the activity is taking the car in for repairs, driving on the interstate, or death by suicide. A similar logic may be useful with regard to the choice of momentous suicide death scenes. In any large group of people, there will be a subset, who, in life, are attracted to cities and scenes associated with beauty, action, prestige, and so forth. In death, for some, this same attraction may be operative.

I don't want to take this "subset" logic too far, however. I think it applies well to the issue of angry suicides and also to the choice of scenic, momentous death locations. But when it comes to the question of life themes and death themes merging in the minds of suicidal people, I want to abandon the "subset" approach, because I think this merging is a universal process in suicide. It occurs in suicide terrorists with little doubt, as their ceremonies of being literally married to death reveal. It occurs in those who choose momentous scenes for their suicides. I think it applies to everyone who dies by suicide, because the act requires a kind of break in natural, usual thought about death. The break is to leave behind evolution's handiwork that we fear and revile death, and instead come to embrace it as nurturing, comforting, even loving. That this is very hard to wrap one's head around doesn't mean that it's wrong; it means that it is intensely difficult to grasp from this side of the break. The only thing that could be construed as a suicide note left by my dad read, "Could this be the answer?" I believe he wrote that as he was traversing the break—he was in between nature's default of "hell no, no way," and the mind of the lethally suicidal, which answers "yes." He eventually answered "yes," to all our detriment . . . and to his detriment, too. He would not have agreed in the moments before his death, however, because in a sense he was already gone. He was beyond that break, to the point of embracing death. This is *not* a point of no return. People can be brought back from this break. But to bring them back, they have to be detected first. Once detected, they have to be understood. And full understanding requires an acceptance of the qualitatively distinct viewpoint from which suicidal people see death.

2 / Suicidal Behavior

I t is difficult to observe fatal suicidal behavior as it occurs; indeed, I think this is in part because people about to die by suicide do not wish to be observed. They feel cut off from other people, certainly, but they also do not want their death to be any harder on loved ones than it already will be. Some fatal suicidal behavior has been witnessed, and some such examples will be touched on in this section, as they have been elsewhere in the book. Usually, though, behaviors have to be inferred in retrospect, through the features of death scenes or occasionally through suicide notes, when they are left. In this chapter, as in the previous one, some effort will be focused on explaining what does and what does *not* count as suicidal behavior. The treatment and prevention of suicidal behavior will get some attention in this chapter as well.

"The Death Scene Shows that the Cause of Death Was Not Suicide"

Let's concentrate first on the most well-characterized scenes in which the cause of death was suicide but might have been mistaken for homicide—those involving gunshots. Reports on this topic abound in the *American Journal of Forensic Medicine & Pathology*. A paper in 2002 examined three death scenes in which Smith & Wesson .38 or .357 revolvers were used. At all three scenes, the guns' cartridges were open. In one scene unspent ammo had fallen from the gun. How could a gun be the cause of death and subsequently be found with its cylinder open, unused ammo spilling out, unless it was homicide or involved a crime-scene meddler? To quote the authors, "Investigation revealed that firing the gun with the thumb on the cylinder release latch could disengage the cylinder. A combination of gravity and recoil impact against the thumb would open the cylinder and even allow the casing and the unspent cartridges to fall from the gun."

A 2001 report from the same journal reviewed over 1,700 cases of suicide by self-inflicted gunshot wound. In sixty-eight of the cases, the entrance wound was to the back of the head, contradicting a popular idea that such cases invariably involve homicide. In over thirty cases, the gun had been fired at intermediate range (e.g., more than two feet away), again contrary to the dictum that this signifies homicide. The majority of deaths by handgun, incidentally, involved wounds to the right temple, which might lead some to speculate on the symbolic meaning of choosing the right versus the left side of the head—indeed, the right side of the frontal lobes are, to simplify greatly, a seat of negative emotion. Shooting the right side of one's head could thus be viewed as an effort to stamp out negative emotions. Like most such speculations, however, it falls to a more sober and sensible one—most people are right-handed.

A report from 1999 adds to the list of "sure-fire" indications of homicide that are not so sure-fire. When people die by self-inflicted gunshot wound, the weapon remains in their hand in only around 25 percent of the cases. In the remaining instances, the gun is usually on or very near the decedent, but around 7 percent of the time, the gun falls from the hand and bounces away from the person, sometimes feet away. A considerable distance between the decedent and the gun is not necessarily suggestive of homicide.

Multiple gunshot wounds to the head have commonly been viewed as signatures of homicide, on the presumption that a first shot incapacitates a person, who then would be unable to fire subsequent shots. This is not always the case, however. In a 1998 issue of the *American Journal of Forensic Medicine & Pathology,* three cases are reported in which decedents had sustained self-inflicted gunshot wounds to the head; they not only survived, but they were not incapacitated by the wound. Each then fired a second shot, which resulted in death. Two of these three cases were initially investigated as homicides, though all three were later conclusively established as suicides.

Differentiating gun-related suicide from homicide can be difficult, as the preceding cases show. This difficulty extends, of course, to differentiating suicides from accidents, including when guns are involved. People do discharge guns by accident, occasionally with fatal consequences. When this occurs, the details of the scene can be suggestive of accident rather than suicide—details, for example, like absence of a suicide note, wound site, distance from which the person was shot, and location of the firearm after death. The problem, as we have seen, is that these are not sure-fire differentiators of suicide from other causes of death.

As noted in an earlier chapter, several instances have been documented in which people have died by self-inflicted gunshot wound while driving their cars on a highway. These initially appear to be single-vehicle, single-occupant accident fatalities—an impression which may be intentional on the part of the decedents. And this initial impression may stand if the investigation is cursory, especially when injuries sustained from the car wreck are extensive. Though it is impossible to tell for sure, it is at least possible that a death by suicide of this sort has been misclassified as an accident.

Of course, there are motor vehicle accidents not involving guns that nevertheless remain complex. In single-vehicle accident fatalities, the cause of death as lacerated organs or brain injuries from the crash is not difficult to establish, but determining whether the crash was accidental or intentional can be. In standard pathology textbooks, it is noted that people who attempt to brake just before the crash—and whose cars thus leave skid marks and whose shoes sometimes have the imprint of the brake on the sole—probably did not intend to die. This is sensible, but overlooks the fact that suicide is a fearsome prospect, and even someone who hurls their car at an embankment at great speed can have a change of heart at the last minute . . . unfortunately too late in some cases. The fact that people change their minds in midact seems to me indisputable, as evidenced by those who have jumped from places like the Golden Gate Bridge and survived. Many of them recall feeling profound regret at their choice in midair. In the case of single-vehicle car wrecks, even instances when people accelerate toward an obstacle can be unclear. One can view acceleration as a sign of intentionality, but acceleration can also occur in people who, in their panic, hit the accelerator by mistake instead of the brake.

In his 1971 book *The Savage God*, Alvarez describes the suicide of Sylvia Plath, whom he knew well. Plath had attempted suicide at least twice before her death, and Alvarez believes that those attempts, though not fatal, were higher in intent to die than her actual fatal attempt, natural gas poisoning. He believes the fatal attempt was actually more of a cry for help because of certain features of her death scene. For instance, she left a note saying to call her doctor. Why, Alvarez wonders, would she leave a note to call the doctor if she did not believe she would be discovered alive? Also, the night before her death, Plath had a long conversation with her downstairs neighbor, part of which involved her lingering over whether he would be awake by a certain time in the morning. Why, Alvarez asks, would Plath be so concerned about what time the neighbor wakes up, if not to ensure that he would be awake in time to let in the nanny who, in turn, would discover Plath in time to save her?

I think, however, that these questions about Plath's death are answerable. In addition to her two serious suicide attempts, the evidence suggests that she was particularly depressed near the end of her life. For example, Alvarez noticed her disheveled appearance before her death—an appearance that for Plath was very unusual. Why did she want the doctor contacted? To let him know she was dead, because he would know what to do. Why ascertain the neighbor's schedule? To make sure he would not interrupt her plan for suicide. In this instance, Alvarez uses elements of a death scene not to mistake a suicide for an accident but rather to mistake an intended suicide for one that was meant to be survived.

Another mistake that can occur regarding death scenes is simply to have a low level of skepticism. In his 1938 book *Man Against Himself,* Karl Menninger describes a newspaper story about a man who shot himself and was discovered soon thereafter when a neighbor heard the shot. The man gasped to the neighbor that he was sleeping and dreaming when he shot himself, and then died. Menninger relates this story as if it were true, when it is far more likely that the attempt was intentional and that the man's gasps about sleeping and dreaming were part of a gunshot-induced delirium or equivocations to cover his motives, or else made up or misunderstood by the neighbor.

An incident that occurred in my hometown of Tallahassee, Florida, illustrates official and public misunderstanding of suicidal behavior, as well as the myth that this or that feature of a death scene does or does not indicate suicide. In March 2007 on a Friday night at 9:44 P.M., a man lying in a fetal position on the railroad tracks was hit by an oncoming train. The man was taken to the hospital in critical condition with fractures to his legs as well as head injuries. The police officer investigating the incident said, "We've had several people struck by a train on the tracks. We need to get the word out to people. Don't sleep on the train tracks."

The local paper that reported the incident has an online reader response section. Suffice it to say that the event and the officer's remarks generated little compassion. For instance, one reader responded, "Thanks officer, maybe we can add some of these 'pointers' to your list: 'Placing a plastic bag on your head is dangerous.' 'Standing in the middle of the interstate is prohibited.' 'Leaping from an airplane without a parachute is going to hurt.' Get the word out not to sleep on the train tracks? Quote of the year!" Another reader stated, "I don't have sympathy for this incident. Perhaps this individual has or had horrible life circumstances which robbed him of house and home, but there are myriad other places to sleep, much more comfortable than a bed of rock and timber and big metal things."

What astounds me about these statements—including that of the officer—is the lack of awareness that this may very well have been a suicide attempt. In my view, the likelihood that one chooses to sleep on the tracks or that one happens to land there in a drunken stupor—at the very time that a train is coming—pales compared to the likelihood that one lies down on the tracks specifically in order to attempt suicide. Indeed, the leader of the American Association for Suicidology's ongoing project to establish the prevalence rate of suicides on railways told me that although there are no precise data on the issue (thus the need for the project), there are at least a few hundred such deaths in the United States each year, possibly more . . . and this does not even include nonlethal attempts, which are also numerous. Indeed, in November 2007, a man in Arkansas was involved in a car accident; he was hospitalized, but soon checked himself out of the hospital against medical advice. A few hours later, police found the man on the porch of a house near the train tracks. The man asked the officers for water, at which point they noticed that one of his arms was missing at the shoulder. The arm was found about an hour later, but was too damaged to be reattached. This story was reported under the premise that the man fell asleep on the tracks, again without mention of the possibility that the incident represented a suicide attempt (perhaps one in which the man changed his mind at the last instant, soon enough to save his life but not in time to get himself fully clear of the train).

These examples demonstrate the fallacious nature of the view that this or that feature of a death scene indicates suicide (or indicates any manner of death for that matter), but I think they show two additional things as well. First, talented medical examiners are invaluable, because much expertise is needed to shed the light of truth on death scenes. Second, to harbor doubts about the manner of a loved one's death only forestalls coming to terms with the loss; many people doubt that their loved ones died by suicide, even when they actually did, and this misfortune can be laid at the doorstep of persistent misunderstandings about suicide death scenes.

"Most People Who Die by Suicide Leave a Note"

Let's get straight to the truth here—no study has found a rate of note-leaving among suicide decedents to exceed 50 percent. Most studies find rates between 0 and 40 percent; a reasonable average would be approximately 25 percent. To give a sense of the low end of the percentage range, a 1997 study in the *American Journal of Forensic Medicine & Pathology* surveyed cases of suicide by self-incineration in Denmark over a ten-year span. They located forty-three cases, none of which seems to have been motivated by political or religious factors (e.g., political protest). In many ways, the decedents seemed similar to others who die by suicide by other means; for example, they were very likely to have been suffering from a mental disorder and to have attempted suicide in the past. They were similar in another way too—no note was found for any of the forty-three. Even allowing for the possibility that some notes may have been lost to fire, this study, like all others, places note-leavers in the minority.

Three-quarters of those who die by suicide do not leave a note. Knowledge of this simple fact could save a lot of heartache and confusion, and probably some money as well. It is not rare for relatives of suicide decedents—and from time to time even experienced investigators—to question whether a death was a suicide or not simply because no note was left. Closure for relatives—and closure of sometimes expensive investigations—can be facilitated by knowledge that suicide notes are rare.

Though the notion that suicide death scenes almost always

include a note is a myth that causes needless distress, I understand why the myth is hard to dispel. When my dad died by suicide in his car, investigators told my mother that there appeared to be no suicide note, though there was a cryptic message scribbled on a small piece of paper near the driver's seat. In the days and weeks following my dad's death, one of the most salient experiences for me was sheer disbelief that my dad would have killed himself, and the fact that he did not communicate to our family before his death—no goodbye, no note—only made things more unbelievable.

What was this cryptic note found in my dad's car? I asked my mother about it, but the investigators did not tell her clearly what the note said, and it was not among his belongings that my uncle and I later retrieved from the morgue. As the months passed and I worked hard to come to terms with my dad's death, I came to view the note as just one of the many things that my dad would often scribble to himself on scraps of paper throughout his life.

Soon after my dad died, I obtained the report from the autopsy that had been conducted on my dad's body. It made for very disturbing reading, but I am completely convinced that facing this extremely difficult aspect of my dad's death, one of the harder things I have ever done, facilitated my recovery and healing from the shock and agony of his suicide. The materials sent to me contained no reference to a cryptic note.

Years later, I reread the report, and for the first time noticed a passing reference to tests that were not part of the report. I contacted the office of the medical examiner in Atlanta where my dad died. This office very helpfully and quickly sent me a few additional pages of material, which summarized toxicology findings (unremarkable), and which included a page onto which a sticky note had been photocopied. The sticky note was the one investigators had mentioned to my mom, and it read, in handwriting that clearly was my dad's, though messier than usual, "Could this be the answer?"

Reading the note fifteen years after my dad's suicide, I remarked that either it was one of the many notes he regularly wrote himself and had nothing to do with his death (he could have been searching for the answer to a career issue, for instance), or it was about his suicide, and if so, I noted the painfully lonely tone of it. It is not a communication to his family or to the world, but only to himself, and only about his own death by suicide. Had I read the note a few days or weeks after his death, I believe I would have viewed it as a suicide note, and though I would have found its brevity and tone heartbreaking, I think it might have been helpful in my coming to terms with his death. Relative to many survivors of loved ones' suicides, I had few questions about whether my dad was killed or killed himself. But I had the occasional question, and this note might have quieted them somewhat.

Thus the power of this particular myth. When a note is present, it has the power to address if not answer urgent questions. When a note is absent, these questions are not only left unaddressed, but they lead to other disquieting questions and doubts, such as the possibility of homicide versus suicide. This emotionally charged symbol, the suicide note, thus has an understandable power, but it is crucial that this power not obscure the equally powerful truth that suicide notes are rare, and that their absence signifies nothing.

Why are they so rare? Some have reasoned that impulsivity is involved in suicidal behavior and that therefore suicidal people often impulsively kill themselves before they have a chance to write a note. There are several problems with this viewpoint, however. A major problem is that it draws on a distinct myth about suicide, that dying on an impulsive whim is common—a myth I discussed and dismissed earlier. Another problem is the lack of empirical support; if it were true that note-leavers are much less impulsive than those who do not leave a note, then this difference should be easy to demonstrate in psychological autopsy studies that examine the lives and characteristics of decedents, including their personalities. But this difference has not been clearly demonstrated.

The life and death of musician Kurt Cobain illustrates some of these points. He was a very impulsive personality, but to say that he died on a whim is to ignore reams of evidence. In his journals, in his songs, and in his conversations, he frequently thought of suicide. He was impulsive, but he did not die impulsively . . . and he left a note.

So the question remains, why is it rare for those who die by suicide to leave a note? It seems unthinkable to many that someone would deliberately choose to leave one's family, friends, and life itself, and not to say goodbye in a note. While this view is understandable, and while I have personal sympathy for it, it represents a line of reasoning that cannot be followed by the person contemplating suicide. That person is in a categorically different frame of mind. To say that people who die by suicide are lonely at the time of their deaths is only to begin to approximate the truth, rather like saying that the ocean is wet. Loneliness, alienation, isolation, rejection, and ostracism are a better approximation, but still do not capture it fully. In fact, I believe that it is impossible to capture the phenomenon fully in words, because it is so beyond ordinary experience, much as it is difficult to conceive of what might be beyond the edge of the universe.

Some verses written by Sylvia Plath come close to articulating this bereft state of mind. "I'm finally through./The black telephone's off at the root,/The voices just can't worm through." These lines suggest a psychological condition that is beyond loneliness, a sense that connections to others are not only absent but are obliterated. And so the answer to why suicide decedents usually do not communicate to others through notes is that the line of interpersonal connection is broken— "off at the root" in Plath's words. The fact that some do communicate before their deaths, either in notes or otherwise, reflects the power of the need to belong and connect. Even when this need is obliterated, it can still wield influence, and can in turn contribute to the ambivalence about life and death that even profoundly suicidal people feel.

It should be remembered, though, that suicide notes are left by people who feel disconnected enough to have carried through with the fearsome activity of causing one's own death. Therefore, it would be surprising if the notes contained a lot of material reflecting emotional connection to those left behind. In fact, many such notes are quite unemotional, and have matter-of-fact tone and content. Suicide notes often contain instructions regarding day-to-day matters, such as the location of keys or a reminder that a bill needs to be paid. My students, colleagues, and I published a study on suicide notes in a 2002 issue of the *Journal of Social and Clinical Psychology.* Some excerpts of the notes read: "I will give you $5000, that's what I figured I owe you. I left your contract and listings on the desk"; "Please call the police before you open the door, I have shot myself"; "Police, my car keys are in my pocket. Please drive my car home. My daughter needs it to drive back-and-forth to work"; and, "You have my permission to withdraw all my savings etc. to pay off bills."

A study in the April 2007 issue of *Archives of Suicide Research* revealed one parameter of suicide notes involving their matter-of-fact tone: sentence length. In this study, genuine suicide notes contained shorter sentences than notes that were simulated—the simulated notes were written by people who hypothetically imagined that they intended to die by suicide and were preparing their suicide note. The short sentences are consistent with the business of leaving instructions for day-to-day matters, but they are also consistent with a phenomenon known as cognitive constriction.

Intense negative emotion narrows attentional focus to concrete thoughts, goals, sensations, and movements. This constricting of cognition takes offline higher-level thinking, like foresight about the consequences of one's current actions. This is one prominent feature of the state of mind of the person preparing to die by suicide. The effort and mechanics of suicide sap attentional resources, so that either there is none left over to even think to write a note, or the note pays little heed to larger, longer-term emotional issues, and focuses instead on relatively low-level trivia like keys and bills to be paid.

Notice, by way of contrast, the "suicide note" left by the man mentioned earlier who, in the dust on the hood of his car, wrote "suicide is painless," and who then disappeared. This is perhaps the most dubious "suicide note" I have ever heard about, for many reasons (including of course that he was later found alive). First, the man had been convicted of fraud and was supposed to report to prison on the day his car was discovered. Second, as I pointed out earlier, people who really intend death by suicide would not write something as flip as "suicide is painless" because they understand its daunting, intimidating quality. Finally, and relevant to the current section on the relative rarity and the usual features of suicide notes, it is unusual for suicide notes to contain abstractions. When they do contain such abstractions, the abstractions are almost always drowned out by more concrete, everyday references. The man's note betrayed him.

We have seen thus far that the absence of notes, as well as their matter-of-fact tone in the relatively rare instances notes are present, indicate key features of the suicidal mind— namely "off at the root" loneliness and cognitive constriction. There is yet another aspect of notes that deserves emphasis, and this one is the most surprising—and to some, disturbing—of them all: It is not uncommon for suicide notes to reflect considerable positive emotion.

In the same study from the April 2007 issue of *Archives of*

Suicide Research that compared genuine to simulated suicide notes, the researchers reported that the genuine notes had approximately two times the rate of positive emotional expressions as compared to the simulated notes. These authors, together with past researchers, attribute these positive expressions to the ambivalence inherent in the suicidal mind, which is a plausible account. However, an important but neglected reason for the expression of positive emotion in suicide notes has to do with the resolution of ambivalence, rather than with ambivalence per se. That is, in addition to ongoing misery, many people who are about to die by suicide have achieved a kind of peace and relief due to their decision, and this peace and relief facilitates the expression of positive emotion. That it is difficult to understand how someone would be in a peaceful, relieved state of mind just before death by suicide shows the light-years' distance between the suicidal mind and the state of mind of everyone else. They are just in a different place than the rest of us—when one is in that state of mind, the answer to my dad's question "Could this be the answer?" can become not just "yes," but "yes" with a sense of steely resolve and calm unity of purpose.

The dissertation of my former student Dr. Foluso Lawal-Solarin demonstrated this increasing sense of resolve in the writings of two people who died by suicide. One was musician Kurt Cobain, whose writings as his death approached are available in his published journals. The other was a diary of a young man who posted his writing to the Web before his death by suicide. These two were compared to two men who were not suicidal. Unlike the writing of the nonsuicidal men, the writing of the two who died by suicide contained increasing expressions of certainty as their deaths neared. This certainty was sometimes couched in religious terms. Religious expressions, too, increased over time in the writings of the suicidal men. These findings not only confirm that suicidal people express a kind of resolve as their deaths approach, but also emphasize that religious expressions do not necessarily signal a reliable buffer against suicidality (as some believe)—indeed, in these two men increasing religiosity seemed related to their increasing resolve to die.

A seeming contradiction may have occurred to you: I have said that suicide notes often contain positive emotional expressions and I have said that suicidal people are flooded with negative emotions—"off at root" alienation and feelings related to being a burden on others. Can both of these emotional states simultaneously characterize those who are about to end their lives?

From the research literature on the nature of emotion, it has been determined that people can simultaneously feel negative and positive emotions. For example, it is not hard to imagine feeling alert and active—states that are positive in nature—and simultaneously feeling distressed and upset—negative states. Research on college students, older adults, and various patient populations has shown this to be true. My colleagues and I have even shown it was likely true throughout history. We focused on letters home from war written by soldiers in the seventeenth and nineteenth centuries, having judges rate the letters on various emotional dimensions. When we subjected these ratings to standard statistical analyses, we showed that the structure of emotion was similar then as it is now. That is, it is not common for people to simultaneously experience positive and negative emotions, but neither is it terribly rare.

One reason it is not rare—and one particularly relevant to the suicidal state of mind—is that attention and emotion do not operate in lockstep. One can be prevailingly distressed about an ongoing personal problem but experience momentary pleasure in the accomplishments of a friend or relative, for example. Similarly, the prevailing emotional state of suicidal people is profoundly negative, stemming as it does from their view that their lives have derailed to the point that they feel their death would represent a contribution to others and from feelings of deep alienation. However, in the moments and hours preceding death—and occasionally in the days preceding death—attention is focused on, constricted to, the suicide plan, and the resolution to die can, in some suicidal people, overlay feelings of calm and resolve on top of the ongoing negative emotions.

The suicide note of Japan's farm minister, Toshikatsu Matsuoka, seemed to contain this positive overlay to a very negative situation. In May 2007, Matsuoka hanged himself in his Tokyo apartment as he faced a series of political scandals that very negatively affected the government of Prime Minister Shinzo Abe. His suicide note was upbeat, including his wish of "banzai," or long life, to Abe's government and to the people of Japan.

Similarly, the South Korean actress Jeong Da-bin, who died by suicide in February 2007, posted a note to her Web site that touched upon ongoing turmoil overlain with resolve and relief. She wrote, "For no reason at all, I am going crazy with anger. Then, as if lightening [sic] had struck, all becomes quiet. Then the Lord comes to me. The Lord says I will be O.K. YES, I WILL BE O.K." Within twenty-four hours of posting these words, she was found dead by hanging in her boyfriend's apartment.

We have seen that suicide notes are relatively rare, and when present, are not what most imagine—for instance, they are mundane and contain a surprising amount of positivity. Knowing some of these basic facts can make a difference in highly emotionally charged real-world cases. Investigators—and families—should pay little heed to the absence of a suicide note; this absence is the norm, and there are tractable reasons for it, including the deeply alienated state of mind of the person about to die by suicide. Those notes that do exist are reflective of the state of mind of someone in suicidal crisis—often the notes are uncommunicative, matter of fact, and may even show positive expressions like resolve and certainty; more rarely, they may show blame or anger. Whatever the expression in the note, it is key for family members to recall that it represents their loved ones in a highly unusual state, one that is very unrepresentative of their lived life. My dad wrote, "Could this be the answer?" and it would be a mistake for me to focus on this lonely question about his death and to forget about the many times when he was thriving and far from alone.

Suicidal Behavior and Contagion

In one sense, suicides do cluster together, an important public health problem, but to call suicide "contagious" is misleading. Imitative learning exists, no doubt, and has been observed across the animal kingdom. In his wonderful book *The Fatal Conceit,* F. A. Hayek mentions "the capacity to learn by imitation as one of the prime benefits conferred during our long instinctual development. Indeed, perhaps the most important capacity with which the human individual is genetically endowed, beyond innate responses, is his ability to acquire skills by largely imitative learning" (p. 21).

But because a learning mechanism exists (and is profoundly important) does not necessarily mean that it applies in every context. In 2005, an 8-year-old girl died by suicide in the United Kingdom. She fashioned a noose from her clothing, fastened it to a curtain pole in her bedroom, and hanged herself. Her mother found her, and, stunned and horrified, called emergency services. They were able to revive the girl, but she died in the hospital a few days later. This tragedy was reported in the *Sun* with the title, "Copycat suicide inspired by film." The film in question, *Girl, Interrupted,* does indeed depict a scene in which a female psychiatric patient hangs herself, and a copy of the movie was found in the girl's room. Misinformed of the facts, the local coroner stated, "An eight-year-old could not intend to take her own life." He went on to say, "She may have been imitating something," and advised parents to be careful about which movies their children see.

As covered later in this book, children can in fact intend

suicide, as hundreds of deaths per year show. But what of the other part of the coroner's statement, that she may have been imitating something? The reporter seems to agree with the coroner in using the term "copycat" in the title of the news article about the girl's death.

The only solid piece of evidence for the claim that the girl was imitating the scene from *Girl, Interrupted* is that the movie was found in her room, along with many others. There is no evidence reported that she saw the movie, and if she did, when she saw it (the film came out in 1999, when the girl was 2; she died in 2005 at age 8). There is no evidence that the movie made a particular impression on the young girl; for instance, there is no record of her talking about the movie with family or friends, no writing of hers showing a particular interest in the film in general or the hanging scene in particular. And yet the coroner and evidently many others attribute the death to the movie.

Why not similarly attribute the death of model Ruslana Korshunova, who jumped to her death in late June 2008 from a Manhattan apartment, to the 1990 movie *Ghost?* The premise of the film was that the character of the husband dies and returns as a ghost to relate to the character of his wife in a very romantic way. The movie is thus open to the criticism that it romanticizes death, and it is clear that the model Korshunova saw it in the hours before her suicide. The reason not to attribute her death to the movie is that it would be inaccurate to do so; she had many ongoing troubles that explain her death much more plausibly. Even though Korshunova definitely saw the movie before her death, uncertain in the case of the young girl, neither suicide can be traced to undue influence of a movie.

The claim that a movie, book, or song led someone to engage in this or that act is fairly common. Before he killed John Lennon, Mark David Chapman was obsessed with J. D. Salinger's novel *The Catcher in the Rye,* and indeed, had a copy with him when the shooting occurred, but in this instance, no one really blamed the book. Should they have? On the one hand, the book really had little to do with the idea of shooting a famous person. Salinger certainly in no way advised or encouraged that readers should hurt someone. On the other hand, in Chapman's mind, the book actually did have a lot to do with it, in that Chapman shared the book's main character's disgust with "phoniness," and Chapman's perception that Lennon was "phony" (e.g., wrote "imagine no possessions" yet owned many houses) was a primary motive in the crime. Still, virtually no one blames J. D. Salinger for Lennon's death; they blame Chapman and his mental illness.

Timothy McVeigh blew up the Murrah Federal Building in Oklahoma City in 1995, killing 168 people, a crime for which he was deeply reviled and for which he was put to death in 2001. Most people remember McVeigh and attribute the bombing to him and his co-conspirator. Fewer may recall that McVeigh was playing out a scene in a book that influenced him profoundly. The book was *The Turner Diaries,* published in 1978 under the pseudonym Andrew Macdonald by a white supremacist named William Luther Pierce. Among many other appalling things, the book describes the bombing of a federal building in terms that have many similarities to what actually occurred in Oklahoma City. It is not unreasonable to say that McVeigh "copycatted" the book. Unlike *The Catcher in the Rye* for Mark David Chapman, *The Turner Diaries* did encourage people to go out and do destructive things, and McVeigh was clear that the book influenced him. The book was in McVeigh's possession when he was arrested on the day of the bombing; in fact, it was the only book in his possession at the time. Few people primarily blame Pierce (though he was hardly a blameless character) or his horrid book for what happened that day in Oklahoma City; rather, they blame McVeigh, his accomplice, and their deluded ideas.

The 8-year-old girl mentioned above had many movies in her possession, not to mention books and other things. She told no one of the movie's influence on her, and yet that one movie is, in part, blamed for her death by suicide. McVeigh had only the one book in his possession at the time of his arrest, told many people of its profound influence on him, and yet the book was mostly not blamed. This strikes me as incongruous.

In the days before her death, the girl wrote "help me, help me" in a kind of health journal project that all the kids at her school were keeping for a class—the notation was not found until after her death. Eight-year-old children can and do develop major depressive disorder, and like many disorders and illnesses, the childhood-onset version is especially pernicious. The terms "major depressive disorder" and "especially pernicious" are like components of a simple math equation, with suicidality being the outcome. The girl died by hanging, which is not at all rare among child suicides, especially girls. Indeed such deaths are on the increase, and have been shown to be the most common method among children ages 10–14 in the United States. The U.S. Centers for Disease Control and Prevention reported that suicides by suffocation (mostly hanging) accounted for about 71 percent of all suicides in girls aged 10–14.

If a person is depressed (as the girl may have been, given her health journal entry and her subsequent death by suicide), then early age of onset suggests poor prognosis. Poor prognosis for major depression almost always includes substantial suicidality. Given that a child has engaged in suicidal behavior, the chances are high that hanging was involved, and this is even more the case for girls. This line of thinking strikes me as a more plausible and parsimonious view of the young girl's tragic death than the idea that a movie she may or may not have watched was to blame.

Whenever cases like this have been litigated, courts seem to agree with the viewpoint advocated here. For instance, both Ozzy Ozbourne and the band Judas Priest have been sued for contributing to deaths by suicide through their music's lyrics. In the Judas Priest case, two young men were smoking marijuana, drinking, and listening to Judas Priest. The young men each had histories of substance abuse and behavioral problems. They formed a suicide pact and shot themselves with a 12-gauge shotgun; one died, the other survived. The families sued Judas Priest for lyrics such as "Keep the world with all its sin/It's not fit for living in." Moreover, the suit claimed that the recordings contained subliminal messages which, when, played backward, stated "let's be dead" and "do it." Judas Priest's manager retorted, in a statement that was not particularly nice but that had a point, "If we were going to do that [subliminal messages], I'd be saying, 'Buy seven copies,' not telling a couple of screwed-up kids to kill themselves."

The claim here, like that in the girl's case, is that people are "copycatting" what they are seeing or hearing, that the media stimulus is a cause of these young people's deaths by suicide. Significantly, Judas Priest won this court battle; Ozbourne won a similar one; and had those associated with *Girl, Interrupted* been taken to court, all indications are that they would not have been held liable either.

Let's summarize: the only case of "copycatting" that would stand up to real standards of evidence that I have discussed thus far is not a death by suicide at all, but the bombings committed by Timothy McVeigh. *The Turner Diaries* very much encouraged and indeed glorified the sort of behavior he mimicked, and it specifically details the bombing of a federal building. McVeigh owned the book; it was the only book on him at the time of his arrest. He openly proclaimed his admiration for it and the effect the book had on him. Crucially, too, McVeigh was fertile ground for this kind of effect; his documented narcissistic and paranoid personality features, his depression about his own life, and his obsession with the government and its excesses (Joiner et al., 2007) opened him to the pernicious effects of a stimulus like *The Turner Diaries,* and 168 deaths resulted.

The example of McVeigh shows that a kind of "copycatting" can and does occur. The perpetrator had specific, pre-existing vulnerabilities, which were activated by a noxious stimulus that fit the vulnerabilities and with which the person had close and ongoing familiarity and contact. None of the other examples discussed in this chapter has this signature. The young girl, Mark David Chapman, and the two young men listening to Judas Priest all had pre-existing vulnerabilities, to be sure. But in each of their cases, a noxious stimulus is not involved in a persuasive way. The courts said as much in the Judas Priest case; in the case of Mark David Chapman and *The Catcher in the Rye*, there simply is nothing in the book about doing such a thing; and in the case of the young girl, there is scant evidence of close and ongoing familiarity and contact with the film *Girl, Interrupted*. Put differently, there is a likelihood that the individuals involved would have done what they did even if Judas Priest, *The Catcher in the Rye*, and *Girl, Interrupted* never existed.

Another version of this myth is that mentioning suicidal thoughts or behaviors in a clinical screening situation will plant suicidality in the minds of patients. If this strikes you as wrong, it should. It is as if a neurologist who asked about migraines could thereby implant them. Unfortunately, this is not a rare belief, even among those who should know better. Madelyn Gould and colleagues have hopefully solved this problem, at least in part; they conducted a definitive study on the topic, described in the *Journal of the American Medical Association* in 2005. In six high schools in New York State, these researchers studied over 2,300 students who participated in a health screening survey over the course of two days. Crucial to the study, half of the students' surveys contained questions about suicidality; the other half's surveys contained no such questions. If suicidality gets implanted in unsuspecting minds, the first group should have higher post-survey suicidality scores, and this is perhaps even more the case if they were distressed to begin with.

What actually happened was that there were no differences between the two groups of students, either immediately after they completed the survey or two days later. The groups showed no differences on general distress, depressive symptoms, and quite important, of course, suicidal ideation. Very intriguingly, there did seem to be some differences between high-risk students who were screened for suicidality versus high-risk students who were not. (In this study, "high risk" was defined as having current depressive symptoms, current substance use problems, and/or a previous suicide attempt.) Among these high-risk students, being asked about suicidality, far from planting the idea in their head and making them worse, actually seemed to improve their state of mind. High-risk students asked about suicidality endorsed *less* depression and *less* suicidal ideation after screening as compared to high-risk students not asked about suicidality. There may have been something actively helpful about being asked candid questions about suicidality, at least for some students, and in any event, the notion that asking backfires was not supported.

My students and I recently reported a similar finding in the *Journal of Social & Clinical Psychology* in 2008. The work was not specific to suicidality but certainly included it. We developed a diagnostic feedback script, which clinicians delivered to patients once diagnoses were established. The script contained candid and no-nonsense descriptions of the diagnosed disorders, what is known about them, and what the treatment options are. We used the script regardless of diagnosis (although of course it was tailored to the particulars of the relevant disorders)—borderline personality disorder, schizophrenia, bipolar disorder, major depressive disorder, bulimia, and on and on, and we used the script regardless of whether suicidality was a major component of the patient's presentation. Whatever the diagnosis and presentation were, we described them to patients with an "all cards on the table" attitude. And patients liked it. Mood ratings improved from before to after the delivery of the script and these improvements in mood did not seem to be fleeting. Moreover, these improvements applied across diagnoses; people who received diagnoses of personality disorders, for instance, experienced the same mood improvement as did patients with other diagnoses.

Marsha Linehan and colleagues reported a similar result in a 2006 paper in the journal *Suicide & Life-Threatening Behavior*. They studied sixty-three women who met criteria for borderline personality disorder and who were also experiencing current suicidality superimposed upon a history of past suicidality—a high-risk group who, one could argue, might be prone to having suicidality triggered by an interviewer asking questions about it. These researchers used a detailed and comprehensive interview-based assessment of suicide risk and found that post-interview changes in suicidality were small in size and fairly rare, and, when they occurred, the changes were if anything more likely to involve decreased suicidality than increased suicidality.

So with this evidence in hand, why are people inclined to believe that a suicidal act can be influenced by something like a book or a movie? Later in this book, I describe a man who believes, among other questionable things, that he is a "witch," and further, that one of the most common sites for suicide in England, the cliffs at Beachy Head, draw people there to die because spiritual energy lines intersect there. In an interview, he stated, "If someone wants to kill themselves, they're going to do it . . . If somebody has that inside themselves, they'll do it, whether it's by gun, whether it's by electricity, whether it's by Beachy Head. My explanation is that it's a kind of paranormal thing, not so much the publicity. I mean, I had a Beachy Head piece in the *Sunday Mirror,* and about seven people jumped off the top after that, but they would have done it anyway."

The man is making an error in logic that is distressingly common in this area. There are times, as the man noted, in which people probably "would have done it anyway." Indeed, I believe the examples of Mark David Chapman, the young men listening to Judas Priest, and the young girl who owned the movie *Girl, Interrupted* are roughly of this type. It is likely they would have acted even in the absence of the purported stimulus. But not all such incidents are of this type, as the example of McVeigh arguably shows. When *vulnerable* people are exposed to a *noxious* stimulus, untoward things may result. Talking about suicide in a way that makes it seem romantic, spiritual, or glorious is a noxious stimulus, and if such talk appears in a newspaper with a large circulation, it will inevitably be read by vulnerable people. This is one reason that the media guidelines put out by the American Association of Suicidology could not be clearer: Do *not* place things in the media that glorify or romanticize suicidal behavior.

In the paragraph above, I italicized the terms "vulnerable" and "noxious" because these are essential to a full understanding of what occurs in any incident involving mass injury, illness, or death. When people in the same general location get sick or die at more or less the same time, it is reasonable to wonder why. Of course, answers can be woefully incorrect and virulent, such as the view, relatively common in the 1300s and 1400s, that various minorities like the Romany and Jews caused the Black Plague—or, they can be true, and save lives, such as when an outbreak of bacterial meningitis is recognized and contained. Notice that in both these examples, contagious agents—bacteria—are at play. And notice too that the cause of death in these examples is passed on from individual to individual in sequential, causal fashion (i.e., a "vector" in public health terms).

But of course, a moment's reflection reveals that, when groups of people fall ill, become injured, or die, the cause need not be bacterial or viral contagions. Many died in the United States on September 11, 2001. Similarly, in the industrial disasters at Chernobyl (nuclear) and Bhopal, India (chemical gas leak), many were sickened or killed in the same locale and at the same time, but the cause had nothing to do with contagions.

In these tragedies, the cause of death was *not* passed on from individual to individual, and a key factor was people's pre-arranged contiguity—people were already in the World

Trade Center and already living near Chernobyl or Bhopal. At Chernobyl and Bhopal, exposure to the lethal stimulus was not perfectly correlated with death, because some stronger, healthier people with high exposure survived, whereas those who were already ill or otherwise vulnerable did not, despite lower exposure.

In what sense is suicidal behavior contagious? Which analogy is better—viral and bacterial contagions, or industrial accidents? In my opinion, many misunderstandings have occurred by likening suicidal behavior to contagious illnesses, when the analogy to disasters like Chernobyl and Bhopal is much more apt.

To get a better handle on this issue, some background is necessary. First we must distinguish between "point clusters"—those occurring in a specific location, often a school or small community—versus "media clusters"—those that affect people across many communities (potentially across the world) who learn about a celebrity's suicide or are otherwise exposed by the media to a death by suicide (Joiner, 1999). An example of a "point" or "local" cluster is several suicides occurring within a few weeks within the same high school or town (like the series of suicides in Bridgend, Wales, in 2007 and 2008). An example of a "media" cluster would be several deaths by suicide occurring around the world within hours or days of the death by suicide of a famous individual.

The bottom line on these phenomena is that "local" clusters occur beyond any doubt, whereas "media" clusters may well exist too, though the claims for them are not entirely persuasive. In the case of a "media" cluster, the viral/bacterial contagion analogy clearly is not apt, because the harmful agent—something that has appeared on TV or in the paper—is not being passed on from person to person. By contrast, the industrial accident analogy fits "media" clusters reasonably well, in that people are being simultaneously exposed to a noxious agent which harms them, especially those who are vulnerable to begin with. Suicides in "media" clusters are not contagious any more than the poisonous gas at Bhopal or the radiation at Chernobyl were contagious.

What, then, about "point clusters"? Might they fit a contagion model, in that one person is affected, and then another person nearby is affected, and so on? It is conceivable, but I don't think this is what is going on. At least, it's not the main thing going on. Rather, the point-clustering of victims may be seen, much like an industrial accident, as the simultaneous effects of some pernicious, external influence on a pre-arranged group of people—pre-arranged either because they live near one another, because they watch or read the same media, or because they gravitate toward the same interests and social circle.

In the case of the industrial accident, the "external, pernicious" agent is not in question—it is radiation or poisonous gas. What is it in point-clustered suicides? The answer, in a phrase, is "severe, personally relevant negative events." Crucially, one example of such an event is the death by suicide of a friend, acquaintance, or a person that one admires but does not know. Consider, for instance, a small group of teenage girls whose fondness for substance abuse and sense of alienation from school and social circles draws them together. One of the girls makes a lethal suicide attempt. The situation of the remaining girls is precarious; not only do they have pre-existing risk factors like substance abuse and alienation, they now have the additional, acute risk of the loss by suicide of a friend. And not only that—they have now learned a lesson, at least implicitly, along the lines of "my friend did that and she is like me; that means that I can do it too if I want." In other words, the remaining girls vicariously habituate, through their friend's behavior, to the idea of death by suicide. As I have argued in *Why People Die by Suicide*, habituation to harming oneself is a key precondition to serious suicidal behavior. This kind of process may have been at play in the two young men who listened to the music of Judas Priest and who made very serious suicide attempts, one lethal.

There was serious concern that a process like this would be at play following the death by suicide of Nirvana musician Kurt Cobain in 1994. Cobain was an extremely well-known figure, widely admired among young people; he was among the leading lights of a kind of music that was popular if not predominant in the early 1990s, and which originated in the U.S. Pacific Northwest, especially in and around Seattle. He died by self-inflicted gunshot wound in Seattle, probably on April 5, 1994. He was discovered on April 8, 1994, and that is when the news story broke about his death.

In response, suicide preventionists rushed to send media guidelines about responsible reporting of suicides to outlets throughout the Seattle metropolitan area. The work seems to have paid off; David Jobes and colleagues reported that there was no detectable increase in the Seattle area in suicides following Cobain's death. This conclusion appears in the Surgeon General's report for 1999 and is affirmed by international experts like Madelyn Gould, who stated "there was no increase in suicide because of a combination of sensible reporting and a strong anti-suicide message from [Cobain's] wife, Courtney Love." In other words, the media reporting of Cobain's suicide was not *noxious,* so it did not have the chance to affect vulnerable people.

In his book *The Copycat Effect,* Loren Coleman strongly disagrees. He writes that all this is "folklore" that "receives routine governmental stamps of approval." He believes that there were actually many "copycats" of Cobain's suicide, because in the years following Cobain's death, Coleman found reports of suicide decedents who had referred to Cobain in some way. For reasons that are not clear, Coleman includes the accidental drug overdose of a musician who was in Cobain's wife's band, noting that the musician, Cobain, and Jim Morrison were all twenty-seven at the time of their deaths. What Jim Morrison has to do with any of this is hard to discern. What Coleman seems not to have considered is that in the four years following Cobain's death, there were approximately 4 million deaths by suicide worldwide. That some of the decedents were Nirvana fans does not demonstrate a copycat effect; it demonstrates that Nirvana was famous. It is the same mistake in logic as occurred when the young girl's death by suicide was confidently attributed to the film *Girl, Interrupted.*

A study in a 1997 *Archives of Suicide Research* supports the views in the Surgeon General's report and those expressed by credentialed experts like Madelyn Gould, and does not corroborate Coleman's opinions. The study evaluated the suicide rates in Australia in late adolescents and young adults during the thirty days following the discovery of Cobain's death. This thirty-day interval in 1994 was compared to the corresponding interval for the preceding five years. There was no evidence whatsoever for increased rates following Cobain's death. In fact, five, ten, and fifteen days following the incident, suicide rates *decreased*. When young men and women were examined separately, there was no evidence of any increase. Perhaps deaths by self-inflicted gunshot wound specifically (the means used by Cobain) increased whereas as suicide by other methods did not? No, not the case.

One of many problems bedeviling "copycatting" kinds of explanations is ignoring alternative, more mundane explanations for spates of death by suicide. For instance, I can forecast as I write in 2009 that, in the spring of 2010, there will be a prominent instance of death or violence reported in the news, and there will also be an increase in deaths by suicide. I can forecast the media report much as I can forecast a sunrise—death and violence are reported regularly in the media, both because they occur regularly and at least a segment of the population finds them newsworthy. I can forecast a spring peak in suicide rates because there is always a spring peak in suicide rates. "Copycatting" need not have anything to do with it.

The "copycatting" of things like Cobain's death—which, it should be pointed out, occurred in the spring—is a facile and unnuanced explanation, as if we were to posit that the victims of Bhopal or Chernobyl were killed by "contagion." If "copy-catting" had any explanatory power, it would be able to explain incidents in which dozens or even hundreds of people simultaneously die by suicide, as occurred in the mass suicides at Jonestown and at Heaven's Gate in California. In Jonestown, over 900 people died, mostly from ingesting a drink that contained cyanide. They did so at the urging of deluded cult leader Jim Jones, and though some were likely coerced (and indeed some were gunned down), the majority of the group seem to have voluntarily ingested the poison. In the Heaven's Gate incident, thirty-nine people died from ingesting a drink containing lethal amounts of phenobarbital, again at the urging of a deluded cult leader, and again apparently voluntarily. They believed that upon their deaths, they would be transported to a spaceship that was near the comet Hale-Bopp. The spaceship, in turn, would be a kind of portal to a higher plane of existence.

These horrors are best viewed not as having anything to do with a simplistic concept like "copycatting," but rather as instances of mass delusion (Heaven's Gate) or of a combination of delusion and coercion (Jonestown) leading people to their deaths. And notice here again the combination of *vulnerable* people exposed to a *highly noxious* stimulus (and notice similarly that not everyone died; some *less vulnerable* people understood that Jones was deteriorating from an already deluded state and escaped). Is it at all arguable that these deranged cult leaders were noxious, and that many of the poor souls they attracted were vulnerable?

It is easy to see that the suicides of the people of Jonestown and of Heaven's Gate were deeply influenced by a clear, discrete stimulus—the cult leaders. It does occur that suicides cluster in time and in space, as these two incidents show. But what also occurs is that people use terms like "copycatting" to misunderstand distinct incidents that really had nothing in common with a true clustering effect. Again, compare the girl who died by suicide, and in whose room a movie, among many others, was found, to Timothy McVeigh, who explicitly attributes his atrocities to one book, the only one he possessed at the time of his arrest. Who was the "copycatter?" The evidence shows quite clearly that it was McVeigh, whereas the tragic death of the little girl is probably best understood as a fatal outcome of a pernicious illness, early-onset major depressive disorder. But in media treatments of these incidents—and, I would argue, in the public mind as well—the girl was the "copycatter." Why this misunderstanding? Is it because, though McVeigh's actions appalled us, we understand his actions better than the little girl's? Is childhood mental disorder and suicidal behavior so misunderstood and stigmatized that we grasp at straws to explain it? If so, this suggests that suicide is, at some level, scarier and less understood by most people than is the terroristic homicide of 168 people.

"If People Want to Die by Suicide, We Can't Stop Them"

Restriction of access to public health menaces has a questionable history, to be sure. Prohibition of alcohol in the United States was an acknowledged disaster. Evidence suggests that it backfired. Not only did people find alcohol despite the ban, but they may have consumed more alcohol because of the ban, in part because stronger liquor was more profitable to smuggle and thus available and popular. Of course, a very violent alcohol black market thrived. More and more resources were allocated to enforcing prohibition just as alcohol tax revenues were drying up. Prohibition may have set back the U.S. wine industry by decades, as productive vines were neglected and as winemakers took their knowledge elsewhere.

This is a very strong cautionary tale about the benefits of restricting access to something that authorities deem dangerous or unhealthy. Online gambling is a more recent example. In late 2006, the U.S. Congress passed a bill that would make it illegal for credit card companies and banks to pay off bets, thus effectively making Internet gambling illegal. This is a true disaster for the Internet gambling industry, in that around 75 percent of all Internet gambling is done by U.S. citizens. Opponents of the ban frequently referred to the prohibition of alcohol and predicted that the gambling law would not affect gambling prevalence or reduce gambling-related disorders because people will just find other ways to bet, including the old-fashioned way of the bookmaker in the corner bar.

Time will tell about the gambling ban. In May 2007, four companies were indicted for violating the ban. The World Trade Organization, on the other hand, issued a ruling that it is legal for gaming operators in Antigua to do business with U.S. customers. Once the dust settles, it is hard to know what to predict, specifically because there is no reliable research to inform expectations. Will restricted gaming increase or decrease gambling? All we have to go on are people's various opinions, which, absent empirical backing, have been shown to be poor guides time and again.

The situation is different, however, when it comes to the restriction of locales and methods of suicide. A moment's reflection might have suggested as much, in that suicidal behavior has many apparent differences as compared to pleasure-inducing activities like alcohol and gambling, and so the restriction of one may not produce similar consequences as the restriction of the others. More important, empirical evidence on restriction of means and locales is available to guide us, although many people choose to ignore it in forming their opinions. Both with regard to the availability and the ignoring of evidence, the Golden Gate Bridge is the clearest example.

The Golden Gate Bridge was completed in 1937, and in the ensuing years, approximately 1,300 people have jumped to their deaths from the bridge. In 2006, over thirty people were confirmed to have died by jumping from the bridge, though an exact number is difficult to ascertain because it is not unusual for people's bodies never to be recovered, and also because there are very likely deaths that occur but are unwitnessed. Crucially in the present context, for every person who dies by jumping from the bridge, the California Highway Patrol restrains two or more people from doing so. It is interesting to ponder what subsequently happens to those who are restrained. As with alcohol and possibly gambling, do people simply go elsewhere, in this case to die? Or does restraint have a more positive outcome?

Much turns on these questions. If it were the case that people simply go elsewhere to die, then prevention efforts on the bridge would be of questionable value. It would certainly be questionable as to whether a permanent barrier should be built, and it would even be questionable as to whether the California Highway Patrol should intervene on the bridge. Alternatively, if it could be established that, after restraint, those who had prepared to jump from the bridge go on to live productive lives, then the fact that barriers were resisted for decades and that we lose around thirty people to suicide from the bridge every year represents a moral outrage.

The answer is that this is a moral outrage, one that I and many others believe would never happen for any other public health problem—only suicide could be stigmatized and thus misunderstood to the extent that thirty people's deaths are ignored year in and year out. The data on this are in, they have been in for around thirty years or more, and they could not be clearer—the vast majority of those who intend to jump from the Golden Gate Bridge but are restrained from doing so go on to live productive lives.

The seminal study on this issue was published in 1978 by Richard Seiden. Seiden located and obtained data on 515 people who were restrained from jumping from the bridge. He compared them to a group of 184 people who had attempted suicide by other means and who had been taken to a San Francisco emergency room. If the view that "they'll just go elsewhere to die by suicide" has any merit whatsoever, one would expect at least half of those restrained to do so. But the actual figure is nowhere close to that. Approximately 95 percent of those who were restrained either were still alive at the time of the study (and in some cases had been alive for decades after being restrained) or had died of natural causes.

The group of people restrained on the bridge, it should be emphasized, had characteristics that made them seem, if anything, more likely than other suicide attempters to affirm the "they'll go elsewhere" myth. First, and obviously, they had initiated a suicidal process involving a very lethal method—very few survive a jump from the bridge. Second, and consistent with their choice of a high-lethality method, the bridge group was preponderantly male, whereas the attempter group who had been taken to the emergency room was preponderantly female. More men than women engage in fatal suicide attempts—in the United States, for every woman who dies by suicide, four men do—and so the bridge group had one of the demographic signatures of a high lethality group (i.e., maleness). Third, the people who were restrained at the bridge had contact with police, but on average, they were rarely referred from police custody to mental health treatment.

To summarize, 95 percent of those who were on the precipice but were restrained did not "go elsewhere," and this despite their demonstrated high-lethality choice of method, the fact that most were men (and thus more likely to die than more gender-balanced samples), and the fact that treatment was not easily accessible to them after having been restrained. Restraint demonstrably saved hundreds of lives.

Imagine if someone had a heart attack or a stroke—let's imagine that it's your loved one—and the public policy was essentially, "Why bother intervening? They'll just have another." Very infuriating. It would be an outrage even if it were true that the loved one would be very likely to have another, and it would be beyond outrageous if it were not true. If you really try to imagine this scenario, then you will have walked at least a foot or two in the shoes of family members who have lost someone to suicide. It is unconscionable that a suicide barrier has not been erected on the Golden Gate Bridge. (As of this writing, one has finally been approved, but nothing has been built.) What has stood in the way of a barrier since the 1930s? Money and aesthetics. It is revolting enough that money and aesthetics have been valued over thirty or more lives per year, but it is worse still. The commission has approved a barrier that prevents people from throwing things from the bridge, and this barrier detracts from the bridge's aesthetics; and they have approved a bike safety lane that cost millions of dollars, despite the fact that no bicyclists have been killed on the bridge. The problem is not money and aesthetics, though if it were, that would be appalling enough. The problem, rather, is ignorance and prejudice. One hopes that this ignorance is dissipating, and there is evidence that it is: The bridge authority voted to approve a barrier in late 2008. If and when a barrier is installed, my generous side will say to the bridge authority, "Kudos, you have saved lives"; my less generous side will say, "1,300 lives too late."

If one were for some reason inclined to defend the commission's uninformed initial stance, one might protest that the Seiden study on those who were restrained from the bridge is, after all, just one study. This is a weak protest, given that the results were very clear and that the study was conducted regarding the very bridge in question. The fact is that suicide barriers work. In his 2008 piece in *New York* magazine on "suicide tourism" in New York City—as many as 10 percent of people who die by suicide in the city are from out of town—Phil Zabriskie tells the story of a young man who loved to travel to New York, and who enjoyed staying at the Marriot Marquis in Times Square. Sadly, the young man jumped to his death from a high floor on the hotel's inner atrium, as had several other people over the years. The hotel remodeled; Zabriskie reported, "No one has died by jumping at the Marriott Marquis since [the young man] took his own life. During renovations of the hotel last year, Marriott erected metal grillwork that impedes access to the atrium."

The effectiveness of simple preventive measures like this has been shown repeatedly, at several different suicide "hotspots," including the Eiffel Tower, the Empire State Building, a volcano on the Japanese island of Oshima, and the windows of a specific U.S. psychiatric hospital. As Seiden stated, "However, these examples differ from the Golden Gate Bridge story in one very significant respect. In every instance the rash of suicides led to the construction of suicide barriers, which dramatically reduced or ended the incidence of suicides" (p. 2).

Perhaps one could protest that these examples do not include bridges. It should be recalled, of course, that the Seiden study measured rates of suicide at a bridge—the Golden Gate Bridge itself. But other bridges have been studied, too, including the Arroyo Seco Bridge in Pasadena, California, and the Duke Ellington Bridge in Washington, D.C. Regarding the latter, an average of four people per year died by jumping from the bridge before a barrier was erected; during the construction of the barrier, there was one suicide, and over a five-year span after completion of the barrier, there were no suicides. Crucially, the construction of a barrier did not cause a corresponding increase in the suicide rate at a nearby bridge (the Taft Bridge). Lanny Berman, the executive director of the American Association of Suicidology, stated, "If you thwart jumpers from an immediately accessible site, you will save some lives."

A position paper on bridge barriers by John Draper, project director of the National Suicide Prevention Lifeline (which, among other important and very useful things, administers 1-800-273-TALK), persuasively corroborates Berman's statement. Draper reviews several clear examples. For instance, Toronto's Bloor Street Viaduct was, alas, a suicide hotspot—in fact, it was second only to the Golden Gate Bridge in terms of the number of bridge-related suicides. The word "was" is key here, because in 2003, a barrier was installed, and there have been no suicides since. A very compelling report from New Zealand (the Grafton Bridge in Auckland to be specific) involved the removal and then the re-installation of bridge barriers. When barriers were removed, the number of suicides from the bridge shot up dramatically. When the barriers were put back again, the suicides stopped, and, as in other studies, there was no subsequent increase in suicides from neighboring bridges. A similar story applies to the Clifton Suspension Bridge in Bristol, England, where a *partial* barrier decreased the suicide rate by half over a five-year span.

Evidently, physical barriers that prevent people from jumping from bridges have saved many lives. Is an actual physical barrier required, however? Would it be sufficient if, instead of erecting a barrier, phones were installed on bridges that, when picked up, directly and immediately connected the caller with a suicide crisis worker? The best available evidence suggests not. As John Draper illustrated in the position paper mentioned above, the effectiveness of bridge phone installations is in question. Such installations have existed on the Golden Gate Bridge since 1993, but there have been at least 380 suicides from the bridge since then. Similarly, more than twenty people have died by jumping from the Sunshine Skyway Bridge in St. Petersburg, Florida, in the three years after phones were installed there. There has been no reduction in the number of suicides on the Coronado Bay Bridge in San Diego since call boxes were placed at the bridge. On June 19, 2008, the Associated Press reported on a death by jumping from the Tappan Zee Bridge in New York. Between April and June 2008, there were at least three deaths from the bridge, and one attempt. The paper stated, "Suicide prevention phones were installed along the bridge last year."

Anyone who is suicidal retains at least a bit of ambivalence about death, and this ambivalence can lead to a change of heart among suicidal people, as well as provide a window of opportunity for others to intervene before people end their lives. But someone who is already on a bridge with high intent to jump may have considerable resolve about death, so much so that only strong measures can capitalize on remaining ambivalence. Call boxes and signs with hotline information may not be powerful enough to exert noticeable influence on those with high intent to die. Physical barriers on bridges are the strongest preventative means available, and these have been shown to work time and again, even regarding people who are presumably resolved to die. I am not stating that measures like call boxes, signs, and public service announcements are summarily ineffective. On the contrary, there is evidence that they are helpful in general. But once someone is far enough along in a trajectory toward suicide that she or he is standing on a bridge with high intent to die, the only documented prevention approach is a barrier.

Given this abundance of evidence, one would think it self-evident that there would have been a barrier on the Golden Gate Bridge all along, given that someone dies there every ten days or so. That there was not is a travesty. There have been other failures of conscience and knowledge involving the issue of suicide barriers on bridges. A June 2005 story in the *Cleveland Scene* focused on Akron, Ohio's All-America Bridge, better known locally as the Y-Bridge. The story's main emphasis was on the neighborhoods and businesses under the bridge. They regularly contend with jumpers falling and dying on their property and even occasionally falling into the structures themselves.

The bridge is situated near an important psychiatric facility, and a former patient, Georgia McLaughlin, attempted to garner support for a protective fence along the bridge's railing. In the words of the reporter, McLaughlin "felt that [the bridge's] closeness to [the psychiatric facility] and to downtown—both saturated with the homeless and mentally ill—was too much of a temptation." Wheelchair-bound, McLaughlin rolled her chair along the bridge carrying a sign that read "Y jump?" She also started a petition and addressed the city council about the issue, all to no avail. In the case of the city council, she was told that aesthetics was the issue, that the fence would affect the bridge's beauty.

The people with homes and businesses under the bridge also lobbied for a protective barrier, also with no results. The president of a neighborhood group was told by the city council that a barrier would be too expensive. In discussing the city council, she stated, "They lazy. They always talking about they budget, so we asked for partial fencing, just to protect the houses. They didn't like that neither. It makes me mad, because I'm a taxpayer, and if you have people jumping on your house, the city should accommodate you to make you safe. But they don't."

And they should accommodate potential jumpers by helping to save their lives . . . but they don't do that either. The same excuses of aesthetics and money are proffered again. And one other excuse too, this in the words of city spokesman Mark Williamson: "It would solve the problem of people jumping off that bridge, but not of people taking their lives. They'll just go somewhere else." Mr. Williamson and the city council, it seems, have fallen behind in their reading—way behind, as Seiden's Golden Gate Bridge study was published in 1978. Some glimmers of hope have developed, however; a barrier for the bridge is now being seriously considered.

As noted above regarding the Eiffel Tower, the Empire State Building, and the Duke Ellington Bridge—and now perhaps the Golden Gate Bridge and the Y-Bridge—there have been some successes. A relatively recent one involves the Memorial Bridge in Augusta, Maine. In late 2004, as reported in the *Kennebec Journal,* the Augusta City Council decided to retain a suicide barrier on the bridge, but also noted that it would be important for the barrier not to detract from the bridge's beauty and its view. To the council's credit, the vote for this decision was 7–1.

One of the council members stated, "This is a case where we are our brother's keeper." Another said, "Some see that fence as something ugly, but I see it as something caring. The fence is a symbol that tells motorists and pedestrians that the capital city is concerned about the mentally ill who live here." These statements are in refreshing contrast to those made by the Golden Gate commission over the years.

The person who cast the lone dissenting vote on the Augusta, Maine council predictably argued that people prevented from jumping from the bridge will just use alternative means, like guns or pills. What is less predictable—and somewhat depressing—is this council member's profession—she is a nurse. Redeemingly, she couched her vote in the context of advocating for more state funding in general for people with mental health problems and had earlier suggested that a better solution for the bridge was to remove pedestrian access to it altogether. The barrier was retained and renovated.

The nurse's assertion contains a point that I have not fully addressed yet—the possibility that, instead of "going elsewhere," people may "do otherwise." That is, if they are prevented from jumping from a bridge, they may not go to another bridge to jump, but they may access alternative means to die by suicide. Many people endorse this mistaken view, including mental health and other professionals.

For instance, in their 1976 book *Suicide: Inside and Out,* David K. Reynolds and Norman L. Farberow, referring to patients on inpatient psychiatry units, state, "Removal of self-destructive materials may be of questionable benefit. The patient's need to kill himself is more important than the symbolism of the method chosen." Referring to sharp objects, they continue, "It is possible that the articles removed from the patient's possession are significant symbols of his contact with others, and their removal may be perceived as similar to being placed in isolation, a validation of the patient's loss of human relationships and ability to control his own actions" (p. 6). The recommendation here is problematic on its face, because it could amount to leaving the patient with a knife so as to enhance his or her sense of connection and control. (I agree, incidentally, that connection and control are crucial factors in suicidal behavior—indeed much of my own work is built on this truth—but of course I don't agree that leaving patients with sharp objects is a proper way to see to their sense of connection and control.)

We might think that an approach like this is from another era, but it persists even today. A *New York Times* article in June 2007 quoted a psychiatrist as saying that "if a patient is determined to kill himself, he can't be prevented from doing it and hospitalization postpones the event." The *Times* also noted some context for the psychiatrist's comments: He had abruptly discharged a patient whom he had tried to enroll in a drug study, and who was very suicidal and deteriorated upon discharge. The patient died by suicide two weeks later. Moreover, the newspaper pointed out that the psychiatrist had "prescribed narcotics and other controlled substances to addicts," and "prescribed narcotics to pregnant patients, one of whom prematurely delivered a baby who soon died." It appears that this psychiatrist holds many mistaken views, one of which is the "go elsewhere" myth.

It has probably not escaped your notice that this view, too, is flatly contradicted by Seiden's Golden Gate Bridge study. Around 95 percent of those restrained on the bridge neither found another bridge nor accessed alternative means. There are additional data. They have been available since even before Seiden's study. From 1963 to the late 1970s, Britain witnessed an approximately one-third decrease in the suicide rate. What could account for the saving of this many lives? In 1963, Britain switched from coke gas to natural gas for domestic use. Coke gas is far more lethal than natural gas. Following this shift, the suicide rate decreased. Moreover, it stayed lower over the ensuing decades, and there was evidence of a close association between the decreasing suicide rate and the decreasing number of homes still using coke gas. Crucially, too, there was no increase in suicides by other means, like hanging, gunshot, and so forth. This latter fact directly contradicts the view that restricting one method will simply lead people to access alternative methods.

U.K. psychiatrist Keith Hawton has done important work on the packaging of analgesics like acetaminophen (called paracetamol in the United Kingdom) and salicylates (e.g., aspirin). On September 16, 1998, legislation in the United Kingdom changed such that the packaging of these over-the-counter agents was restricted to packs of thirty-two pills for pharmacies and twenty-four pills for other retail outlets. A main idea behind the change was to decrease household stores, and thereby restrict a potential means of death by suicide.

The legislation appeared to work. In a 2004 *British Medical Journal*, Hawton and colleagues reported a 22 percent reduction in deaths by intentional overdose of acetaminophen or salicylates in the year following the change in legislation, and this reduction was maintained in the years afterward. They also found that acetaminophen-related admissions to liver units and liver transplants were reduced by approximately 30 percent (an overdose of the drug can destroy the liver), and this decrease was also maintained in the subsequent years.

A different legislative effort, this one targeting guns in Australia, also appeared to work. Automatic and semi-automatic guns were banned in Australia in 1996 following a man's shooting rampage that killed thirty-five people. A 2006 paper in the journal *Injury Prevention* evaluated the firearm suicide rate (as well as the rate of other firearm incidents) before and after the ban. Several interesting results emerged, including that firearm suicides were by far the largest cause of total firearm deaths in Australia, accounting for more than 75 percent of all deaths involving firearms. In addition, the researchers reported that, in the eighteen years before and including the year of the rampage, there were 8,850 firearm suicides, for an average of 491.7 such deaths per year. In the seven years after the ban, there were 1,726 such deaths, for a yearly average of 246.6. A decrease from an average rate of around 492 firearm deaths per year to around 247 is substantial. This study also found no evidence for the "go elsewhere/do otherwise" myth. If this myth held truth, then in Australia the decrease in firearm-related suicides should be offset by at least some increases in other methods of death. But no such increases were detected, again disaffirming this unfortunate myth.

Restriction of the number of pills per package can save lives, as can a switch to natural from coke gas, barriers on bridges and buildings, and automatic gun bans. Why do these things work? In his 1978 Golden Gate Bridge study, Seiden articulated a view that answers this question and that has universal consensus among those who study suicidal behavior. He said, "there are those who hold [the] view . . . that a switch to less lethal agents would reduce suicides or that when a person is unable to kill himself in a particular way it may be enough to tip the vital balance from death to life in a situation already characterized by strong ambivalence."

This ambivalence is crucial to understanding those who attempt and die by suicide. Of the very few people who survive a jump from the Golden Gate Bridge, virtually every one of them recalls experiencing profound regret at the decision to jump during the four seconds it takes to reach the water. That is, within a span of five seconds, a person experiences both a deep wish to die (thus the jump) and a strong urge to live (thus the regret immediately after the jump). To experience these strong and competing feelings within such a brief timeframe demonstrates the extreme ambivalence inherent in the suicidal mind and illustrates why things like a bridge barrier may tip the balance in favor of life. In fact, it *does* tip the balance in favor of life, as shown by the Seiden study and several other sources of information.

Another instance of life and death wishes competing and occurring within a brief time interval is noted in Loren Coleman's *The Copycat Effect.* Coleman describes a man who doused himself with gas, struck a match, and was badly burned. On the way to the hospital, he repeatedly asked for water. He wanted to die badly enough that he set himself on fire, and soon after, the urge to live predominated, leading him to be desperate for water. Soon thereafter, he was interviewed in the hospital by psychiatrists, who asked him if he wanted to live. He nodded affirmatively, but died a few hours later.

Tad Friend, in his 2003 *New Yorker* article on suicide at the Golden Gate Bridge, quoted psychiatrist Jerome Motto on a death by suicide that affected him deeply. Motto said, "I went to this guy's apartment afterward with the assistant medical examiner. The guy was in his thirties, lived alone, pretty bare apartment. He'd written a note and left it on his bureau. It said, 'I'm going to walk to the bridge. If one person smiles at me on the way, I will not jump.'" The man did jump, so one presumes that no one smiled at him on the way. This is a poignant and sad anecdote for several reasons, one of which is that it demonstrates how easily the life and death balance can be affected—one smile might have saved a man's life.

If one smile might have saved a life, then it stands to reason five police cruisers with a minimum of six officers, one of whom is a trained negotiator, and a medical unit should save lives for sure. This is the team that is sent by Akron police when they are dispatched to a local bridge to talk down a potential jumper, and, according to an article in 2005 in the *Cleveland Scene,* the team has never lost a would-be jumper during negotiations. This intervention, like others noted earlier, is effective and saves lives, and it does so at least in part by nudging a deeply ambivalent person, who is tottering on the precipice between life and death, back toward life.

I am aware of at least one legal case in which a man's family is suing a business over the man's death by suicide. One element of the defense in this case is that sending rescue in a timely manner would not have made any difference. But it would have, as the record of the Akron team shows, and as stands to reason once the deep ambivalence of the suicidal mind is taken into account. Someone having an internal debate about whether or not to die is much more likely to be dead in an hour if that debate runs its course than if it is interrupted immediately.

Consider the death of a California state official who was having a severe conflict at her workplace. In May 2005, she was supposed to attend a meeting to discuss the matter but did not show up. She sent a long e-mail instead. The e-mail was not explicit about suicide but contained passages such as "I cannot take any more . . . of the humiliation I have had to endure for the past year." To their credit, those who received the e-mail understood that she might be at risk, but there were delays in sending help, in part because the woman lived seventy-five miles away. Authorities reached her house two hours after her e-mail was sent. There, in the front yard of the house, they discovered the woman's two dogs, both dead from gunshot wounds, and the woman herself, also shot but still alive. She was airlifted to a hospital, where she died less than an hour after she was found. It was later discovered that she had been preparing for suicide for days at least. Her possessions were packed up and labeled, and she had left labels differentiating her computer and other personal possessions from those owned by her workplace. A lengthy suicide note was also found.

This is a very lethal scenario—many days of planning and preparation; dogs shot dead; the woman herself gravely wounded. Despite all this, one wonders, what would have happened had rescue occurred not two hours later, but one hour later. Even with the two-hour delay, she was alive when emergency personnel arrived. An hour could have made a considerable difference. Sending rescue, and sending it earlier, likely would have saved her life.

A very different incident from the Salem/Beverly area of Massachusetts in 2007 illustrates some of the same principles; rescue helps, or would help if accessed. A 19-year-old woman called her boyfriend stating that she was going to kill herself. The boyfriend called 911 and asked them to send help to the woman's apartment. Three officers arrived at the apartment; the woman was distraught but uninjured, and the officers escorted her to a local hospital.

She and the officers were met at the hospital by the woman's father, who was also a police officer. Daughter and father had a verbal disagreement, after which the woman left the hospital before registering there. She went home to her apartment, where her boyfriend found her a few hours later, dead by hanging. Approximately two years earlier, in this same area, a policeman in the same department went against the department's policy by handling a 911 call about his own son's domestic disturbance incident. Two days later, a murder-suicide occurred in which the officer's son killed his girlfriend and himself.

According to newspaper accounts, both of these are cases in which rescue started off well, or at least by the book. In the domestic disturbance incident, authorities were called, but the process was, it appears, interrupted by the young man's father, with a tragic ending involving two deaths. In the case of the young woman, a person threatened suicide, a concerned individual called for help, help soon arrived, and the uninjured person agreed to go to the hospital without incident. The process appears to have been interrupted, and in this sense, rescue was incomplete. Hospitalization—or even evaluation in the emergency room to see if hospitalization was warranted—was aborted, and the incident ended very badly. Just as one wonders what would have happened to the California woman if rescue had not been delayed by two hours, one wonders what would have happened to this young woman in Massachusetts had the rescue process not been short-circuited.

Rescue is a sensitive issue in some quarters, because sending rescue when it is not necessary can be intrusive and otherwise unfortunate. Also, it takes specialized training to be able to conduct rescue in a safe, respectful way, and this training is not available to many of the frontline people who need it. Therefore incidents in which rescue is sent to someone who does not want it or even need it, or in which rescue is done in a coercive, disrespectful way, do unfortunately occur. This is a shame and an urgent training issue. I have also seen it become a distraction from the real issue: Competent rescue saves lives, as I think the incidents noted above illustrate.

In his 2006 book *Cliffs of Despair,* Tom Hunt interviewed a man named Kevin Carlyon who is a self-described witch. Among other improbable things, Carlyon believes that energy lines running back and forth between sites like Stonehenge intersect at England's Beachy Head cliffs—a suicide hotspot—creating a kind of energy that lures people to jump. Referring to a newspaper article Carlyon had published in a prominent British paper, Hunt quoted him as stating, "If someone wants to kill themselves, they're going to do it . . . If somebody has that inside themselves, they'll do it, whether it's by gun, whether it's by electricity, whether it's by Beachy Head. My explanation is that it's a kind of paranormal thing, not so much the publicity. I mean, I had a Beachy Head piece in the *Sunday Mirror,* and about seven people jumped off the top after that, but they would have done it anyway." The evidence suggests otherwise. The publicity Carlyon generated, romanticizing an already dangerous spot, represented the real public health menace. That a person without a shred of evidence but access to a major media outlet says and does such things is outrageous enough. It is compounded by the fact that city commissioners, health professionals, and public health officials say and do them too.

"It's Just a Cry for Help"

"Talk is cheap." This is one of my favorite sayings, as my Ph.D. students and clinical supervisees can attest. I like it for a lot of reasons, including, in the case of Ph.D. students, that replacing talk with action (in the form of writing articles and grant applications) will enhance their careers, and in the case of clinical supervisees, helping their patients replace talk with action (in the form of behavioral change) is almost always the quicker path to lasting relief.

The difference between talk and action is very apparent in various sports. In football, each play starts with both the offense and defense huddling together to, in a sense, talk, but when the ball is snapped, talk is cheap and it's all action. In golf, player and caddy will talk at length about club selection, lie, shape of the shot, distance, wind speed, and so on, but then talk stops (indeed it is forbidden except for the whispering announcers), and it is all up to the action of the golfer. In baseball, there sometimes are conferences involving many people on the mound, and there is constant "talk" of a sort—

in the form of signals—between catcher and pitcher, between manager and various players, between second baseman and shortstop, and so on. As with football and golf, in baseball there is a time for talk, and then a time for action.

But every now and then in baseball, this progression from talk to action is not so neat, because the need for talk arises during the action, when a kind of change in plan is needed. When a runner is stranded between bases and the other team is chasing him down, communication is necessary. When a runner is trying to steal a base, communication to the catcher is necessary. Baseball, then, is like a lot of sports, in that it usually follows a talk-then-action rule. But complications arise in baseball that make this rule unworkable.

I believe the useful saying "talk is cheap" and the usual rule of talk then action have had a role in producing the myth that when people talk about suicide they are not serious about actually doing it (else they'd be doing it instead of talking). The saying should be "talk is usually cheap," and the rule should be that talk usually precedes action, because there are exceptions—baseball contains a few such exceptions, and suicidal behavior can represent an exception too.

Baseball is occasionally an exception because the plan for action can change suddenly, necessitating communication between the players to know how to change course. A roughly analogous situation pertains to suicidal behavior. It is common for a person to have a resolved plan for suicidal action and to have even started to enact that plan. Then something comes up and tips the decisional balance back toward life. This ambivalent see-sawing between urges toward death and toward life is characteristic of the suicidal mind, as we have seen. It is during these times of indecision, when life and death forces are battling it out in the minds of suicidal people, that such people often talk to others about what they are going through. Talking to others, especially about something painful and personal like ideas about suicide, represents a reaching out to others, a questioning about whether reliable social ties are there and can be counted on. Much can depend on the answer to this questioning. If the answer is understanding, encouraging the person to access care, life may prevail; if the answer is dismissive—"you're all talk" or "you're just trying to get attention"—it may not.

The myth that suicide talk means low risk is directly repeated or indirectly perpetuated constantly, not only in the media, but in scholarly and professional venues too. Consider this statement, which contains a certain truth but also may be misinterpreted to indirectly perpetuate the myth: "While in most suicide cases people have given verbal or behavioral clues that they intend to take their lives, suicide researchers agree that most people expressing verbal threats will not in fact attempt it" (Timmermans, 2006, p. 184). The first part of the sentence is clear and right on target: When people give off clues about their impending suicide, it is a serious situation indeed. The second part of the sentence, read closely and literally, is true as well: Of all the people who experience the desire for suicide, even to the point of voicing it to others, only a proportion go on to actually die. This is quite right, just as it is quite right that, of all the people who experience severe chest pain, only a proportion (and a pretty small proportion at that) will go on to die from a heart attack.

A key point is that, in the case of severe chest pain, it is relatively rare for the reaction to be "He's faking!" or "She's just trying to get attention!" Indeed, most people would find these reactions cruel, rightly. And this despite the fact that a sizable proportion of chest-pain scenarios actually are false alarms, with the discomfort caused by anxiety, a panic attack, esophageal problems, and so forth. In the case of suicide threat, it is common for the threat to be dismissed, and an underappreciated fact is that this represents playing with fire, just as ignoring or dismissing chest pain can be.

Relatedly, heart disease can be a chronic, progressive illness. Someone who has a heart attack at one point in time is vulnerable to another in the future because of the ongoing nature of the condition. It would be ridiculous to say something like, "If the guy were going to die from heart disease, he would have done it already; he's been having heart problems for years." But this very thing is frequently said about suicidal people, including by trained mental health professionals, who should know better. The logic is something along the lines of this: "They have tried suicide before and did not die—if they were serious about dying, they would have already done it." This represents a profound misunderstanding of the trajectory of suicidal behavior over time. Suicide is a daunting and fearsome prospect, even if one desires it. To overcome the natural barriers and restraints takes time; to feel beaten down and demoralized to the point that one feels that death will be worth more than life takes repeated experience and time . . . just as the progression of heart disease takes time.

Ignoring or otherwise mishandling suicide-related communications can have tragic consequences. As an illustration of this point, recall the man who had written a note and left it on his bureau. It said, "I'm going to walk to the bridge. If one person smiles at me on the way, I will not jump." The man did in fact jump to his death. Now, this fellow was not exactly talking to others, but according to what he wrote in his note, he was communicating in a way, looking into the faces of passersby and nonverbally asking, "Do you care?" He claimed in his note that an affirmative response, in the form of a smile, would have saved his life—that the decisional balance between life and death rested with something as simple and easy as a smile. His death in the waters beneath the Golden Gate Bridge suggests that saving smiles were not forthcoming. The young man communicated, not by talking openly to loved ones or friends, but by looking—or perhaps more accurately furtively glancing—into the faces of strangers. He says a smile would have saved him; if a smile from a stranger can have this effect, then it follows that caring words, affection, and help from a loved one or friend could be even more positive still.

One may legitimately wonder whether a few caring words can make a difference. Happily, this question has been addressed in a fairly definitive way. The study, conducted in 1991 by Jerome A. Motto and Alan Bostrom, involved over 3,000 people hospitalized because of suicidal thoughts or behaviors, or because of depression. Approximately one month after discharge from the hospital, patients were contacted about follow-up treatment, many of whom refused it (a common occurrence, unfortunately). Of those who refused follow-up treatment, the researchers divided a total of more than 800 patients randomly into two groups. People in one group received a "caring letter" a few times per year for five years, and the other group received no further contact.

The "caring letters" received by the first group were not lengthy or involved; on the contrary, they consisted of quite brief expressions of concern and reminders that the treatment agency was accessible when patients needed it. Care was taken to individualize the letters; the letters received by a given individual were, when possible, signed by the professional who was in charge of the person's care; subsequent letters were always worded differently than previous letters, and they included responses to any questions or comments made to previous letters. The researchers always included a self-addressed, unstamped envelope. They provided this example of a contact letter: "Dear_____: It has been some time since you were here at the hospital, and we hope things are going well for you. If you wish to drop us a note we would be glad to hear from you."

The study produced a very important finding: Patients who received the letter had a lower suicide rate in the five-year interval after discharge as compared to patients in the control group. Indeed, to date, this is one of only two clinical interventions subjected to a randomized controlled trial that has produced an effect on deaths by suicide (some other studies have produced effects on suicide attempts or suicidal ideation). The other study also involved caring follow-up contact (Fleischmann et al., 2008).

The "caring letters" researchers specifically attributed this finding to patients having felt cared about. They described this as "a feeling of being joined to something meaningful outside oneself as a stabilizing force in emotional life . . . it is this force that we postulate as having exerted whatever suicide-prevention influence the contact program might have generated." They continued, "[an earlier paper] expressed this concept clearly after recounting suicide prevention measures over 600 years and contemplating what is really new, observing that 'there is surely at least one common theme through the centuries—it is the provision of human contact, the comfort of another concerned person, often authoritative but maybe not, conveying a message of hope consonant with the assumptions and values relevant to that particular time.'" The findings and explanations provided by the researchers are quite consistent with the importance I ascribed to failed belongingness as a primary suicide risk factor in my recent theory of suicidal behavior.

In the "caring letters" study summarized above, the letters were personalized—they were signed, with original signature, by the person in charge of the patient's care, and any note the patient sent in response to the previous letter was answered in the subsequent letter. The researchers believed this level of detail was important, because without it, the letters may not have conveyed enough genuine care and concern. But this does raise a question—how much of this kind of detailing is necessary to make the letters have that feeling of caring, enough of such feeling to make a difference in people's suicidal behavior?

A study from Australia suggests not much. The study was designed to replicate the one described above and so was structured similarly. But there was an intriguing difference, and it had to do with the "caring letters" themselves . . . or actually, in the case of the Australian study, they might more accurately be described as "caring automated postcards." The postcards were printed out by a computer, had no personalized features at all, and did not contain any reference to previous comments or questions patients may have had. What they did contain was an expression of caring and availability, along the lines of "we hope you are doing well, and wanted to remind you that we are here if you need us." And each postcard also contained a simple, computerized image of a dog (which might lead me, if I received one of these, to assume the postcard was from the Humane Society or a veterinarian's office).

The effects of these postcards—both anecdotally and in terms of overall findings—were, as in the study with personalized caring letters, positive. Those who received the postcards engaged in fewer suicidal behaviors than those who did not receive them. This occurred despite the fact that the postcards were, in some ways, impersonal. Crucially, though, study participants did not experience them as impersonal. The expression of caring and availability, even though written by a computer in standardized phrasing, got through to the participants.

Anecdotally, many of the participants in the study affirmed that they noticed the computerized nature of the postcards but nevertheless found them a pleasant lift. Many referred to the image of the dog, referring to it as cute and saying things like "it brought a smile to my face." It is almost as if the participants were inviting care and were prepared to accept even relatively small doses of it as sufficient. The results of this study suggest to me that the man who claims he would have been saved by just one smile might have been telling the truth—if a computerized postcard with an image of a dog on it can convey enough caring to make a difference, then I buy that a smile from a stranger can too.

Indeed, humans (and other primates) seem innately prepared to find even minimal caring to be "good enough." One of the most memorable images from twentieth-century behavioral science research is that of monkeys clinging to artificial mothers, made either of wire or of cloth. In these famous studies conducted by Harry Harlow and colleagues, rhesus monkeys were separated from their mothers a few hours after birth and were raised by inanimate "mother machines" that dispensed milk. Monkeys were randomized to two conditions in which the machines differed. Both machines looked more or less like monkeys, but one was covered with terry cloth, the other with wire mesh. Monkeys "raised" by the terry-cloth machine were generally healthy, whereas those "raised" by the wire machines were less so (e.g., were fearful, stress reactive, unable to calm themselves, prone to outbursts). The studies show there is a limit to what sort of caring is "good enough" (a wire mother won't do), but that the limit is surprisingly low (a terry-cloth machine will do). Humans (and rhesus monkeys) are ready to be cared for, and it doesn't take much to do it—some terry cloth, or a postcard, or a smile, as minimal as they are, may suffice.

The moral of this story thus far is that when people talk about suicide, it likely reflects the fact that they are thinking about actually enacting suicide—not the fact that they are just talking or crying out for attention (more on this shortly)—and, crucially, that a simple word or two from a caring other can make a real difference. Indeed, this point has reached such consensus among the suicide research and prevention community that the American Association of Suicidology (AAS) has listed "talking about suicide" at the very top of its list of suicide warning signs. The list is divided into two sections—those signs for which help should be accessed immediately, and those for which help should be accessed in the near future. "Talking about suicide," along with such signs as "threatening suicide" and "looking for ways to die by suicide," were deemed warning signs for which help should be sought immediately. Some signs for which help should be sought soon were marked hopelessness, agitation, and feeling trapped. (The full list of AAS suicide warning signs can be viewed through the Web site www.suicidology.org.)

The "talk means inaction" myth has been perpetuated by the real but misunderstood phenomenon of using self-injury as a ploy for attention or a cry for help. Lots of people need and want attention and help, but many of those who use self-injury to obtain them suffer from a condition called borderline personality disorder, and this condition, like "self-injury for attention," is both real and misunderstood. The disorder is defined by longstanding patterns of markedly labile emotions, interpersonal storminess, behavioral impulsivity, self-injury, and feelings of emptiness. The condition is real, agonizing, and associated with a lot of difficulties in social, work, and family domains. It is also associated with nonsuicidal self-injury, serious suicide attempts, and death by suicide.

This last sentence contains the source of much of the misunderstanding of borderline personality disorder. People with the condition engage in self-injury that is not intended to end in death *and* in self-injury that is intended to be fatal. They thus can be very dangerous, but they can also come across as if they are not really dangerous at all. Why, one might reasonably ask, would one engage in self-injury if the point were other than death? Or, one might skip the question and just assume that the answer is "for attention" or "a cry for help." The answer, as it turns out, is that people engage in nonsuicidal self-injury mostly for the purpose of controlling their own negative moods. It is hard to believe and understand at first, but it is the case that if one is in a negative mood, and one for instance cuts one's wrists, the negative mood dissipates. It dissipates for a few reasons: the physical pain distracts from the emotional pain; the novelty of the wound and the blood distract from the negative mood; and the release of endorphins (our own natural internal painkillers) in response to the injury lessens the negative mood.

Of course, self-injury is, for a number of reasons, not an optimal means of regulating negative moods. In addition to physical injury and possible subsequent events (e.g., the risk of infection), self-injury is a quick, short-term fix that does not represent a long-term solution to underlying problems and can in fact make things much worse. A main goal of psychotherapy for this condition is to replace mood regulation strategies like self-injury with more adaptive ones like mindfully thinking through problems and their solutions, perhaps by bouncing ideas off a trusted friend.

Another disadvantage to self-injury as a form of self-regulation is that it starts people on the trajectory to frank suicidal behavior. If someone can cut severely for the purposes of mood regulation, then, should the purpose of death arise, the individual can cut (or do other lethal things) severely too. It is here where dismissing self-injury as merely a ploy for attention is doubly wrong; first, even if the intention is not death, the motive is not primarily attention but mood regulation; second, whatever the motive, intentional nonsuicidal self-injury lays the foundation for later self-injury with death as the purpose. This fact is consistent with my recent theory of suicidal behavior, which emphasizes that injury of any sort, but especially intentional self-injury, habituates people to the pain and fear of suicide; therefore, should a serious desire for death arise, these individuals do not have the natural barriers of pain and fear to stop them from enacting their own deaths.

The fact that suicide-related tragedies are regularly preceded by suicide-related communications is borne out by news articles virtually every day of the week. I have already mentioned the young man who walked to the Golden Gate Bridge, saw that no one smiled at him on the way, and jumped to his death. Here, the communication was indirect (looking at others' faces to see a smile), but in many cases, it is far more direct. For instance, in an incident that occurred in 2007 in Idaho, a man attempted suicide in February of that year by overdosing on anti-anxiety medicine. He survived the attempt and was hospitalized. In the hospital, he stated that were he to attempt suicide again, he would first kill others in a mass shooting or perhaps a bombing. Three months later, he went on a shooting rampage, discharging over 200 gunshots. The first shot killed his wife; subsequent shots were sprayed at the sheriff's dispatch center and into a church for which he worked as a janitor. These shots killed a police officer and wounded several others. Approximately three hours into the rampage, he died from a self-inflicted gunshot wound.

As documented in Lee Whittlesey's *Death in Yellowstone*, a young man who worked in the park in the 1960s "had mentioned suicide," although "his fellow employees had not known him to be depressed" (p. 178). He was later found dead in the park's Canyon Village bunkhouse from a self-inflicted gunshot wound.

Another, very different tragic example occurred in Australia in 2007. Two teenage girls' bodies were found hanging from a tree in a remote area; the girls had been dead for days. This tragedy garnered many headlines, in part because the girls had obtained information from the Internet on step-by-step instructions for suicide by hanging. A somewhat less-publicized aspect of the girls' deaths was that they were frequent participants in chat rooms, and in the weeks preceding their deaths, each had posted many dark messages, including very clear references to suicide. Moreover, the girls had spoken directly to their friends, making statements like "Things are f'ed up . . . I'm going to die." One of the girls' friends remarked that the group felt that telling parents about the girls' comments was not the thing to do, a decision they now deeply regret. The friend said, "I reckon if I did say something, they would still be here."

Hospitalization as a Treatment for Suicidal Behavior

First, some facts: Thousands of people die by suicide in the United States every year either while hospitalized for psychiatric conditions or days after being discharged from the hospital. There is an association, therefore, between being hospitalized and dying by suicide.

But, of course, to conclude that a treatment such as being admitted to the hospital backfires is to neglect alternative explanations; in this case, underlying severity of illness both increases the likelihood of hospitalization and increases the likelihood of suicide. The causal arrows go not from hospitalization to suicide, but from serious psychiatric illness to both hospitalization and to suicide. This same issue arises in the discussion of whether antidepressant medicines or flu treatments cause suicidal behavior (e.g., the flu virus itself may cause both abnormal behavior and induce flu treatment)—a topic to which I will return in a subsequent chapter.

With this crucial caveat in mind, it is important to acknowledge that we do not know with certainty whether hospitalization is an effective treatment. The way we know if any treatment is effective is via the randomized, placebo-controlled clinical trial, and hospitalization has not been subjected to such a trial. Given the ethical dilemmas inherent in randomly assigning seriously suicidal patients to the hospital versus some kind of placebo condition, this trial may never be conducted.

A clinical trial of this sort is clearly the gold standard in evaluating the effectiveness of treatments, but the absence of such a trial does not imply a full vacuum of knowledge. Several studies have compared newly developed, intensive psychotherapeutic treatments to "treatment as usual," which usually involves inpatient psychiatric hospitalization. I was involved in one such study, led by David Rudd and published in a 1996 issue of the *Journal of Consulting & Clinical Psychology.* In our study, the intensive psychotherapy primarily focused on teaching patients behavioral, problem-solving skills, mostly regarding interpersonal issues like conflict resolution and clear communication. And the word "intensive" definitely applied: Over the course of two weeks, patients spent approximately nine hours per day in treatment in a day hospital. Excluding nights and weekends (which they spent at home), patients therefore completed approximately ninety hours of psychotherapy within a two-week timeframe. For purposes of comparison, in the usual psychotherapy setting (i.e., weekly psychotherapy with some weeks missed due to vacations and practical issues), ninety hours of psychotherapy would occur over two years.

We randomly assigned over 300 suicidal patients (those who either had recently attempted or had ideated severely enough that they were of clinical concern) to either this intensive, problem-solving treatment or to treatment as usual, which commonly involved the initiation of antidepressant medicines and some generic counseling over the course of a weeklong hospital stay on an inpatient psychiatry unit.

The point of the study was to demonstrate that the intensive psychotherapy was at least as effective as the usual inpatient stay of several days plus antidepressants. The study accomplished this aim and then some—for instance, although both treatments demonstrated clear effectiveness, there was evidence that the psychotherapy outperformed the usual treatment with regard to retaining in treatment the highest risk patients, not a trivial feat. From another perspective, however, one of the most surprising findings from the study was how well the usual treatment fared. Many of the study's outcome indices showed that treatment as usual did as well as a treatment that included two straight weeks of cutting-edge psychotherapy, nine hours a day . . . not a trivial feat.

This brings us back to the question of the effectiveness of hospitalization. Our study (and others as well) suggested the usual treatment scenario for severely suicidal patients—of which hospitalization is frequently a primary component—performed pretty well. Indeed, regarding both treatment conditions from the study, post-treatment occurrences of suicidal behavior were very rare, so much so as to prevent meaningful statistical analyses, and certainly there were to our knowledge no deaths by suicide in the study's two-year follow-up interval.

Of course, as with any treatment, for hospitalization to be effective, it has to be done reasonably competently; it cannot lack what treatment researchers refer to as "treatment fidelity." There are instances in which such integrity was clearly lacking, with very unfortunate consequences. In December 2007 at a state-run psychiatric hospital in New Jersey, a patient who in 1996 had killed his parents with a knife simply wandered away from the hospital. He was found a day later and returned to the facility, where he was supposed to be on round-the-clock suicide watch. (What this means is unclear—checks every fifteen minutes, constant video monitoring? Indeed, woefully little research has been done on how such watches should be structured.) During this watch, the patient hanged himself in a bathroom using a bedsheet. This resulted in the firing of workers who were supposed to be monitoring the patient as well as in the suspension of a worker who noticed that the patient was missing but did nothing about it, and suspensions for clinical professionals who did not conduct a thorough risk assessment when the patient was returned to the facility—each assumed that the other had done so.

A case from Michigan bears some unfortunate similarities to this one. A man in his twenties, diagnosed with bipolar disorder, was involuntarily admitted to a state psychiatric hospital after refusing to take his medicines, making threats against others, and experiencing suicidal ideation. In the hospital, he hanged himself with his belt, which had not been taken from him. The patient's mother alleged that this oversight was compounded by an effort on the part of staff to cover up her son's suicide by placing his body in his bed and hiding his belt. The mother sued in federal court, and the case was settled in late 2007 for $725,000.

Both of these tragic cases involve inept hospital care. Some would use cases like this to infer that hospital care is useless or worse. It is unfair and illogical to do so. *Inept* care is useless or worse by definition; the issue at hand is not about inept care, however. It is about hospital treatment that meets professional standards of care. Regarding the latter, there is no evidence of the treatment making people worse, and there is some evidence, albeit imperfect, that the treatment is helpful.

Even when done well, hospital treatment is not always effective; it would be surprising if it were, given that no treatments in this domain are completely effective. Few treatments for anything are. Like the red herring of inept treatment, the lack of perfect effectiveness should not deflect from the possibility that hospitalization can be therapeutic. Mental health professionals who harbor the view that hospitalization is not helpful therefore may endanger patients; not only this, they may open themselves up to considerable legal peril in the event that a patient under their care attempts or dies by suicide. As my own legal consulting work and that of my colleagues will affirm, there are a few stock phrases that would save clinicians a lot of legal risk, one of which is to say to patients, "Have you considered the possibility of a brief stay in the hospital?"

In this context, it is important to point out that there are patients whose clinical condition is dangerous enough that this question needs to be replaced by an assertion: "You need to go to the hospital." For patients who represent a clear, imminent, and physical danger to themselves (or others), involuntary hospitalization for a period of at least seventy-two hours (in most states) can and should be initiated by appropriately credentialed clinicians. Ideally, such hospitalizations allow for crisis intervention, clinical stabilization, evaluation of the need for medication, and if indicated, starting or adjusting medications, and treatment planning for when the patient leaves the hospital. Given the state of mental health care in the United States and elsewhere, it is true that this ideal is not realized as often as it should be. It is also true that inept versions of hospitalization occur and that even when the standard of care is met, patients will still die by suicide during and just after hospitalization (and clinicians will still get sued for it, even when they do everything right, though being sued and losing the suit are two very different things). This is the nature and severity of the illnesses that underlie suicidal behavior. None of these gainsays the essential point, however: These conditions can make people acutely ill, and, as in other areas of health care like infection or heart disease, acute and severe illness often necessitates hospitalization.

"Rational" Suicide

In Tom Hunt's book *Cliffs of Despair,* he states, "According to [a doctor near the Beachy Head cliffs], a fifth of the people who jump off the cliffs suffer not from mental illness but from 'exogenous stress, varying from impending court proceedings to unrequited love'" (p. 143). This puts the estimate of suicide decedents who have mental disorders at 80 percent—too low as I will argue—and also overlooks the point that things like "court proceedings and unrequited love" can trigger mental disorders (especially mood disorders). The majority of people who undergo these stressors do not die by suicide. Writing in the *American Journal of Insanity,* which he edited in the 1800s, John Gray stated that "in the large proportion of cases, if not the majority, [suicide] is committed by sane people." One wonders how many misinterpreted such statements to mean "most people who die by suicide do not have mental disorders." This is not what Gray meant; what he intended was that most who die by suicide do not necessarily have particular *kinds* of mental disorders (those with delusional or otherwise psychotic features, for instance).

In *The Diary of a Writer,* Dostoevsky recorded his own views, stripped down from and unfiltered by the characters in his novels. Regarding the logic of suicide, he wrote, "I will not and cannot be happy on the condition of being threatened with tomorrow's zero . . . therefore, in my unmistakable role of a plaintiff and of a defendant, of a judge and of an accused, I sentence this nature, which has so unceremoniously and impudently brought me into existence for suffering, to annihilation, together with myself . . . because I am unable to destroy nature, I am destroying only myself." In the same work, he states, "It is clear, then, that suicide—when the idea of immortality has been lost—becomes an utter and inevitable necessity for any man who, by his mental development, has even slightly lifted himself above the level of cattle."

Dostoevsky was an accomplished writer, the author of extraordinary novels like *Crime and Punishment.* And it is only through writing that he in any way acted on his logical resolve for suicide. Dostoevsky did not "destroy" himself—he died at age 59 from a lung hemorrhage—and thus on his own very dubious logic remained at "the level of cattle." He had one of his fictional characters, Kirilov, enact "logical suicide" in the novel *The Possessed.* As has been mentioned throughout this book, at least when it comes to understanding the facts and truth about suicide, it is crucial to remember the clear line that separates fiction from reality.

My view is that the vast majority of deaths by suicide, approaching 100 percent, involve a combination of learned fearlessness with two simultaneous, long-lasting states of mind: 1) the view that one burdens others to such a degree that one's death will be worth more than one's life; and 2) the view that one is profoundly alienated from others. It is difficult if not impossible to hold these states of mind and to be "rational" in the sense that most people mean when they use the term "rational suicide."

Consistent with this, my view also is that virtually everyone, approaching if not 100 percent, who dies by suicide had a mental disorder or a subclinical variant thereof at the time of death. If "virtually everyone" is defined as greater than 90 percent, then this statement is not controversial, as numerous rigorous studies have shown (thus the British doctor's estimate of 80 percent, noted above, is too low). At least 90 percent of those who die by suicide have at least one *full syndrome* mental disorder (not partial syndrome or subclinical variant) at the time of their suicide. The question is about the remaining few, at most 10 percent.

It is my view that these 10 percent have partial syndrome or subclinical variant versions of mental disorders. For the sake of clarity, by "partial syndrome or subclinical variant," I mean symptoms of mental disorders that, though they do not meet full criteria for diagnoses as spelled out in the psychiatric nomenclature, nonetheless cause noticeable distress and impairment. In the lexicon of the *Diagnostic and Statistical Manual (DSM)*, soon to appear in its fifth edition, such clinical presentations often carry the moniker "not otherwise specified" (NOS). For example, a person who experiences suicidal ideation, sleep disturbance, and sadness, but does not experience any of the other six symptoms specified by *DSM* as constituting major depressive disorder (i.e., anhedonia, appetite disturbance, concentration problems, energy problems, guilt, psychomotor retardation/agitation), does not meet diagnostic criteria for major depressive disorder because at least five of the nine symptoms are required. Assuming the three symptoms of suicidal ideation, sleeplessness, and sadness are causing marked distress and impairment, however, the person would meet criteria for depressive disorder not otherwise specified (NOS).

Note in the example of a person with depressive disorder NOS that the symptoms may not necessarily be readily apparent to most or even to any of the people in the individual's life. People can feel sad, think about suicide, and not sleep well without anyone else knowing, in part because they are "getting by" and functioning reasonably well. Should someone die by suicide under this scenario, many would claim that the individual had no mental disorder. The more accurate claim would be that the person had no mental disorder as far as anyone knew. When deaths like this are investigated using "psychological autopsy" (interviews with surviving family and friends; comprehensive record review), what often emerges is a partial syndrome mental disorder that none of the family or friends recognized as such.

My suspicion is that this is exactly what happened regarding the death by suicide of the private high school's president in January 2008, mentioned earlier. He gave a very capable and indeed enthusiastic speech to students and staff to kick off the new year. Those who heard the speech reported that the man seemed to be functioning well, as usual. A few hours later, he checked in to a room on the upper floors of a downtown hotel, left a suicide note there, and jumped to his death. Looking back on the man's life, there were indications that mild to moderate depressive symptoms had affected him, off and on, over the previous years, and these may very well have figured into his death, but these symptoms were not apparent to the people in the audience who heard him talk, fluently and competently, in the hours before his suicide.

A further important consideration: If one is suffering from a partial syndrome mental disorder (or a full-blown disorder, for that matter) and one is therefore considering suicide, it is quite possible that one might want to rationalize the choice, especially in light of the stigma surrounding mental disorders and suicide. Statements in suicide notes along the lines of "For the record, I do not have a mental disorder; I am doing this for rational reasons with sound mind" are not rare. They are also not necessarily true—people who really do have mental disorders can and do make such statements regularly.

One issue—really the only issue—that tempts me to back off the position that fully 100 percent of those who die by suicide have mental disorders is physician-assisted suicide. Since Oregon passed its Death with Dignity Act in 1997 and the procedure became available in 1998, 341 people have died by physician-assisted suicide (this figure of 341 is through 2007), an average of approximately thirty-four people per year, 86 percent of whom had terminal forms of cancer. The procedure involves prescriptions obtained from physicians that are self-administered, lethal doses of medication. There are many safeguards built into the process, including the requirement that the patient make two discrete written requests to die, separated by at least fifteen days, a determination by a physician that the patient is mentally competent to make the decision to die, and an evaluation of whether the patient has a mental disorder like depression.

By definition, then, none of these patients has a full-blown mental disorder like major depressive disorder, else they would be screened out by the process. This does not of necessity prevent the possibility, however, that they have partial syndrome conditions, such as two or three prominent depressive symptoms; they indeed have at least one by definition, namely, the desire to die. I am inclined toward the view, though I acknowledge it is debatable, that those who choose physician-assisted suicide have partial syndrome mental disorders (virtually all depressive disorder NOS) for three reasons.

First, it is crucial to understand that only a proportion of people with terminal illnesses want to die. In a study of patients with amyotrophic lateral sclerosis (ALS) disease, one of the main predictors of desire for assisted suicide was distress at being a burden on others. In these kinds of studies, progression of illness and factors like amount of pain are accounted for, and so it is not that these factors explain why some feel a burden and want to die and others do not. Among similarly ill and pain-affected individuals, some want to die and some do not, and perceived burdensomeness seems to differentiate the two groups. To understand this difference, one could attribute particular resilience and strength to the group that wants to live, a very plausible view. But it may be just as plausible to attribute subthreshold depressive symptoms to those who desire death. And note, in this context, that it should make no difference if such symptoms are understandable given the circumstances. According to *DSM*, depressive reactions are depressive reactions regardless of the trigger (e.g., a man who is severely depressed about loss of job, marriage, and home is nonetheless diagnosed with depression).

Second, it is interesting that, of all Oregonians who go through the process to obtain physician-assisted death, only a proportion (approximately 60 percent) actually use the lethal prescriptions provided to them. One reason for this is that some die from the underlying illness (usually cancer) before they are prepared to use the prescription. But another reason is that some decide not to use the prescription. To my knowledge, there are no systematic data comparing those who obtain the prescription and then use it versus those who do not use it, but my guess is that one predictor of this difference would be factors like perceived burdensomeness, purpose in life, connection to life, and so on.

Third, in 2007 the most frequently mentioned motivations among those who died from the prescriptions in Oregon were loss of autonomy, decreasing ability to participate in activities that make life enjoyable, and loss of dignity. Most people readily understand these motivations, but again, it must be remembered that there are many people, equally ill and in pain as those who decide to die, who do not endorse these motivations.

And so I am prepared to defend the view that 100 percent of suicides are characterized by the combination of learned fearlessness, perceived burdensomeness, and profound alienation from others, and that these factors, in turn, arise from underlying mental disorders, mostly of the full-blown type, but sometimes of the partial syndrome variety. As discussed in detail in other sections of the book, people can have these conditions, especially depression, and not be psychotic or deluded, and, certainly in the case of people with terminal illnesses, people can have subsyndromal depressions that most of us can readily understand, sympathize, and even identify with. But none of this changes the fact, in my view, that mental disorders represent the matrix from which serious suicidal behavior emerges.

"Slow" Suicide

As a recent biography shows, the comedian Chris Farley was a good-hearted man, and a very gifted actor and comedian (*The Chris Farley Show*, 2008). He also was badly addicted to drugs and alcohol. His intake of alcohol and numerous other drugs was prodigious and frequent. Farley did many stints in rehab settings, a few of which he was able to follow with months, and in at least one instance, around two years, of sobriety. Ultimately, he would return to heavy use of drugs and alcohol, which badly affected his career (major studio films take out insurance policies on their stars to protect their investment, and Farley became uninsurable), and in the end, it killed him. He died of opiate and cocaine intoxication, with coronary atherosclerosis as a significant contributing condition. His autopsy showed cocaine, heroin, and marijuana in his system at the time of his death. The last person to see this loving and friendly man was a female escort he had hired.

Did Farley have a "death wish?" After all, he had been told by family, fellow and former *Saturday Night Live* cast members, and many health professionals that his pattern of behavior would likely kill him, as it did one of Farley's heroes, John Belushi. Still, he willingly continued, often with obvious relish. Moreover, in his biography, one of his friends stated, "He called me late one night and told me why he wasn't going to stay sober anymore, and, at that point, we both knew what that meant. The thing is, Chris actually had great willpower, and great strength. Once he decided something, it was done." The implication is that Farley had decided on death, a gradual, self-inflicted death, with drugs and alcohol as the means.

Tellingly, however, this view seems to be the minority opinion among Farley's friends. One friend said, "I don't buy that it was a death wish, that it was a slow suicide. I just don't." Another stated, "Any idea that Chris wanted to die is bullshit. Chris was so full of life, and he had a boundless enthusiasm for everything and everyone. He enjoyed his life and savored it."

As I explain further below, I think Farley's friends who believed he loved life and wanted to continue living (and doing drugs and drinking) were almost certainly correct. But some of the reasons that Farley's friends marshal for this view sound a lot like another myth covered in this book: "It could not have been suicide because the person had future plans." As I discussed, such plans are not probative regarding whether a death was caused by homicide, suicide, accident, or natural causes. People who die from each of these causes regularly express plans to go shopping the next day, interview for a job the next week, or sell or buy a car or house the next month. Farley's friends fall into this same logical trap, believing that his plans and hope for the future rule out suicide; they do not.

But other things do. In the days before his death, if Farley had been interviewed by a psychologist who (as some do) employed a "sentence completion test," it is interesting to ponder what his reaction would have been to the stem phrase, "I enjoy ____." All indications from Farley's life, including accounts of his final days, suggest that he would have responded along the lines of "everything, I enjoy everything—my family, my friends, my profession, my faith (Farley was an observant Catholic), and I enjoy having fun too, including alcohol and drugs." Contrast this with the response to the same stem phrase of someone on the verge of suicide. The response would be empty and bleak; something like "I enjoy nothing" or "I enjoy death."

It is the difference between Farley's hypothetical response and that of the suicidal person that, I believe, falsifies the notion of "slow suicide." Why do people who know they should not smoke anymore do so anyway, at great risk to their lives? It is not because they like death, it is because they like *smoking;* the risks they are willing to take show just how much they like it. Why did Farley (and so many others, famous and lesser known alike) continue the very extensive use of drugs that he had been told and understood might well kill him? It was not because he liked death, it was because he liked *drugs*—he liked them so much that the risks be damned.

If, in some fantasy world, you offered the severely addicted smoker a deal in which he or she could continue to smoke without limit, as well as the assurance of no health effects, you would be hard-pressed to detect any disappointment. On the contrary, the smoker would have a "cake and eat it too" feeling, characterized more by mirth than anything else. If, in this thought experiment, the intent of the smoker was really "slow suicide," they would feel (at least a little) thwarted and not so mirthful. Judging by the smokers I know, I am confident how this little fantasy experiment would turn out.

Consider also people who *both* liked drugs *and* who died by suicide by means other than drug overdose. Indeed, this is a common pattern among chronic heroin abusers (who have above-average rates of death by suicide but whose suicides often do not occur via heroin overdose), and it clearly was the case with musician Kurt Cobain, who fronted the group Nirvana. Cobain was a daily self-injecting heroin user and used many other drugs too. Unlike Farley, Cobain was not a contented man, enthusiastic about everyone and everything. One need look no farther than the lyrics he wrote to see this fact, and if still unconvinced, a glance at his journals, now published, will confirm it. At the end of his life, Cobain was in misery, and this of course was a main factor in his death by suicide, which occurred, not by heroin overdose, but by self-inflicted gunshot wound.

There are two separate processes at play in Cobain's life (though it is the case that the two can get intertwined). The first he shared with Farley—both men enjoyed drugs, so much so that they were willing to take great risks to use them. The second process is suicidal in nature—Cobain had thought about suicide many times over the years before his death (as his journals and lyrics show) and had attempted suicide at least once. Using heroin is like playing with fire, and certainly, the troubles it causes can contribute to people's misery and fearlessness, a lethal mixture for suicide. But to say that heroin is primary in deaths like Cobain's—or to say that its use represents a "slow" suicide in deaths like Farley's—is to misunderstand the nature of suicidal behavior, substance abuse, and accidental death. Cobain did not die by heroin overdose, accidental or otherwise; he died quite intentionally by self-inflicted gunshot wound. Farley did not intentionally die; he died by accidental drug overdose, and the evidence indicates that his last words and gestures conveyed that he desperately did not want to die—reports are that, in the moments before he lost consciousness, he pleaded with the escort who was with him to help him, and gasped "don't leave me."

People with anorexia nervosa—essentially a self-starvation syndrome—have also been viewed as engaging in "slow suicide." It is not difficult to see why this has come up. Self-starvation can result in death, and indeed, there are documented instances in which people—nonanorexic people—have retreated to isolated areas like remote woods, denied themselves water, and thereby died by suicide. People with anorexia nervosa are at high risk for death by suicide. Indeed, anorexia nervosa is the most lethal psychiatric syndrome of all, and if a person with anorexia has died prematurely, chances are that the cause of death was suicide (as opposed to the consequences, often cardiac in nature, of self-starvation, though this can be a cause of death too).

Despite all this, it is a mistake to view anorexia nervosa as a form of suicide per se. The crucial point is that anorexic people are not getting thin to die, they are "dying to be thin." Thinness is the goal, and people with the syndrome crave it much as people crave a substance to which they are addicted. This can be seen rather clearly on "pro-anorexia" Web sites

(Web sites aimed at helping people with the condition maintain their disorder by viewing it as a life choice rather than as a disorder). Virtually all of these sites include "thinspiration" images, pictures of emaciated models, celebrities, and other women (almost all images are of women). Studies of such sites show that visitors spend a lot of time examining these images, and many leave comments like "I love those ribs" and "One day I will be thin enough. Just the bones, no disfiguring flesh." This last comment seems to involve death, but death is not mentioned; thinness is.

What anorexic people are doing is dangerous, no doubt, just as what Chris Farley was doing was dangerous. In the minds of these individuals, the goal is not death, but the goal, whether of thinness or of drug use, is, to them, worth the danger of death.

Another important point is that, in absolute terms, most people with anorexia nervosa do not die. As noted in an earlier section, my colleagues and I published a paper relevant to this topic in the *Journal of Affective Disorders*, which involved a sample of approximately 250 anorexic individuals followed from around age 20 to around age 35. Eleven of the 250 died during the follow-up study, most by suicide, a staggering rate of early mortality in *relative* terms (matched samples without anorexia would have no deaths, or perhaps one). In absolute terms, however, the vast majority did not die. I believe this is because the point of anorexia is not to die, and so most anorexics do not. The point is extreme thinness, a side effect or byproduct of which can be death, and so the condition is associated with high rates of early mortality.

Still another angle on "slow suicide" and self-starvation is that there are people who eat extremely restricted diets in order to *extend* their lives. There is some evidence that a very low-calorie diet—one that causes body mass index numbers that are similar to those of some patients with anorexia—causes longevity (the evidence is not totally consistent, and is clearer in animals than in humans); it also causes things like frequent chills, low endurance, and orange skin (due to the ingestion of large amounts of carotenoids found in low-calorie, high-nutrient foods like carrots and kale). The connection between anorexia and calorie restriction has occurred to adherents of the latter lifestyle (there is a society called the Calorie Restriction Society)—in a 2006 *New York Magazine* article, a calorie restriction (CR) enthusiast stated, "The focus of CR is health. Nobody here is trying to figure out how to eat less and disappear. The constant thought is, 'How can I pack more nutrition into my calories?'—and that's not something an anorexic is doing. Anorexia is slow suicide."

But anorexia is not slow suicide. Anorexics are not focused on health, true, but they are not usually focused on death either. They are focused on emaciation. (Whether or not calorie restriction is all that different from anorexia is somewhat arguable—both groups are obsessed with food and with body impacts, both groups prize appearance-related effects of low food intake, both groups are thin to the point that some untoward physical effects occur.)

The concept of "slow suicide" has also emerged regarding a phenomenon referred to as "passive suicide." The notion is that a person might cause his or her own death, but in a way that requires little initiative or effort; in addition to such things as anorexia and excessive substance use, other examples that have been proffered include a severe diabetic who does not adhere to treatment and a person who steps into traffic without looking at a time when there are relatively few cars. The concept of "passive suicide" overlooks the key idea of suicidal intent. If someone intends to die by suicide and enacts his or her death by refusing medicine, food, or water, what is "passive" about that? If someone wanders into a street with no cars and little chance of being struck, what is "suicidal" about that?

The distinction between suicidal intent and the idea of "passive suicide" has been supported empirically, including by studies using factor analysis of questionnaires and interviews assessing suicidality (factor analysis is a statistical method that sorts like with like). These analyses produce two factors; one is made up of items reflecting serious intent and planfulness to die (an ominous factor); the other is made up of items reflecting a wish not to live, a desire for death, and so on (a less ominous factor). Which factor does "passive suicide" go with? It goes with the "desire not to live" items, not with the more serious intent or plan items. Intent and planfulness are essential aspects of serious suicidality, and the fact that "passive suicide" does not group with such items indicates that "passive suicide" is separable from truer, more ominous forms of suicidality.

Freud posited a life instinct *(eros)*—eminently sensible. He also proposed a death instinct *(thanatos)*—less sensible and less in accord with data from the natural world, although perhaps understandable to those, like Freud, who lived through the death and destruction of the First World War. Picking up the theme, Menninger wrote, "There is a little murder and a little suicide dwelling in everybody's heart." Menninger is impressed in this context with ascetics who retreat to the desert, whose self-denial represents to Menninger a form of suicidality. He believes that the proclivity to retreat to the arid desert represents an infantile wish to return to the mother's womb. So, he claims, do fantasies of drowning. Similarly implausibly, Menninger wrote, "In the end, each man kills himself in his own selected way, fast or slow, soon or late." This is just not so, for all the reasons articulated above.

3/ Causes, Consequences, and Subpopulations

I n the preceding two chapters, seventeen separate myths or misunderstandings have been addressed. That's a lot, but there are many more, and these remaining topics involve claims like "this or that thing causes suicidal behavior" or "suicidal behavior does not occur in this or that group." Some interesting points and distinctions will emerge—for instance, suicidal behavior occurs across nature, including animals and even plants. Young children die by suicide, too. The comings and goings of the seasons can spur suicidal behavior, as can rhythms inherent in the days of the week and in menstruation. Regarding consequences of suicidal behavior, those have been referred to throughout the book and will be referred to throughout this chapter too, though one consequence in particular gets specific and, I believe, needed attention, and that's the issue of lying to young ones and others about the cause of death in instances when someone has died by suicide. In this chapter, as in others, the truth can be as interesting and surprising as the myth, as illustrated by the view that suicide is a uniquely human act—as we will see, it is not.

"Animals Don't Die by Suicide"

Of course people are animals, and it is abundantly clear that people die by suicide. This may seem like a technicality or wordplay, but it is not. Most life or death things that apply to people apply to other animals too. Just scan down the leading causes of deaths in people—the top three are heart disease, stroke, and cancer—sure enough, these kill animals too. The Bible gets this right; from Ecclesiastes, "That which befalleth the sons of men befalleth beasts . . . as the one dieth, so dieth the other."

But suicide? Many have thought not. In his *Conceptions of Modern Psychiatry,* the American psychiatrist Harry Stack Sullivan stated, "So far as we know, there is nothing remotely approaching [suicide] in the infrahuman primates or any of the lower animals. It is a distinctly human performance." Highlighted on the back cover of Ed Shneidman's book *The Suicidal Mind* is the statement, "Suicide is an exclusively human response to extreme psychological pain." Georges Minois, in his *History of Suicide* (1999), put it even more emphatically (and as we will see, incorrectly), "Suicide is an exclusively human behavior: Both animal suicides and suicide epidemics are myths." Minois was doubly mistaken—as we will see, self-sacrifice is pervasive across the animal kingdom;

moreover, suicide epidemics, at least in the form of spates of suicides in a given locale occurring far beyond chance rates, clearly exist. The people of Wales can attest to this, as they lost at least seventeen young people to suicide in the single area of Bridgend, almost all in 2007.

When I mention the issue of suicidal behavior in animals to people who do not study suicidal behavior for a living (and even to some who do), by far the most common reaction is something along the lines of "lemmings, of course." Lemmings, members of the rodent family, engage in mass migrations when their numbers outpace their food source (usually a kind of moss). These migrations can be very chaotic and can therefore lead to the deaths of many lemmings, though these deaths are accidental, not intentional. Interestingly, lemmings can swim, and if a migration leads them to a cliff overlooking water, many of the animals will leap into the water, urged on by the press to find food and also by crowding against the cliff's edge. Many do not survive the plunge and many of those who do later drown. This phenomenon no doubt led some to imagine that they were intentionally leaping to their deaths. Such imaginations have been fueled over the years by various shows and films. For example, the documentary *White Wilderness,* produced by Walt Disney in 1958, shows footage of what appears to be lemmings running over a ledge to their deaths. A later investigation showed, however, that the footage was faked; lemmings were purchased by the filmmakers, and some of them were thrown by the crew into the sea.

These kinds of incidents propagated the lemmings myth,

but I think another factor perpetuates it—the similarity of the story to one that appears in the New Testament, in slightly different versions in the gospels of Matthew, Mark, and Luke. Jesus comes upon a man whose behavior has been very disturbing to his community, so much so that he is put in chains in the cemetery—chains that he regularly breaks. In chapter 5 of the gospel of Mark, verses 4 and 5, it reads, "Whenever he was put into chains and shackles—as he often was—he snapped the chains from his wrists and smashed the shackles. No one was strong enough to subdue him. Day and night he wandered among the burial caves and in the hills, howling and cutting himself with sharp stones." The man's self-injury, incidentally, is one of several instances of such in the story of Jesus in the New Testament, perhaps foreshadowing the resolution of that story. The man saw Jesus as he approached, and began to beg Jesus not to torture him. Jesus asked the man's name, to which he replied, "My name is Legion, because there are many of us inside this man." The spirits spotted a herd of pigs nearby, and asked Jesus to send them into the pigs. Jesus obliged, at which point the 2,000 pigs plunged themselves into a lake and drowned. The man was left calm and "perfectly sane."

In modern terms, this is likely a story—and one full of hyperbole at that—about schizophrenia and the effect of a charismatic person on vulnerable people and perhaps on animals too. I think it is largely fiction, and I mean that as a compliment—it is great literature. This story tells of the agony of mental disorders, and also of their power. The man's distress was so powerful that the community could not contain it, not even with chains. That the distress had suicidal elements is evident from the man's self-injury, as well as from the ultimate fate of the herd of pigs. That the "spirits"—that is, the man's illness and suicidality—were sufficient not only to "infect" 2,000 pigs but also to drive them to suicide, shows, I think, the writer's understanding of the power of conditions like mental disorders and associated suicidality.

It also shows a two-thousand-year-old belief that at least some forms of suicidal behavior exist in animals. In fact, there is a substantial amount of and diversity in self-sacrifice in nature. The diversity of the phenomenon is clear in humans: People not only die by suicide in the conventional sense, but there are quasi-suicidal phenomena like suicide terrorism, kamikaze pilots, and self-sacrificing heroism. Regarding the amount of self-sacrifice in nature, insects provide probably the clearest example.

For readers who have not lived south of a line that extends approximately from North Carolina to central California in the United States, the "fire" in the term "fire ants" may not provoke a visceral response. It refers not to their color (though they are red) but rather to their sting—when a nest is disturbed, the ants swarm and sting, leaving painful welts. Their mode of self-sacrifice involves their mating behavior. Like so much in ant life, reproduction is a function carried out only by specific individuals, the "sexuals." These sexuals, despite being ants, grow wings. Somewhat romantically, these wings are used only once, for mating. Both the male and female sexuals take flight, mostly in the spring, and mate in midair (Tschinkel, 2007).

There is a romantic quality to this, but also a graphic one. Once the male and female are coupled, the male's entire genitalia quite literally explode into the female's. This has two major consequences. First, it delivers 7 million or so sperm into the female, all that she will need for the rest of her life. Second, it kills the male. Why does the male engage in this fatal flight? Specifically because the ant's death will be worth more than his life to his genes. That is, the sacrifice of the genes that reside in him is very well compensated, in evolutionary terms, by the millions of copies of his genes that will persist in his mate—a future queen—and in her offspring.

Self-sacrifice in fire ants is a male phenomenon occurring in the spring. In humans, far more men than women die by suicide, and there is a spring peak in suicides as well as a winter low point. Perhaps these are just coincidences, but in my view, they reach the threshold for a "damn strange coincidence"—a designation coined by eminent psychologist Paul Meehl for situations in which a weird coincidence may shed new light on the underlying nature and structure of a phenomenon of interest.

Male honeybees, too, experience death in midair during copulation. In his excellent book *The Buzz about Bees: Biology of a Superorganism,* Jurgen Tautz writes of male honeybees' aerial pursuit of a queen:

> They catch up with her, they grasp the queen with their legs, and latch on to her genital organ with their mating apparatus. They extrude about 50% of [their genital organ], and then just hang passively on the queen . . . the

complete extrusion of the [male's genital organ] is undertaken by the queen herself, through a strong contraction of her abdominal muscles. It is not unusual for this process to result in the explosion of the [male's] abdomen, with a sometimes audible snap while still in the air. The bursting of the [male's] abdomen results in his immediate death. (pp. 120–121)

Another clear example of self-sacrifice in the course of reproduction, all for the good of one's genes, occurs in the Australian redback spider. After sex the male redback is eaten by the female, and the male puts up little struggle. Male redbacks do this apparently to gain advantages in the competition for females, and thus to win in the effort to pass on genes: Cannibalized males copulate longer and fertilize more eggs compared to males that survive copulation. Also, after consuming their first mate, female redbacks are likely to reject subsequent males—and thus reject their genes in favor of those of the original male redback. There is some evidence, although it is not as clear as in the case of the Australian redback spider, that some male praying mantises adopt the same self-sacrificial reproductive strategy.

Other insects sacrifice themselves for the good of their genes' persistence as well, but not all of these strategies directly involve reproduction. Like the stories of the fire ants, honeybees, and Australian redback spiders, pea aphid self-sacrifice has some grim elements, but the underlying motive would seem to have redeeming properties too. One of the life worries of pea aphids involves wasps. The problem is that the wasps use the pea aphids as a kind of incubator for their own offspring. A wasp will inject an egg into a host aphid, and as the young wasp matures, its food source is the host aphid's insides. Eventually, the now mature wasp chews its way out of the aphid's body and flies off, leaving the host aphid dead. Of course, this now mature wasp will go on to victimize other pea aphids in just the way that the wasp's parent did. Multiplied over many wasps and aphids, this entire affair can devastate pea aphid populations.

To survive, the pea aphid needed to evolve a breaking mechanism, so that wasps would not wipe them out. The breaking mechanism is self-sacrifice. When injected with a wasp egg, the aphid will kill itself soon thereafter. The method of self-sacrifice is dropping from plant stalks and leaves (where pea aphids spend their lives) to the ground, where they are soon preyed upon by ladybugs and other natural predators.

Why do pea aphids do this? Why do they willingly give themselves up? They do it because their deaths will be worth more than their lives . . . to their genes. Just as a male fire ant self-sacrifices because the loss of his copy of genes is compensated for by the millions of copies of his genes that his queen will go on to produce, so pea aphids self-sacrifice because the loss of their copy of genes is compensated for by the survival of their genes in their many pea aphid relatives, who will live on due in part to the self-sacrifice. Aphids' self-sacrifice kills not only themselves but the parasite as well, sparing the rest of the population, where the majority of copies of the self-sacrificing aphid's genes reside. In the animal kingdom as in humans, the motivating force appears to be "my death will be worth more than my life." Fire ants and pea aphids are correct in their calculations, which imparts a kind of redeeming selflessness to their behavior; humans are incorrect in their calculations, as their devastated families can assure you.

Amazingly, pea aphids have evolved yet another defense, this time not against parasitization, but against direct predators, particularly their nemesis, the ladybug. Aphids have the ability to transform what they eat into a chemical irritant, mustard oil, which they can use as a kind of chemical bomb against ladybugs. When an aphid explodes the chemical bomb, three things happen: 1) the ladybug is either killed, badly injured, or else scurries away; 2) other aphids scatter, making them harder to prey upon; and 3) the original aphid dies from the explosion of the mustard oil bomb, the insect world's version of the suicide bomb. Again, the calculation is made to sacrifice self for the good of one's genes, which live on in others.

Unless, that is, there's another solution . . . and there is for at least some pea aphids. Those that are mature enough can simply fly away instead of exploding the chemical suicide bomb. Flying away makes evolutionary sense, of course, because the aphid that does so lives another day—a day in which the aphid can see to passing on its genes directly through its own reproductive behavior.

This may seem selfish, at least compared to the aphids who sacrifice themselves either through dropping to the ground or through detonating a chemical suicide bomb, but really, all these behaviors are selfish. They are all selfish in the sense that they are motivated by the quest to preserve and sustain one's own genes. This kind of self-sacrifice is sort of what the eminent sociologist Emile Durkheim had in mind (though from an entirely different perspective) when he wrote about "altruistic suicide," which he defined as self-sacrifice for the good of the group. But Durkheim may have had this at least partly wrong—it is possible that this kind of behavior in nature, at least with regard to its evolutionary origins, is not really done for the good of the group, but for the good of one's own genes.

Worker bumblebees are another group that escape parasitization through self-sacrifice. They are parasitized by a specific species of fly, and in response, they fly off and abandon their nest. Bees cannot survive away from the hive; the behavior of cutting themselves off from the hive ensures their death. The motive for this death should be familiar now— the parasitized bee's premature death kills the parasite and avoids its spread in the bee colony, thus sparing the doomed bee's own genes, which persist in multiple copies in the saved colony.

Thus far, the examples have involved aphids, bees, spiders, and ants—a little hard, perhaps, for a human to identify with. Well, then, consider lions. Male lions will willingly give themselves up on the "battlefield," much as will humans on occasion. For the lions, the battlefields are usually the savannas and grasslands of sub-Saharan Africa, and their enemies are other male lions, who are trying to raid and steal their pride of lionesses. Now, it does not take a lot of imagination to understand why a male lion would protect his mate. But, interestingly, the battle is joined not just by male lions protecting their own mates, but also by male lions that have no mates themselves. The presence of these mateless lions is, at first glance, perplexing. Why would they sacrifice themselves to protect other lions' mates? Packs of male lions are mostly brothers; defending the brothers' pride ensures spread of one's genes through one's brothers. Is it possible that the same motive for self-sacrifice is at work in aphids, fire ants, honeybees, spiders, lions, and humans?

Why do humans self-sacrifice? Suicide terrorists and kamikaze pilots could not have been clearer that, at least in part, the motive was to benefit family and society (e.g., Reuter, 2004). Self-sacrificial heroism has been described similarly by those who engage in it and survive. The data suggest that those who engage in conventional death by suicide are also spurred, at least in part, by the opinion that their deaths will be worth more to others than their lives. A calculation that carries validity in cases like fire ants and pea aphids represents a tragic and sometimes fatal misperception in modern-day humans.

If suicidal behavior exists in species like fire ants and lions, one may legitimately wonder whether it exists in animals that are more closely related to humans. In fact, self-injurious behavior has been documented to occur in nonhuman primates; the most well-studied examples are rhesus monkeys. At times of distress, some monkeys will bite themselves, usually on their arms or legs, sometimes leaving visible injury. It is very interesting to note that the locations of these self-injuries in rhesus monkeys are not random; rather, the monkeys tend to bite themselves in body locations that are associated with acupuncture/acupressure-induced pain relief (Marinus, Chase, & Novak, 2000). These body locations are similar in humans and other primates, and humans' self-injury tends to target these areas too. It is thus possible that humans and rhesus monkeys engaging in nonsuicidal self-injury are doing so as a means to self-administer a crude form of acupuncture.

In both humans and nonhuman primates, the serotonin system appears to be involved in self-injury. In humans, there is some evidence that drugs that target the serotonin system lead to decreased self-injury. In rhesus monkeys, administration of l-tryptophan has been documented to decrease self-biting (l-tryptophan is a serotonin precursor, a building block for serotonin).

Much of this work suggests that self-injury in rhesus monkeys (and in other nonhuman primates) is motivated by stress or mood regulation, and indeed, it has been shown that for monkeys who engage in self-biting at times of stress and thus of accelerated heart rate, their heart rate decreases after self-injury. Interestingly, animals that experience stresses like separation from their mother early in their lives are especially vulnerable to the phenomenon of self-injurious behavior, suggesting that these early adverse experiences interfered with the development of more normal stress-regulation abilities. Self-injury as a means to regulate emotions has been documented in humans also. The most well-studied group are people with borderline personality disorder, many of whom have also been documented as having experienced very adverse early environments.

Astoundingly, suicidelike behavior may extend not only across the animal kingdom but to plants as well. There is an extremely rare and relatively newly discovered palm tree called the "suicide palm." A biblical quotation attributed to Jesus in the New Testament (John 12:24) describes the behavior of the palm well: "I tell you the truth, unless a kernel of wheat falls to the ground and dies, it remains only a single seed. But if it dies, it produces many seeds." This verse appeared to have impressed the Russian novelist Fyodor Dostoevsky (who was preoccupied with suicide but did not die by suicide), who used it as the epigram to *The Brothers Karamazov* and had it inscribed on his tombstone.

The "suicide palm" grows, on the island of Madagascar, to a height of around fifty feet and has huge, fan-shaped leaves. The tree gets its name from the fact that, every fifty years or so, it flowers itself to death. That is, for the only time in its fifty-year life, it bursts into bloom, showering down thousands of small flowers for pollination. The flowers develop into fruits with seeds, and these fruits are eaten by animals and birds, which disperse the seeds. Just as the male sexuals among the fire ants take one and only one fatal flight, during which they deliver millions of sperm to the future queen, so the suicide palm bursts into bloom in one and only one fatal explosion, passing on the means for its reproduction.

From these examples it is pretty clear that self-sacrifice is a common phenomenon across the animal kingdom, and its motive, consistent with the calculation "my death is worth more than my life," is to increase the chance that an individual organism's genes will persist. This is why male fire ants fly off to their deaths; why pea aphids fall to their deaths or self-detonate; why lions fight to the death on behalf of their brothers' mates; and why certain palm trees explode into flowers every fifty years or so.

But is it why humans die by suicide? Does the death of a severely depressed man, alone in his apartment, by self-inflicted gunshot wound "increase the chance that [his] genes will persist"? In one sense, no, of course not. His reasons involve feeling deeply alienated from others and feeling profoundly burdensome toward others, accompanied by a kind of learned fearlessness of self-injury. But is it more than a "damn strange coincidence" that the calculation underlying that man's feeling that he is a burden, namely, "my death will be worth more than my life," functions not only in humans but elsewhere in nature?

This pervasive calculation may exist across species as a kind of evolved behavioral module, one that has been conserved even to this day, even among humans. Of course, an evolved module that was adaptive over the course of evolutionary history may no longer be so. A complex animal like a human can take an ancient, evolved template and do any number of novel things with it. This is one view of human suicide with which I have sympathy—the fundamental calculation that self-sacrifice was evolutionarily adaptive for many animals under certain circumstances. So it may have been in the course of human evolution. But no longer. What it is now is an agonizing tragedy—a horror that may involve, in part, a kind of misfiring of a behavioral module that had adaptive properties in ancestral times but has since become a bane.

"Young Children Do Not Die by Suicide"

I certainly wish this were true, but it is not.

It is relatively rare for children to die today by any cause. This is, in part, because children have not had the time for the "slings and arrows" of life to affect their physical health. Deaths due to causes like heart disease occur rarely. Of course, wear and tear and related illnesses and problems are common in older people.

Similarly, the risks that lead to death by suicide—fearlessness about pain and death, perceived burdensomeness, and social isolation—are rare in young children as well (and common in older people, as is death by suicide). Of these three risk factors, all are rare in youth, but not equally so. Social isolation, unfortunately, affects a fairly substantial number of children, especially those who are neglected. The sense that one is a burden on others is probably a little less common in young children, but it can still occur, again especially in children who are mistreated, including being told directly that they are a burden. By contrast, fearlessness of injury and death is something that is quite rare in children because of the simple fact that the learning of such fearlessness takes time and experience. Thus, even in the rare instance that a child develops suicidal desire, enacting such desire is even more difficult for a child than it is for an adult.

Nevertheless, it happens. In the United States in 2005, there were 272 deaths by suicide in the 14-year-old and under category, approaching one death every day. The vast majority of these deaths occurred in children between the ages of 10 and

14, though some deaths were in children 9 and younger. Of this entire group, 204 were boys and 68 were girls, for a gender ratio of 3:1. This same ratio appears in a 1962 study of death by suicide in U.S. youth. Interestingly, this ratio is relatively low; the gender ratio regarding deaths by suicide across all ages in the United States was closer to 4:1 in 2005. There is a sense, then, in which male lethality accelerates over the life course, and I believe this is due to male fearlessness further outpacing female fearlessness as the years pass and experience with injury and pain accrues in males more than females.

Of the 272 deaths by suicide in U.S. children in 2005, the majority, around 65 percent, were classified as "suffocation"—mostly hanging. A paper in the March 2006 issue of the *American Journal of Forensic Medicine & Pathology* reported on deaths by hanging in South Africa in the 1990s and found several such deaths in youth, including two who were 9 years old or younger. Of the 272 U.S. youth who died by suicide but not by hanging, almost all were by self-inflicted gunshot wound. The tendency for males to use firearms can already be detected in this age group. Well over a third of all male youth suicides involved a gun; the corresponding figure for female youth suicide is well under one-fifth. If past patterns are any indication, this difference will only grow over the ensuing decades. Across all ages, around two-thirds of all male suicides in the United States involve guns; the corresponding figure for females is approximately one-third.

In a previous discussion, I described the tragic case of an 8-year-old girl who died by hanging; the allegation was that she imitated a scene in the movie *Girl, Interrupted,* an allegation that I doubt. In discussing the case, the local medical examiner stated, "An eight-year-old could not intend to take her own life"—again, as I pointed out, a ridiculous claim, as those with experience on child inpatient psychiatry units know. Worse, the coroner in question used this inaccurate view as a basis for his verdict—he ruled the death an accident, when it was almost surely a death by suicide. This suggests the possibility that suicide rates in young people, at least in some areas of the world, are underestimated because deaths that are actually suicides are being classified as accidents (this may happen from time to time with adult suicides, too, though probably less so). In his 2006 book *Postmortem*, Stefan Timmermans described two such possible incidents. In both cases, the decedents were teenage boys, and in both cases virtually all the evidence pointed to suicide. Nevertheless, in the case of an older adolescent who jumped from a high place, the medical examiner's team decided that, although the act was clearly self-caused, it was not intentional, essentially because "a teenager wouldn't do that." They ruled the death accidental. In the second instance, a younger teen died by hanging, and the staff deemed this cause of death "undetermined" because they did not know why the boy had engaged in the act. It should be emphasized that both of these cases involved teenagers. If this kind of thinking can apply to teenagers, it surely applies to children, likely leading to the misclassification of a fair number of youth suicides as either accidents or as "undetermined" deaths. A 1984 article in the *American Journal of Psychiatry* stated, "Suicides among preschoolers probably go unrecognized given the incredulity of parents and physicians." The article then refers to a chief medical examiner who said "he never records a child's death as suicide whatever its age even if a suicide note is left because he does not want to stigmatize the parents" (p. 520). Years earlier, James Toolan wrote in that same journal, "Contrary to popular opinion suicide and suicidal attempts are not rare in childhood and adolescence" (1962, p. 719).

One wonders where a belief like this would come from? Why would someone think that a young person could not intend suicide? One source, at least in part, is psychoanalysis. The view was that children could not even be depressed—much less suicidal—because they lacked a mature superego, which was the source, according to the psychoanalysts, of the excessive guilt and self-criticism characteristic of depression. Mahler stated in 1961, "We know that systematized affective disorders are unknown in childhood. It has been conclusively established that the immature personality structure of the infant or older child is not capable of producing a state of depression." This view is now discredited, but unfortunately, that does not mean that it does not persist—the remarks of the coroner in the death that was blamed on *Girl, Interrupted* show as much.

In fact, it seems that most media coverage of suicide raises the possibility that children cannot know what they are doing when they attempt and die by suicide. As reported in *People* magazine in September 2003, an 8-year-old girl died by hanging in her bedroom in New York state. The medical examiner ruled the death a suicide. And yet, the reporting of the tragedy repeatedly emphasized the possibility that the girl did not understand what she was doing. An expert interviewed for the article identified this as a possibility, and it is the explanation that the girl's devastated mother embraced, as the article makes clear.

By way of contrast, the death of a fourth-grade boy in Indiana—like so many child suicide cases, by hanging in his bedroom closet—was reported by the *Evansville Indiana Courier* (May 2007) with great skill and accuracy. As with the other cases, the death was a suicide, but unlike the other cases, this fact was affirmed by the medical examiner and was accurately (and compassionately) reported in the news article. The article describes the child's escalating behavior problems, such as sneaking out of his apartment against his mother's wishes, frequent arguments with his mother, and many problems at school. The child also expressed that he felt that nobody liked him and that he wanted to change his misbehavior. This mixture of conduct problems with depression-spectrum symptoms—feeling down on oneself, lonely, and guilty—is a common precursor to suicidal behavior for youth and adults alike.

The first patient I ever encountered in my role as a student-clinician in the 1980s was a boy about 10 years old who had nearly died by hanging. He survived and was doing relatively well a week after the incident, when I encountered him. The remaining concern with the child was mild to moderate brain damage, as the oxygen supply to his brain had been severely reduced for an unknown amount of time before he was discovered (probably not much more than two minutes, judging by his survival and relatively good recovery).

Though I had not read it at the time, a study from the

1980s on the existence and features of suicidal behavior in youth was available. In fact, this study, reported by Rosenthal and Rosenthal in a 1984 issue of the *American Journal of Psychiatry,* focused not just on youth, but on *preschool* children, average age 3.5 years old. This paper provided several illuminating findings. First, of course, the very existence of genuine suicidal behavior in children as young as 3 years flies in the face of the notion that young children cannot develop suicidality. Second, and relatedly, the majority of the suicidal preschoolers in this study viewed death as permanent, which contradicts the common claim that children who attempt suicide do not understand the irreversible nature of death. Third, the signature of suicidal behavior in the preschoolers resembled that shown in adults; specifically, as compared to a matched child psychiatric control group, the suicidal children had higher pain tolerance, less crying, more aggressive and other provocative kinds of behaviors, and also were very likely to have experienced interpersonal disruptions (loneliness, rejection) stemming from abusive family backgrounds. Children in the suicidal group were also very likely to have been multiple attempters despite their young age—in fact thirteen of sixteen had made at least two attempts.

Previously in this book, I have been critical of overreaching attempts to attribute deaths to causes like copycatting. But it should also be made clear that clusters of suicides do occasionally occur. In Japan in April 1986, pop singer Yukiko Okada jumped to her death from the seventh floor of the building that housed her recording studio. There were several suicides afterward, which is only to be expected, given the fact that deaths by suicide peak in the spring regardless of what famous people do. But some deaths appeared to be clearly linked to Okada's, including the deaths of children. About a week after the singer's death, a sixteen-year-old girl in Korea expressed to her friends that she wanted to be like Okada and later jumped to her death from a tall building. A very similar scenario unfolded in Tokyo about two days later, this time involving a 9-year-old girl. Young children do die by suicide, and suicide's features and character are more similar to adult suicide than most have realized. As with so many other myths disputed in this book, the truth is not easy. But it is better than the myth, because it allows people (including devastated parents of youth who die by suicide) to accept the truth and to start in on the journey, long and difficult to be sure, of adapting to the staggering loss of their loved one.

"Young Ones (and Others) Should Be Lied to about Deaths by Suicide"

Nine years ago, I was presented with a choice. The person who presented the choice was my son Malachi, three years old at the time. The choice was whether to lie to him or not. He said something along the lines of "I have a father; why don't you?"

Some background: This child lifted his head off my shoulder and looked me square in the face on the very day he was born—we have a picture of it. He said his first word about three and a half months later, "da da." He was and is precocious and perceptive, and this entered into my thinking about what to tell him. I realized I would not be able to keep the truth—any truth—from this child for very long. A lie would have bought some time, but only a limited amount. What else might it have bought? Here's what: A lie told by a father to a son about something deeply meaningful to both their lives, a lie that, when found out, would send this message from father to son: "I don't think you're strong enough to handle this truth." Such a lie would also generate a question—a very legitimate one—from son to father: "What else are you lying about?"

I concluded that this was a terrible bargain, and one I did not make. Not that it was easy to tell a three-year-old, gently but honestly, what happened to his granddad; why he's never met him and never will. Like any genuine work, it was hard, but like any genuine work, it paid off. Both my sons are at peace with their grandfather and educated about mental disorders. They know more or less what they look like, and they understand that they are relatively common, nothing to be ashamed about, and treatable. My hope is that this knowledge will help my sons help others in the future—their friends, their families, perhaps even themselves.

I am confident that this decision was the correct one. Not all make the same choice to be honest about death by suicide—sometimes with devastating consequences. One such unfortunate tale is told by Paul Hoffman in *Wings of Madness*, a biography of the early-twentieth-century flight pioneer Alberto Santos-Dumont. Relatively few people in the United States have heard of Dumont, but in the early 1900s he was as famous as the Wright Brothers. Indeed, there was a priority dispute regarding manned flight between him and the Wrights (with the dispute settled in the latter's favor). Today he is well known in Europe and a national icon in his native Brazil (where many would still dispute the Wrights' priority).

In his young adulthood, Santos-Dumont flew hot-air balloons around Paris, including around the Eiffel Tower. As he aged, however, he became increasingly unstable (possibly due to a condition in the bipolar spectrum, although that is not entirely clear). He checked himself in and out of various asylums in Europe. After having checked out of one of these, he was staying with his nephew at a hotel. The two were in the hotel's lobby, from which Santos-Dumont sent his nephew on a brief errand. Just after his nephew left the hotel, Santos-Dumont went up to his hotel room and hanged himself with two red ties knotted together—ties that represented one of his trademarks during his ballooning days.

In the days following his death, top Brazilian officials, possibly including the country's president, ordered that the details of Santos-Dumont's suicide be suppressed and that the cause of death be listed as cardiac arrest. One wonders if, in the early twentieth century, the frank and respectful reporting of the death by suicide of an internationally known adventurer would have contributed to a reduction in the stigma we currently attach to death by suicide.

Of course, Brazil's leaders were following a very old precedent in viewing Santos-Dumont's death as something to be lied about. In his *History of Suicide*, Georges Minois documents several such examples. For instance, in 1830, Louis Henri II, duc de Bourbon, prince de Condé, hanged himself.

In the papers, cause of death was reported as assassination. The truth had been discussed, though, prompting one of the duc's countrymen to write fourteen years later, "It is impossible to announce that the duc de Bourbon committed suicide, that the last of the Condé's hanged himself. In pronouncing these words we would believe we were unworthily calumniating the memory of that prince" (p. 316). Truth will out sooner or later, as evidenced by the fact that someone found it necessary to argue against that nobleman's suicide—fourteen years after it occurred.

But there is another way of looking at the issue. Not only will truth out, it can set you free. In a more recent case, a child had witnessed a long history of domestic violence between his parents. The violence escalated and ended in an incident in which gunfire occurred, with no injuries to anyone. The mother fled the domicile with the child, and some minutes or hours later, the father died by self-inflicted gunshot wound.

What to tell the child? Needless to say, the child was disturbed by the original incident and felt afraid of what his father might do to his mother and him. The mother was hesitant to disclose to the child that his father had died by suicide, not because of the death per se, but because of the cause. Might it be better and easier to let the child imagine that his father left the country on a long trip, she wondered? She was gently counseled to reconsider, and counselors assisted in her in talking openly with her son, who, upon learning of his father's suicide, was understandably saddened, but visibly relieved to know the threat to him and his mother no longer existed.

I recently sent out an e-mail to a listserv focused on suicide-related topics, asking for people to send me e-mail if they or a loved one had been lied to about someone's suicide. The theme of the responses was remarkably uniform, given the variety of individuals who responded: People felt that, once they finally found out about a death by suicide that was kept from them, puzzle pieces began to fall in place. This was certainly true about family relationships and family patterns, but it was also true about individuals' own histories. For example, a common kind of reaction was, "Once I found out that my mother's death was not an accident after all, it put my and my brother's long history of depression in different light, a little more sympathetic light, actually."

Research studies on this topic have found that stating the facts about a relative's death by suicide comes hard to many people. A representative study found that approximately half of those with a relative who had died by suicide hid the fact at least some of the time—this as compared to those with relatives who died by accident or from natural causes, who never hid the fact from others (Range & Calhoun, 1990). This statistic used to bother me, and I suppose it still does somewhat—close to 50 percent feel the need to deceive about suicide, whereas no one does about other causes of death. Indeed, in what I've written above, I've revealed some of my annoyance by using terms like "lying" and "deceive." Is that fair?

I don't think it is, at least not always. My dad died by suicide in 1990, almost nineteen years ago as I write this, and when I heard of people's lies about what happened to my dad,

I could barely conceal my contempt. I started doing research on mood disorders and suicidal behavior even before my dad died, and in the years since then, I have done quite a bit of work on the topic, including the book *Why People Die by Suicide,* in which I discuss my dad's death at some length.

But through all those years and through all that work, I never knew, not until 2008, that my maternal grandfather died by suicide too. I don't feel actively lied to about that, and I'm not angry about it. My mother lost both her dad and her husband to suicide, and yet is doing well—that stirs both sympathy and pride in me. It also humbles me a little and reminds me that though I found my dad's death agonizing, there are many others with heavier burdens still. Also, might her previous experience with her dad's death have helped her cope with my dad's death?

Though the genetic contribution to suicidal behavior should not be overplayed—it exists but is by no means determinative—my sisters and I are, relatively speaking, genetically loaded for problems, which puts our struggles and accomplishments in a somewhat different light. And if we're genetically loaded (again, only relatively speaking), then our children are to a degree as well. So I told mine the truth as a hedge against risk, and have never looked back.

Suicide and Genetics

It is remarkable how many instances occur throughout the literature asserting with total confidence that "suicide is not genetic." This is made all the more remarkable given how frequently over the centuries the connection between heredity and suicidal behavior has been noted (e.g., it is reiterated in editions of Isaac Ray's *Treatise on the Medical Jurisprudence of Insanity,* which was published between 1831 and 1878). Not having read or believed this work, Karl Menninger, in his 1938 book *Man against Himself,* stated, "There is no convincing scientific evidence that the suicidal impulse is hereditary and there is much psychoanalytic evidence to show that the cases of numerous suicides in one family may be explained on a psychological basis." When a loved one dies by suicide, Menninger believed, a relative's unconscious death wish is suddenly gratified, creating a wave of guilt that may culminate in another suicide. Note in passing the view of human nature implied here: Not only are people unconsciously pleased when a loved has died by suicide, but they are so hapless that the ensuing guilt overwhelms them and leads them to suicide as well.

As what he apparently viewed as very persuasive evidence, Menninger described an anecdote involving a Countess of Cardigan (p. 53, footnote). The countess's mother had died by suicide, and the countess regularly felt suicidal herself, especially on the anniversary of her mother's death. Ultimately, the countess died by suicide on the eighth anniversary of her mother's passing. Menninger remarked, "Even the most ardent believer in heredity would not expect the suicidal impulse to recur in annual cycles." This statement is ignorant of two fundamental facts: Suicidal impulses do recur in annual cycles, as evidenced by suicide's "spring peak," and genes do not code for such ideas as, "I believe I will kill myself on the anniversary of a parent's death." Rather, they code for general tendencies—in this case, toward suicide—tendencies that are shaped, exacerbated, and mollified by a diverse array of other influences (including, for some, anniversaries).

Menninger was working many decades ago and was under the sway of a pervasive but dubious theoretical framework. Thus we might hope that such dismissals of the role of genetics in suicide are a thing of the past. But in his 2004 book *The Copycat Effect,* Loren Coleman writes, "The fact that learned behavior, rather than genetics, may lie behind the 'suicides running in families' is clearest if one compares the Fonda and Hemingway situations," referring to the families of actor Henry Fonda and writer Ernest Hemingway (p. 220). Coleman suggests the Fondas are good at coping with suicide and good at surviving suicide, whereas the Hemingways are not. He states, "The Fonda family has embraced and understood that suicide is pervasive, and their copycat behavior has come as survivors, not victims" (p. 221). According to Coleman, the Hemingways copycat dysfunctionally; the Fondas copycat functionally; both families have a lot of suicides, but Coleman believes none is genetically influenced. To imagine in 2004 that suicide does not have a genetic component is astounding. Menninger (in 1938) and Coleman (in 2004) mention family after family in which suicide runs— at least suggestive of a genetic effect—and then both retreat from genetics, mostly, I believe, to support other positions—psychoanalysis, for Menninger, and "copycatting," for Coleman.

What do the actual data say? Anecdotal data, though open

to doubt, can be intriguing. Suicidal behavior runs in my family, as I have mentioned. Would Menninger really want to claim that my dad's death was due to the guilt he felt about feeling gleeful over his wife's dad's death twenty years earlier, a man he really did not know? Or would Coleman really want to argue that my dad copycatted his father-in-law's suicide after an interval of twenty years, again a man my dad barely knew? (Or was it some other suicide my dad copycatted, one that occurred in 1990, the year of my dad's death—it would not be hard to find one, in that there are a million suicides to choose from in 1990, not to mention 1989.) And who did my granddad "copycat"?

Of course my dad and maternal granddad were genetically unrelated, but that does not provide positive evidence for a nongenetic view. There is no doubt of a genetic component to heart disease, for example, and if the many millions who die from it each year are genetically unrelated, the fact nonetheless stands. Menninger noted "a highly regarded family [that] contained five sons and two daughters; the oldest son killed himself at 35, the youngest developed a depression and attempted suicide several times but finally died of other causes at 30, a third brother killed himself in a manner similar to that of his older brother, still another brother shot himself to death, and the oldest daughter took poison successfully at a party. Only two children remain living of this entire family." The plight of this poor family is at the very least suggestive of the possibility of a genetic effect.

How to demonstrate an effect? We might begin by asking two questions: As demonstrated by what, and as compared to what? Again, families like the Fondas, the Hemingways, and the remarkable family described by Menninger show, in their high rates of suicide, that genes may be involved. The suicide rates in these families are compatible with a genetic explanation, but these families' suicide rates are compatible with other explanations too. We have seen two such accounts from Menninger and Coleman. A more plausible view—and one that is still nongenetic—would involve the environmental (emotional, verbal) transmission from parents to children of factors that confer risk for suicidal behavior. Examples might include a pessimistic world view, or a view that family members are defective and blameworthy (these things can and do have a genetic component also, but that unnecessarily complicates the story for now). The aim, then, would be to separate out the effects of genetics from the effects of environmental factors like these. The trouble, of course, is that in most families, both genes and environmental factors are shared; they are entangled, or, in a favorite term of scientists, confounded. How to disentangle these effects?

The field of behavior genetics has developed persuasive methods of accomplishing this very thing, the strongest of which is the twin adoption approach. It occasionally happens that individuals within twin sets—both identical twin sets and nonidentical or fraternal twin sets—are adopted away at birth to different homes. From a behavior genetic standpoint, this situation produces a natural experiment in which genetics and environment are disentangled: The environments are different, but, in the case of the identical twins, genes are not. In the case of the fraternal twins, genes overlap by an average of around 50 percent, just as they would in any pair of siblings. If genes are operating on a certain behavior, the identical twins should be more similar on that behavior as compared to the fraternal twins.

This kind of study is difficult to conduct for obvious practical reasons. But it has been done regarding some personality and behavioral characteristics, and the genetic effect on such characteristics is now beyond dispute. This type of study has not been attempted on suicidal behavior to my knowledge because of the relative rarity of such behavior.

Studies on suicidal behavior in twins raised together, however, have been conducted, and these show a clear genetic effect. The nonadoption twin methodology has solutions to disentangling the effects of genetics and environment, comparing identical to fraternal twins on an outcome of interest like suicidal behavior. With regard to death by suicide, such studies show that, if one identical twin has died by suicide, chances that the other has too are clearly elevated. Similarly, if one fraternal twin has died by suicide, the chances that the other twin has as well are somewhat elevated, but not to the level seen with identical twins. The ones with more genes in common have more of the behavior in common.

A very interesting group to study with regard to the genetics of suicidal behavior (and of much else) is the Old Order Amish. One reason for this is their very careful and comprehensive genealogical records; another is that they have relatively high rates of serious mood disorders and suicidal behavior. In one study looking at Amish family trees over a 100-year period, twenty-six suicides were identified. Of these twenty-six, the vast majority belonged to one of only four Amish families. Death by suicide aggregated in just a few families and left many other families totally unscathed.

Danish researchers have provided still more evidence, using a large register of Denmark's adoptions. From this register, the researchers found fifty-seven adoptees who had died by suicide. From the remaining thousands of people in the register, the researchers then selected a group of fifty-seven adoptees who had not died by suicide. They selected these latter fifty-seven to be similar to the fifty-seven who had died by suicide regarding things like age and gender (in other words, they were "matched controls"). The point of the study was to compare these two groups regarding suicidal behavior among the adoptees' *biological* parents—not the parents who adopted them, but rather the parents who bore them in the first place. Notice how neatly this design removes the effects of environment and isolates the effects of genes. All of the participants had been adopted, and the variable of interest in the study was the suicidal behavior of all the adoptees' biological parents. The researchers reasoned that if there is a genetic component to suicidal behavior, then the biological relatives of those who had died by suicide should engage in more suicidal behavior than the biological relatives of those who had not. Indeed, this was the finding; approximately 4 percent of the decedent adoptees' biological parents had died by suicide—a very high rate when compared to the worldwide population average of around .01 percent. By contrast, well under 1 percent of the comparison adoptees' parents had died by suicide.

Most reasonable people find studies like this very compelling and clearly demonstrative of a genetic effect. Of course, it is very important to be careful with terms—what is meant by "a genetic effect." It does *not* at all mean that genes are the only factors; if they were, identical twins would always have identical outcomes, and they certainly do not. It does mean that genes are part of the story of suicidal behavior, though they are probably the lesser part of the story compared to other, nongenetic factors. The genetic studies themselves show this, in that they usually estimate that around 40 percent of the effect on suicidal outcomes is carried by genes . . . which of course leaves around 60 percent to be explained by nongenetic factors.

What does this mean for the biological relatives of those who have died by suicide? Should I be worried about the risk conveyed to me or my sons? The answer to this question—a question that is understandably very common among suicide survivors—is no. My sons are at least two generations removed from the individuals who died by suicide, and risk fades considerably. Even for me, the genetic risk is not especially substantial. Assume that the population risk—that is, the risk for anyone picked randomly out of the phonebook—is 10 per 100,000 (which it is, more or less, in the United States). In these terms, my risk due to my dad's genes is around 12 per 100,000. That's an elevation in risk, but it is moderate; certainly it is nowhere near the five-, ten-, or even one-hundred-fold risk people routinely ask me about at speaking engagements on suicide (the modal worried person being a mother asking about her children's risk due to their dad's, her husband's, suicide). Suicidal behavior is genetic, modern science has made that fact unmistakable. It is so unmistakable that people exaggerate it routinely—for instance, I have experienced at least one conversation on speaking tours in which a person implies some surprise (pleasant surprise, it should be noted) that I have not yet died by suicide, given my family history.

People shouldn't take the genetic effect to mean more than it does. Of course, parents will still worry, so instead of worrying about a child's genetic predisposition (which again has relatively modest impact and about which nothing can be done anyway), solid advice is to monitor potentially vulnerable children for mental disorders that precede suicidal behavior (e.g., serious depression, severe sleep problems, marked behavioral disruptions), and, should they occur, take the child to a pediatrician or mental health professional. In addition to the development of the symptoms of serious mental disorders, parents should also be aware of the suicide warning signs mentioned throughout this book, especially the ones involving talk about suicide or preparations for suicide. These are indeed worrisome and require quick action . . . much more so than genetic effects, which, while a contributor to risk (not to mention a fascinating window on human nature), fade very much into the background—or should—when compared to imminent warning signs.

"Breast Augmentation Causes Suicide"

Lest you think I am jesting, there are people who fervently believe this. Indeed, enough people think it that the American Association of Suicidology has posted a position paper on its

Web site, and the American Society for Aesthetic Plastic Surgery was concerned about the issue as FDA hearings were occurring in 2003 on the safety of silicone breast implants.

In the 1980s and 1990s, there were several lawsuits that claimed that silicone breast implants, manufactured by Dow Corning, caused several types of health problems, including breast cancer, lupus, arthritis, and several neurological conditions. These repeated lawsuits led to a multi-billion dollar settlement in 1998, which put Dow Corning into bankruptcy for years. The trouble with all this is that the implants actually do not cause health problems according to independent studies, including one organized by the National Academy of Sciences' Institute of Medicine. Silicone implants have several aesthetic advantages over the alternatives, which are saline-filled, and so plastic surgeons, many of their patients, and others were eager for them to be re-approved. The initial hearings were set for 2003.

I testified at these hearings on the issue of breast augmentation's association with suicide, which I will discuss shortly. Attending the hearings allowed me not only to speak on this particular issue, but also to observe the many aspects of the hearings in general, which in some respects were very dramatic.

On the point of the association between breast augmentation and suicide, there is no doubt at all that there is an association. Surprising but true, and yet, as we will see, deceiving. In four separate studies on women in the United States, Canada, Sweden, and Finland, it has been established that women who had breast augmentation were significantly more likely than other women who did not have breast augmentation to die by suicide.

A somewhat hackneyed truism of scientific research is that correlation does not prove causality. That is, even if there is a significant correlation between breast augmentation and suicide, that does not necessarily mean that breast augmentation in any way causes suicide. But why the association? A likely explanation is that breast augmentation patients differ from other women in important ways—differences that may be relevant to suicidal behavior—and these differences, as opposed to breast augmentation per se, may elucidate the link.

For example, breast augmentation patients in the United States are overwhelmingly white. Estimates in the literature exceed 95 percent, and in at least one study on breast augmentation, so few nonwhite patients were available that the researchers were forced to focus only on white women. By contrast, of course, the general U.S. population is racially diverse, increasingly so. Recent estimates indicate that approximately 75–80 percent of the U.S. population is white.

A sample in which white people are over-represented will have more deaths by suicide than a representative sample simply because white women are more than twice as likely as other women to die by suicide. Breast augmentation patients are not more prone to suicide than others because of breast augmentation; they are more prone to suicide, in part, because almost all of them happen to be white, and white people die by suicide at higher rates than most other groups. This same logic can be applied to other variables—for instance, smoking. Breast augmentation patients are somewhat more likely than others to be smokers, and death by suicide is more common in smokers than in others. The likelihood is, then, that the association between breast augmentation and suicide is not causal, but instead is due to a host of other variables to which they are both linked and which explains their association.

Moreover, whenever there is a true causal association between two things, it is almost always possible to specify the mechanism of the causal connection; put differently, one can usually spell out the steps that lead from the cause to the outcome. For example, phenylketonuria (PKU) is a subtype of mental retardation caused by a genetic problem on chromosome 12. There is a causal association between the genetic problem and PKU, and its mechanism is as follows: the genetic problem leads to an inability to produce sufficient levels of an enzyme called phenylalanine hydroxylase, which, in turn, leads to an inability to break down phenylalanine. Phenylalanine builds up in the body, disrupting the proper development and functioning of brain tissue. The companion account of the possible mechanism of causation of breast augmentation on suicide (which causation, it should remembered, is illusory) is far less impressive. The account would be something along the lines of: "breast augmentation is hard on women's minds and bodies, which in turn, demoralizes them, which then leads to suicide."

It is the inanity of this account that compelled me to get involved in the controversy and to testify to the Food and Drug Administration (FDA). Suicidal behavior is a massive international health problem that kills thousands of people daily, and when it does not kill them, it often maims or otherwise ago-nizes them. This is not even to mention the effects on family members. To assert that breast augmentation is an important cause of women's suicide—to assert that it is a cause at all—trivializes suicide by using a false claim (breast augmentation leads to suicide) to prop up a false agenda (chemical compa-nies and plastic surgeons are antiwomen and so greedy that they would gladly harm women for financial gain).

To top it all off, there is evidence that the effects of breast augmentation on the women who choose to have it—far from demoralizing them—enhances their satisfaction with their bodies. For those who choose the procedure—grown women who can see to their own needs and decisions—that is the point after all, and many studies affirm that this is the usual result.

The FDA hearing on silicone implants was an illustration of how not only various interest groups but the FDA itself can easily be swayed by emotional testimony and other perfor-mances about facts that are simply untrue or at best irrele-vant. I sat in on most of a day's testimony, which gave me the opportunity to hear a substantial portion of the proceedings. By far the most memorable and gripping of the testimony came from family members who had lost a wife, mother, sis-ter, or daughter to a disease they believed had been caused by silicone breast implants. One's sure knowledge that the testi-mony's premise is mistaken does not change the fact that one's heart pours out. A tricky thing, though, is that this sym-pathy can affect one's view of the facts. It took active men-tal work not to let that change my knowledge of the facts.

In another emotional incident at the hearing (which I only heard of secondhand), a woman brought a container of spoiled breast milk to the hearing, slammed it down on the table, and claimed that breast implants were responsible for affecting her milk. Some associated with the FDA evidently were swayed by the various testimonials, because the ultimate decision from the 2003 hearings delayed the approval of silicone implants. This was overturned in 2006, and the implants are now FDA-approved.

In the wake of the hearings, I took some e-mailed heat from women who are convinced that breast augmentation causes suicide, never mind what the evidence indicates. I was told by one woman, for instance, that "Our blood is on the hands that do harm," implying that I was one of those harmdoers. Another informed me that I did not understand the issues, that I did not understand what it was like to lose a family member to suicide, and concluded, "This is war. You're so sick it's just sad. You care not what you do to the families of those poor women victims. I would be ashamed."

Although, based on the totality of the evidence, I dismiss the view that breast augmentation causes suicide (and although I do in fact know what it is like to lose someone to suicide), I did not feel dismissive or otherwise combative toward the women who contacted me. I told each of them how sorry I was for what they were going through, and I invited each to carefully read my paper on the issue of breast augmentation and suicide and to report back with any mistakes of logic or fact in the paper. I got no replies, and my suspicion is that this is not because they read the paper and were convinced. Rather, even though at least some of them seemed to hate me, I suspect they were surprised and in part satisfied that I replied at all, and especially that my reply contained a genuine expression of sympathy. As many psychologists and others have indicated, a little empathy can go a surprisingly long way.

But empathy need not cloud our command of the facts (and, it should be admitted, psychologists and others have at times been too unaware of this truth). The claim that breast augmentation causes suicide is not only factually untrue, but like many untrue things, it is especially pernicious because it becomes fruitful and multiplies. It leads people to misunderstand the true facts and circumstances of their loved ones' deaths and to thus prolong their mourning, it leads others to misunderstand the deaths of those who die by suicide in general, it removed or made difficult a healthcare choice for women (including women who had had mastectomies and very much wanted the option of silicone implants), and it cost our society substantial resources in the form of lawsuits, bankruptcies, and the like.

"Medicines Cause Suicidal Behavior"

In January of 2002, a 15-year-old child stole a Cessna plane near Tampa, Florida, and flew the plane into the forty-two-story Bank of America building in downtown Tampa. He was killed instantly. It later emerged that the teen had a problem with acne, and had used the acne drug Accutane®. Could the acne drug have led the young man to steal a plane and cause his own death by crashing it into a downtown building? As implausible as this sounds, this was a usual claim in the coverage following the event.

As has been seen many times throughout this book, just because two things co-occur does not imply the one thing caused the other. An individual used Accutane and died violently by suicide—a co-occurrence. But to demonstrate causality in an incident like this, the least one would want to do is ask a few questions. Did the young man have Accutane in his system at the time of his death? Are there other, more likely explanations for what he did?

The teen, it turned out, was a great admirer of Osama bin Laden. In the young man's suicide note, recovered from the plane, he wrote, "Osama bin Laden is absolutely justified in the terror he has caused on 9-11. He has brought a mighty nation to its knees! God blesses him and the others who helped make September 11th happen." The note goes on to speak against "monstrous Israelis" who "want nothing short of world domination," claims that al Qaeda has met with the teen several times to persuade him to join them, and closes with the statement, "Osama bin Laden is planning on blowing up the Super Bowl with an antiquated nuclear bomb left over from the 1967 Israeli-Syrian war." These statements put the claim about acne drugs in another light. In addition, his autopsy showed that he had no Accutane in his system at the time of his death. The boy's family later dropped their lawsuit against the makers of Accutane.

If the acne drug was not to blame, what is? A very solid guess would be mental illness, more specifically a serious mood disorder. The young man's claims that he was regularly courted by al Qaeda, that he had inside knowledge about a nuclear device that bin Laden would detonate at the Super Bowl, and his use of statements in his suicide note such as "You will pay—God help you—and I will make you pay!" suggest the grandiosity, anger, and psychotic features of bipolar disorder.

To the degree that people remember a connection between Accutane and suicidal behavior, this event is probably a main source, and yet it was clearly spurious. Accutane, like virtually all medicines, has side effects, to be sure. The most serious issue with Accutane is its teratogenicity—it can cause birth defects if ingested or handled by pregnant women. Side effects can also include depressive reactions.

The drug Tamiflu®, which is a key tool in fighting influenza and has been stockpiled in case of an epidemic, has also been subject to scrutiny because of possible associations with depressive-like reactions and suicidal behavior. Concerns arose after the deaths by suicide of Japanese teenagers who had taken the drug. As is so often the case in these situations, there is no systematic evidence of a link between the drug and suicidal behavior, and credentialed authorities, in this case the Japanese Health Ministry, have clearly said as much. Furthermore, as in the case of the young man who flew a plane into a building, there is an alternative explanation—the flu virus itself can cause disturbances in behavior.

This last fact—that the flu itself, rather than its treatment, can cause behavioral problems—deserves underscoring, because it is widely underappreciated, and a version of this same issue comes up time and again with regard to all sorts of medicines. Of course, if one has a condition like the flu, one is likely to experience both the effects of the flu as well as treatment for it. There is nothing necessarily causal about the treatment on the effects; both the treatment and the effects stem from the prior fact of having contracted the flu virus.

Consider antidepressant medicines in this regard. The overwhelming majority of the evidence indicates that these medicines, though imperfect, have prevented and reduced enormous amounts of human suffering. They represent reasonably effective treatments for, among other things, major depressive disorder, and this is of extreme importance, because studies have shown that major depressive disorder causes sufferers comparable amounts of impairment (e.g., spending days in bed, not functioning at work, or neglecting family duties) as heart disease. In fact, the condition is always included among the top five health problems in terms of its global burden, and in some such tallies, it is the leading illness. Antidepressant medicines have done much to reduce this burden, and have the potential to do more with further advances in the underlying science and especially advances in access to treatment.

But they have their critics. And though there are many strands to the criticism, perhaps the aspect that has received the most attention is that they cause suicidality in some people. In October 2004, the U.S. Food and Drug Administration (FDA) put out a public health advisory about this risk and issued a black-box warning for all antidepressants, which is the strongest measure the FDA takes, short of withdrawing a drug's approval altogether. The warning was the result of evidence from placebo-controlled clinical trials of antidepressants. When pooled together for one analysis, a significant difference emerged between children and adolescents who had been prescribed an antidepressant versus those who had been prescribed a placebo, with the former showing more suicidal ideation and behavior (no deaths by suicide were reported in these analyses). There is very little evidence for a similar effect among adults; in fact, there is evidence of the opposite effect (i.e., antidepressants reducing suicidality more than a placebo).

What has been the impact of the FDA's black box warning on the prescribing of antidepressant medicines? Multiple studies have shown that the warning decreased the numbers of prescriptions written for antidepressants, especially for youth. The crucial issue is whether this has had any effect on suicide rates or on suicidal behavior and ideation. The majority of the evidence suggests not, and some of the evidence indicates a backfiring effect, in that fewer prescriptions for antidepressants may have resulted in more suicidality. There have been no clear decreases in the U.S. suicide rate from 2004 to 2006 (the last year for which numbers are available), when the FDA warning was in effect. A 2007 study in the *American Journal of Psychiatry* reported that prescriptions to youth for a certain class of antidepressants, selective serotonin reuptake inhibitors (SSRIs) like Prozac®, Paxil®, and Zoloft®, decreased substantially in both the United States and the Netherlands following the black-box warning. Furthermore, researchers found that youth suicide rates increased by 49 percent in the Netherlands between 2003 and 2005 and by 14 percent between 2003 and 2004 in the United States. Although the change in the United States is not as large as that in the Netherlands, it is nonetheless notable—in fact it is the largest recorded increase since the Centers for Disease Control and Prevention began collecting rigorous data on the issue in 1979. In both countries, as the numbers of SSRI prescriptions for youth went down, the number of deaths by suicide in youth went up.

A 2007 study by the National Bureau of Economic Research examined the association between use of SSRIs and suicide rates in twenty-six countries over twenty-five years. They reported that an increase in sales of one pill per capita was associated with a decrease in suicides of about 5 percent. Compared to other interventions, the study indicated that the medicines were a cost-effective way to deal with the massive public health problem of death by suicide.

A study from Denmark published in the *Archives of Suicide Research* in 2007 corroborates this result. A great advantage of doing this kind of research in Denmark is the existence of national registers, which collect information on wide swaths of the entire population with regard to many things, including prescribed antidepressants and suicide rates. This particular study focused on patients with a mood disorder diagnosis severe enough that they were hospitalized for it. The number of post-discharge antidepressant prescriptions filled was a robust predictor of suicide rates: Those who filled the fewest prescriptions had the highest rates of death by suicide.

Another study from the *American Journal of Psychiatry* in 2007 provides some of the most informative results of all on the topic of antidepressants and suicidality. The study examined the time pattern of suicide attempts as it relates to the start of treatment for depression, whether that treatment included antidepressant medicines, psychotherapy, or both. Regardless of treatment type, the most common timeframe for suicide attempts was *before* the initiation of treatment. Once treatment began, suicide attempt rates fell by 50 percent in the next month, and then continued to decline in subsequent months. Importantly, this was true across the age span; it applied to youth and to adults.

Also very intriguing was the fact that those most vulnerable to suicide attempts were those who received an antidepressant prescription specifically from a psychiatrist; such patients were more likely to attempt than those receiving psychotherapy, for example. The critics of antidepressant medicines may view this finding as supporting their concerns, but on closer examination it does not. Those who received an antidepressant from a psychiatrist were more likely to have attempted *before* treatment started. What is going on here is that, of depressed patients, the most severe (as reflected by suicide attempt) are being seen by psychiatrists (as opposed to family physicians and other mental health professionals), and when seen, are more likely than other patients to be put on medicine.

This brings us back to the example of mixing up the flu, its treatment, and its effects. Just as the flu might bring on a dose of antiviral and may also initiate behavioral side effects—with the antiviral having nothing to do with the behavioral side effects—so may major depressive disorder lead to taking anti-depressant medicine and also to suicidal behavior (a common feature of the disorder)—with the medicine having nothing to do with the suicidal behavior.

Antidepressant critics, perhaps the most vocal of whom are associated with the Church of Scientology, seem not to understand this logic. In some of their materials can be found headlines like "Analysis Reveals Suicide Victims Have Psych Drugs in Blood Stream," the implication being that the drugs caused the suicide. But that's not necessarily so—it is expected that those who die by suicide will have above-average rates of antidepressant use, because those who die by suicide frequently have serious mood disorders and are being treated for them—unsuccessfully, unfortunately. Such medicines are not magic bullets, it should be pointed out, and do not work for everyone.

Another critic of antidepressants claims: "psychiatrists indiscriminately prescribe the drugs to millions, based on subjective diagnoses made without any physical tests such as blood tests, brain scans or X-rays." This is deceptive and thus unfair, because *all* diagnoses for mental disorders—schizophrenia, bipolar disorder, anorexia nervosa, you name it—are made without lab tests or scans. This does not make them any less real—ask someone who has experienced them if the tons of scientific literature are not persuasive enough—and that which causes real agony deserves real treatment (not to mention real compassion). Drugs like antidepressants are real treatments, and like all such interventions, have a track record of good (though not perfect) effectiveness, along with a profile of side effects.

This brings us back to why the FDA would issue a black-box warning for antidepressants. This warning was based on clinical trial data showing that young people who took antidepressants experienced higher rates of suicidal ideation and behavior as compared to young people on placebos. The bottom line is that we do not know for sure why this occurred, but there is a leading explanation. Many people find antidepressant medicines activating—they can help with energy problems and can alter flat moods into more positive ones. In most instances, this represents welcome relief from fatigue, lack of energy and focus, and low mood. But can there be too much activation? The answer is yes, and when this occurs, it can lead to agitation, restlessness, anxiety, and insomnia. These can comprise acute risk factors for suicidal ideation and behavior, as agitation and insomnia are ranked among the most serious suicide warning signs. The upshot of all this is that medicines which prevailingly lead to relief from depression can, in a small subset of people, potentially lead to overactivation and thus to increased suicidality. What to do? What should always have been done and what the FDA advisory urges: people starting on an antidepressant medicine should be closely and regularly monitored to make sure that the usual therapeutic response and not the unusual over-activation response results.

Sleep and Suicidal Behavior

Anyone who has followed the history of scholarship on mental disorders is impressed with Emil Kraepelin. He was a German psychiatrist who lived in the latter part of the nineteenth and the first part of the twentieth centuries. He may have been the world's best psychiatric nosologist, ever. He understood the structure of mental disorders deeply—he knew how to define particular disorders and how to accurately differentiate them from one another. Moreover, he saw clearly the crucial role of course of illness in differentiating one from another mental disorder—a fact that remains underappreciated to this day. He is the intellectual forefather of today's *Diagnostic and Statistical Manual of Mental Disorders (DSM)*, which, though imperfect, is a staggering achievement of scholarship with no legitimate rival. When psychiatry began to depart in the 1960s and 1970s from psychoanalysis, it was to the ideas of people like Kraepelin that they looked, rightly. Freud, the father of modern psychiatry? No, it was Kraepelin.

Kraepelin understood the important role of sleep in mood disorders. In this passage from his 1921 *Manic-Depressive Insanity and Paranoia* (p. 44) he notes the role of sleeplessness in both mania and depression:

> The attacks of manic-depressive insanity are invariably accompanied by all kinds of bodily changes. By far the most striking are the disorders of sleep and general nourishment. In mania sleep is in the more severe states of excitement always considerably encroached upon; sometimes there is even almost complete sleeplessness, at most interrupted for a few hours, which may last for weeks, even months . . . In the states of depression in spite of great need for sleep, it is for the most part sensibly encroached upon; the patients lie for hours, sleepless in bed, . . . although even in bed they find no refreshment.

This last phrase—"even in bed they find no refreshment"—represents a very keen observation, as I think it's an important key to the association between sleep problems and suicidal behavior. And, although Kraepelin did not emphasize the connection between sleep and suicidality, the connection no doubt exists.

Sleep disorders and complaints have been linked in multiple studies to the entire spectrum of suicidal thoughts and behaviors, including suicidal ideation, suicide attempt, and death by suicide (for a review, see Bernert & Joiner, 2007). Indeed, as was noted in the section on the myth of "aggression turned inward," sleep problems are listed among the suicide warning signs endorsed by many prominent organizations; in the mnemonic IS PATH WARM, the first "A" is for "anxiety and agitation, including being unable to sleep." A fair criticism of this mnemonic is that sleep problems are important enough in suicidal behavior that they should be represented separately from anxiety and agitation. Researchers have shown that general insomnia in severely depressed patients at one point in time predicts death by suicide over the ensuing year or so (Fawcett et al., 1990); that community participants' poor self-reported sleep quality at one point in time predicts death by suicide over the ensuing thirteen to fourteen years (Turvey et al., 2002); and that depressed patients rate their sleep quality as poorer if they are also suicidal than if they are not (Agargun et al., 1997).

These studies show an association between the sleep problems people *say* they are having and suicidality, but, as the sleeping partners of loud snorers can attest, there can be a difference between what people say about their sleep and what actually occurs. To address this issue satisfactorily, objective sleep studies are required, in which people's brain waves and other physiology are monitored as they sleep. Studies like this have shown the same link between sleep troubles and suicidal behavior. For instance, depressed patients with a history of suicide, as compared to those with no such history, experienced less delta wave (slow wave) sleep, which is the most restorative kind (Sabo et al., 1991). As another example, it has been shown that the rapid eye movement (REM) sleep of suicidal patients has more negative, dreamlike qualities than that of nonsuicidal patients (Agargun & Cartwright, 2003).

The link between sleep problems and suicidality has been documented using both self-reported and objective sleep indices. However, both sleep problems and suicidality are associated with depression, so maybe all this is simply one outcome of people having ongoing depression. A person with depression is, after all, very likely to develop insomnia and also likely to have suicidal ideas and behaviors. Researchers have tested this possibility. For the most part, evidence suggests that depression is not the whole story. To take one interesting example, among patients with psychotic disorders, those with a history of suicidal behavior showed more REM sleep abnormalities on objective assessment than did those with no history of suicidal behavior, and this relationship held even when depressive symptoms were accounted for (Keshavan et al., 1994). That is, in this study as in others, even when depression is held constant (using research techniques like statistical controls), the relationship between sleep difficulties and suicidal thoughts and behaviors persists.

"Sleep difficulties" can mean a lot of different things—

trouble falling asleep in the first place, trouble maintaining sleep once asleep, breathing problems during sleep, getting sleep but not feeling rested from it, and disturbing nightmares that interrupt sleep. Are any of these facets more likely than others to confer risk for suicidal thoughts and behaviors? Intriguingly, there is evidence that nightmares confer such risk. A large study in Finland showed that those who reported having nightmares at one point in time were more likely than those who reported no such troubles to die by suicide over the ensuing fourteen years (Tanskanen et al., 2001). This pattern was particularly clear regarding those who endorsed having *frequent* nightmares; they were 105 percent more likely than others to have died by suicide over the course of the follow-up interval. Bernert and colleagues (2005) assessed self-reported sleep complaints and suicidality among 176 psychiatric outpatients. Various sleep complaint indices (general insomnia, sleep-disordered breathing, nightmares) displayed significant associations with suicidal ideation. However, these researchers' approach included statistical control for depressive symptoms (as referred to above), and when this was done, the association between nightmares and suicidality persisted, whereas associations between either insomnia or sleep-disordered breathing symptoms and suicidality did not. A similar pattern of findings was obtained by an independent research group who were studying sleep, mood, and suicidal ideation in adolescents (Liu, 2004).

Why would nightmares be the specific aspect of sleep difficulties that confers risk to suicidal ideation and behavior?

There are two leading explanations, and both hearken back to Kraepelin's comment that "even in bed [depressed patients] find no refreshment." First, most vivid dreams, including nightmares, occur during REM sleep. Episodes of REM sleep occur throughout the night, but their length changes as the night progresses. A REM sleep episode early in the night might last approximately ten minutes, whereas the last REM sleep episode in a night's sleep might last six times as long. Therefore, most dreaming, including nightmares, occurs in the last half of a night of sleep.

Those who are having a lot of nightmares are thus having them relatively close in time to when they wake in the morning; the fact that depressed people often experience early morning awakening (e.g., waking at 4:30 A.M., not rested but unable to go back to sleep) makes this all the more true. In an intriguing study relevant to this point, researchers studied a sample of depressed women over the course of a year (Cartwright et al., 1998). Women who reported nightmares and other negative dreams early in the night but fewer negative dreams later in the sleep period were more likely than others to be depression-free at the end of the yearlong study. By contrast, women who experienced relatively few negative dreams at the beginning of the night but more as the night progressed were not likely to be depression-free a year later. A person in this latter scenario has his or her first waking moment affected by the terrors and helplessness of a nightmare. Indeed, there is a severe form of major depressive disorder that is characterized by, among other things, noticeably worse mood in the morning, and at least one research group has hypothesized that this may have to do with nightmares preceding awakening (Agargun et al., 2007). It is not difficult to imagine that this would be demoralizing to the point of worsening depression and increasing risk for suicidal behavior. To use Kraepelin's phrasing, far from finding refreshment in bed, such individuals are finding its opposite.

The second explanation for the association between nightmares and suicidality is related to the first, and it is that frequent nightmares, regardless of when they occur during the evening, encroach upon people's last refuge for peace and rest. A typical comment from someone in this plight would be, "My life was bad already, but now it's bad even in my sleep." This is what I believe Kraepelin had in mind, and I might put it even more emphatically: To discover that a place that was supposed to be an inviolable, refreshing refuge has turned instead into a seat of horrors is a kind of "final straw" that can break people's will to live.

"Suicidal Behavior Peaks around the Christmas Holidays"

The *Cleveland Scene* (June 2005) published a piece on suicides occurring from Akron, Ohio's Y-Bridge that stated, "officers are dispatched to the bridge at least once a week to talk down potential jumpers. Holidays are the worst." Holidays are the worst how? The worst for the officers, whose holiday plans are disrupted? Or the worst in the sense that bridge incidents occur more frequently during holidays?

My guess is that most who read the piece inferred the

latter—a suicide peak around the holidays, specifically the winter holidays—because it conforms to an entrenched myth that suicide rates peak then. In fact, this myth runs so deep that it wouldn't surprise me if bridge motorists *do* alert authorities about people on the bridge more around the holidays, not because of an actual increase, but because of the myth making them more vigilant.

This myth pops up everywhere; for instance, in his book *The Savage God,* Alvarez cites an early-eighteenth-century French novel, which begins, "In the gloomy month of November, when the people of England hang and drown themselves . . ." (p. 102). The fact is that there is a seasonal peak, and it is in the late spring. This translates to May-June in the northern hemisphere (information which, to his credit, Alvarez gets right). During the 1990s in the United States, for instance, the overall daily number of suicides was in the low eighties. The daily average during May and June, however, was closer to ninety. And when was the daily average at its nadir? December, by a long shot, with an average of approximately seventy-seven per day, the only month to average less than eighty daily deaths by suicide. And evidently, it has been this way for centuries, at least. In his *History of Suicide,* Georges Minois cites a summary of fifty-four deaths by suicide during the Middle Ages. Then, as now, there was a spring peak.

Knowledge of the spring peak in suicides could do a lot of good. It would offer one explanation for why suicides can seem to run in clusters. There are lots of reasons this happens, but a major one is seasonal. There will be "clusters" or "spates" of suicides in spring, independent of outside events. A recent April news report from India began, "There have been a spate of suicides in the city by elderly over the past week." It went on to summarize the details of some of the deaths. The report suggested a mystery about the "spate," but the mystery would be mostly solved by a glance at the calendar combined with the knowledge that older people represent one of the most at-risk groups for suicide.

The truth about suicide and seasons is thus the polar opposite of the common belief; far from representing the peak in suicides, the time around the winter holidays represents the low point in suicide deaths, probably because it is a time of togetherness.

My research group placed a paper in the journal *Suicide & Life-Threatening Behavior* in 2008 specifically examining the hypothesis that seasonality and suicidality are associated at least partly due to seasonal fluctuations in togetherness. Consider a large college campus in this regard. College campuses provide numerous activities for belonging; anyone who doubts this should check out a nearby university's online master calendar. Day after day, there are artistic, musical, theatrical, dance, museum, academic, athletic, and other events —many of them free of charge. There are organizations like fraternities and sororities (and at least one study has documented lower suicidal ideation among these groups). There are groups organized around hobbies, interests, and political issues, not to mention good and relatively easy access to student support, counseling, and health-care services. Perhaps partly as a function of this high level of belongingness, college students have relatively low rates of suicide as compared to their same-aged peers not at college.

Opportunities for belonging and togetherness are thus high on a college campus, but they are not uniform throughout the calendar year. At most campuses, during the standard academic year (the fall and spring semesters, roughly September to May), school is clearly "in," and chances for social engagement abound through classes, dormitory and apartment life, sport fandom, and so on. The summer is different, though; activities continue but they ebb considerably. Those who earn their livelihoods on college campuses come to expect the summer-emptying of campus much as they do spring rains or winter cold. Therefore, it is conceivable that students' sense of belongingness may be lower in the summer than in other semesters. Consequently, we reasoned, suicidal ideation may be higher in the summer than during the regular academic year, and this association may be partly explained by fluctuations in belongingness.

And indeed, this is what we found. Among over 300 university students, some assessed in the summer semester, others assessed in the fall and spring, we showed that mean scores on a measure of suicidal ideation were higher in summer than in the other semesters—approximately three times higher. We also showed that scores on a measure of social connection followed the same pattern—lower feelings of social connection in the summer than in the other semesters. Moreover, using a set of statistical procedures, we were able to document that one reason that suicidal ideation fluctuated over the semesters was *because* social connectedness fluctuated over the semesters—low levels of belonging in the summer led in part to high levels of suicidal ideation.

This study was conducted in the northern hemisphere, where of course spring corresponds to April through early June. If there really is a genuine spring peak in suicide rates, then shouldn't things be shifted six months in the southern hemisphere? That is, because spring in the southern hemisphere occurs between October and early December, this should be the time when the most suicides occur in that half of the world. Indeed, it is. A study from South Africa, for example, published in a 1997 issue of the journal *Psychiatry Research,* affirms the spring peak in October-November, and a corresponding winter trough in the southern hemisphere's winter, which occurs in May or so.

Why is there a universal spring peak? Seasonal variations in belonging may be a part of it, as the study on college students discussed above suggests. And in the northern hemisphere, the winter trough in suicides corresponds to times of high social connection; in the United States, Thanksgiving and the winter holidays. But in the southern hemisphere, these holidays are disentangled from the literal season (in addition to the fact that not all of these holidays are celebrated there)— December 25 in South Africa, for example, falls in the spring-summer, and spring-summer is a time of high suicide rates. Holiday-related social connection therefore cannot constitute a full explanation.

In his book *The Savage God* (p. 103), Alvarez speculated that the spring peak occurs because some people remain depressed from the winter; as everyone else and nature are active and blooming, the subset of depressed people remains down, and it is this contrast that demoralizes the persistently depressed to the point of suicide. One advantage of this explanation is that it applies plausibly to both the northern and southern hemispheres.

My preferred explanation differs from this one somewhat. I agree that the increased activity and energy accompanying spring play a role, but I think the role is even more fundamental than to serve as a basis for contrast. A repeated refrain throughout my scholarly work on suicidal behavior and throughout this book as well is that suicide is fearsome and daunting enough that it requires a kind of energy, concentration, and focus. Human biorhythms are such that people become more active in the spring; for a subset, this activation may enable suicidal behavior.

The concept of activation—and of overactivation—arose in the section on medicine-induced suicidal behavior. There it was noted that, for most people, antidepressants are activating in a therapeutic way, but, in a small subset of individuals, antidepressants may be overactivating, leading to agitation and insomnia and thereby elevating suicide risk. Spring may operate much like an antidepressant—most people feel a little more energetic in the spring, but for some, overactivation may occur.

Two strands of evidence support this view, one conclusive, the other less so. The conclusive aspect has to do with the incontrovertible fact that, for people who have bipolar disorder, the manic phase of the condition is very likely to occur in the spring. Manic episodes are time-limited, usually lasting days or weeks, so not only is the onset of the episode likely to occur in spring, so is its resolution. As manic phases begin, endure, and then fade, overactivation symptoms like insomnia and agitation are common. Some of the spring peak in suicide is accounted for by those with bipolar disorder becoming manic and then coming down off of the mania into depression—the combination of depression with the overactivation left in the wake of a manic episode can constitute a window of very elevated suicide risk.

The less conclusive strand of evidence is that people in general (not just those with bipolar disorder) may have more trouble sleeping in the spring. Systematic and pointed data on this topic are hard to come by, but clinically, one certainly can observe this in some psychotherapy patients. If there is somewhat of a spring peak in sleep problems, this could in part explain the spring peak in suicide, because insomnia is a clear risk for suicidal behavior, as described in another section of this book.

In this context of overactivation-induced suicidality, a common piece of clinical lore should be discussed; namely, that as severe depressions lift, a window of suicide risk emerges because people are gaining the energy to act while possibly still suffering from the other symptoms of depression. In a 2004 paper in the journal *Professional Psychology: Research & Practice,* my colleagues and I studied this issue in a sample of over 100 suicidal people. We identified a subsample of around 10 percent who experienced renewed energy in the context of otherwise persistent depression. These people did show elevated risk, but so did people who showed distinct patterns of incomplete remission; for example, renewed concentration in the context of otherwise persistent depression, or renewed confidence in the context of otherwise persistent depression. We concluded that incomplete remissions of any sort probably indicate severity of underlying illness (the reason why the remission may be incomplete), which, in turn, may account for elevated suicide risk.

This is a sensible conclusion that is backed up by much empirical data in addition to clinical wisdom. But I do not counsel abandoning altogether the notion that severe depression with renewed energy can equal serious suicide risk, for several reasons. First, though this involves an appeal to authority, arguably the most eminent clinical psychologist of all time, Paul Meehl, as well as the German descriptive psychiatrists he was fond of (eminent in their own right), endorsed the view. Second, our paper showed that forms of incomplete remission signal more severe illness and thus high suicide risk, and renewed energy in the context of persistent depression does indeed represent one form of incomplete remission (albeit only one). Third, there is evidence that people about to die by suicide can experience a change in demeanor in the hours before their deaths that can involve states like relief, resolve, even optimism. Much of this evidence is anecdotal, and it should be noted that most deaths by suicide are preceded by misery, certainly in the days and weeks before the death, but in the hours and minutes too. Still, as was noted in the section of this book on suicide notes, one of my students' dissertations showed that the writing of two people who died by suicide contained increasing expressions of a kind of positive certainty as their deaths approached—a certainty couched in religious terms. Other studies have shown that displays of positive emotion are surprisingly common in suicide notes.

There are other time-related cycles that are relevant to suicidal behavior, in addition to the seasonal pattern. There is a clear weekly pattern, with deaths by suicide more likely to occur earlier in the week, especially on Mondays. Like the spring peak, this pattern appears to be at least centuries old, in that the series of fifty-four suicides occurring in the Middle Ages also exhibited a Monday peak. For more current data revealing other such cycles, consider the figure here. My students and I included a similar figure in our 2006 paper on sport fandom and suicide rates published in the *Journal of Social & Clinical Psychology*. It shows the number of suicides (on the vertical axis) that occurred on each of the February 22nds on record from the 1970s and 1980s.

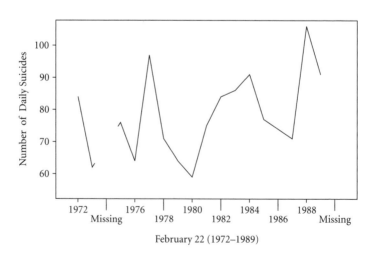

February 22 (1972–1989)

Why February 22nd? Because that was the date of the Miracle on Ice, the very unlikely upset by the U.S. hockey team of the Russians in the 1980 Lake Placid Winter Olympics (a victory made all the more salient by its geopolitical resonance—the Soviets were in Afghanistan at the time and U.S. hostages were still in Iran). We expected that the day of the Miracle on Ice might represent the February 22nd on record with the fewest number of suicides, and our expectations were supported, as the figure shows. (We expected this to be the case due to "pulling together" effects touched off by the Miracle on Ice.)

The figure shows some other interesting facts, too, including that the daily U.S. mean was around eighty suicides per day, and that there is considerable variation around this mean, as the peaks and valleys illustrate. When I present this figure at speaking engagements, I ask the audience to guess what accounts for the two peaks in 1977 and 1988. The usual (and reasonable) answer has to do with economic downturns, but actually the answer is more mundane—those dates are early weekdays, either a Monday or a Tuesday.

The audience usually groans in recognition, murmuring things like, "Oh, I know, I just hate Mondays." Their reaction is a natural one, attributing the Monday peak to the angst and stress of starting the work week. This may have something to do with it, but I think there is another element that is under-recognized, and it draws on the same logic mentioned above regarding the spring peak. Specifically, just as the spring peak occurs just after a period of relative inactivity (and thus a period of, in a sense, rest), so too does Monday occur after the weekend, for some a period of relative inactivity and rest. Suicide is an activity that requires reflection, planning, energy, and a kind of determined resolve. Monday may represent a weekly suicide peak because those who die on Monday may have spent the weekend building up their will to do a very daunting and difficult thing.

There are still other cyclical qualities to suicidal behavior. Some may expect that the phases of the moon would influence rates of suicide, but they would be wrong. As one of many examples of such studies, a paper published in the journal *Chronobiology International* in 2005 examined over 3,000 deaths by suicide in a region in Germany from 1998 to 2003 and detected no association whatsoever between lunar phases and the occurrence of such deaths. The belief that suicides peak under a full moon—a belief that is common among many, including emergency room and inpatient psychiatric facility personnel, is very likely fuelled by the times when a peak associated with early weekdays or with spring happens to coincide with a full moon. That is, the myth persists because of confirmation bias—a tendency to attend to supportive instances and discount instances that do not conform to expectations, such as the early-week and spring peaks that occur when there is *not* a full moon. This logic, of course, can apply to any seeming spate of suicidal deaths. Before they are attributed to clearly false things like lunar cycles or often misunderstood things like copycatting and contagion, very simple things like the spring peak and the early-week peak should be considered first.

Still another suicide-related cyclical phenomenon, in addition to early weekdays and the season, is menstruation. This one may sound dubious, in the same category as the lunar myth, but it is real. A 2006 paper published in the journal *Psychological Medicine* reviewed and compiled the results of forty-four different studies. The review revealed that, across studies, there was an association between specific menstrual phases and suicidal behavior, and this association was particularly apparent when the review was limited to studies with the most rigorous methodologies. More specifically, suicidal behavior seemed to be more common during the late luteal and follicular phases, when estrogen levels are comparatively low. The reasons for this association are not clearly understood, though it is notable that premenstrual dysphoric disorder (irritability, restlessness, tension, and so on; colloquially known as "PMS" or premenstrual syndrome) occurs during the late luteal phase and indeed was known in previous versions of the psychiatric nomenclature as late luteal phase dysphoric disorder.

It is notable that this syndrome can include restlessness, feeling "on edge," insomnia, and agitation. It is therefore possible that, just as people become overactivated by spring and by days early in the week (and thus more vulnerable to suicidal behavior), so some women with this condition may experience overactivation and thus suicidality.

In this context, it is interesting to consider the phenomenon of menstrual synchronization. It has been documented in many studies that, among women in close proximity to one another for extended periods of time (e.g., college roommates, best friends, sisters), menstrual cycles synchronize; that is, they come to occur at the same time for each of the women.

This could represent one contributing factor in the occurrence of clusters of suicidal behavior in young adolescent and adult women. If the women are close for long enough, menstrual cycles may synchronize, which means that the phases of highest risk, late luteal and follicular phases, will coincide for the women. Menstrual synchronization would have the effect of pre-arranging a potential cluster. The coordination of acute risk factors could cluster suicidal behavior in time. This is only a speculation about one of many factors implicated in clustering; it is tentative even with regard to women, not to mention the clustering of suicidal behavior among men.

Temporal cycles involving reproduction and seasons influence all life, and humans are no exception. Anything of importance to human functioning, then, should be affected to a degree by these cycles, and suicidal behavior is a thing of life-and-death importance; it should be no surprise that it is subject to temporal fluctuations. What may be more surprising is the mechanism behind temporal fluctuations in suicide. Most would assume that it would have something to do with depressed mood, and indeed, depression is a key risk factor for suicidal behavior. But the temporal fluctuations—the genuine ones having to do with season, day of week, and even menstrual phase—probably do not arise because of depressed mood, but rather, because of in a sense its opposite—over-activation, which includes states like agitation, restlessness, insomnia, and what some might refer to as "nervous energy." Suicide requires resolve, fearlessness, and a kind of energy, and, because these things are to a degree cyclical, so is suicide.

Conclusion
Stigma—The Future of a Partial Illusion

am often asked by those who know I have a family history of suicide (or perhaps because I do) why I would study suicidal behavior. Isn't it too morbid?

My ready answer is, "No, there's nothing morbid about working to prevent an agonizing cause of death and a massive public health problem." Put differently, *Hic locus est ubi mors gaudet succurrere vitae,* or, "This is the place where death rejoices in helping the living," which is the inscription above the door of Vienna's Anatomical Institute, where autopsies are performed.

The answer that I am tempted to give is consistent with this one, but longer and somewhat more strident. First, in pondering the nature and causes of suicide, I am hardly alone. Not only have many colleagues I know and admire studied the topic (Roy Baumeister, Aaron Beck, Yeates Conwell,

Madelyn Gould, Marsha Linehan, and David Rudd would represent a partial list), but so have, in one way or another, Plato, Kant, Rousseau, Hume, Pascal, Voltaire, Goethe, and Shakespeare (another partial list). Second, heart disease and cancer claim far more lives than suicide, and so in that sense are more "morbid" than suicide, and yet my strong suspicion is that few ask heart disease or cancer researchers why they have chosen such a "morbid" field.

In compiling his 2001 book *The Art of Suicide*, Ron Brown sent inquiries to galleries and museums in the United Kingdom, asking about art that depicts suicide. He writes, "I have kept their letters of reply, some of which expressed horror or disgust at my topic, some even hinted at a morbid desire on my part" (p. 19). Again, it is hard to imagine similar responses to requests for art depicting other forms of human illness and suffering.

Other reactions I have encountered include this: "You must be depressed or suicidal—or at least your family must be—to want to study suicidal behavior." There may be a grain of truth here—it is a point of honor for me to combat suicide because it runs in my family—but I am not certain how big this grain actually is, for two reasons. First, I started the scientific study of mood disorders and suicidality *before*, not after, my dad's suicide, and I was unaware at the time of his risk as well as of my maternal grandfather's death by suicide approximately twenty years earlier. Second, I know many specialists in suicidal behavior, and it is my impression that less than half have a personal or close family history of suicidal behavior. It is possible that they have not disclosed such a history in part because of the very stigma discussed here, but my intuition, for what it is worth, is that most choose to study suicidal behavior for other reasons.

But for the sake of argument, let's assume that there is a grain of truth in the idea that those who study suicidal behavior mostly do so because they have been personally affected by it. In that case, their career choice is in danger of being overwhelmed by a dismissive public attitude, which might be paraphrased as: "You're just trying to fix your own psychological problems, just like all mental health professionals." It is not insulting to have psychological problems—indeed, a mantra of mine is that mental disorders are common, have tractable causes, are treatable, and are nothing to be ashamed of. But it *is* insulting to have one's life work reduced to an unfounded accusation of various neuroses. Cancer and heart disease researchers, I suspect, rarely experience similar treatment by the public. Both the questions I get and the reactions that Ron Brown got to his inquiries to museums and galleries, to lesser or greater degrees, are related to the deep stigma attached to suicide. It is instructive to parse the concept of stigma into its constituent parts.

First, that which is stigmatized is feared. Fearing something is not bad in and of itself; fear can be quite healthy and adaptive. Infants, for example, instinctively shy away from crawling off a ledge. This fear might also be called "taboo"; things that are taboo are often so for a good reason. The universal taboo on incest, which prevents a number of potential birth defects, is a good example. In the 1950s, economist and Nobel laureate Thomas Schelling understood that the taboo against using nuclear weapons was sensible and should be maintained. As Tim Harford pointed out in his 2008 book *The*

Logic of Life (p. 51), Schelling saw this differently than did President Eisenhower's secretary of state John Foster Dulles, who argued that nuclear options should be "on the table" for strategic reasons. President Eisenhower apparently agreed— he approved the doctrine that nuclear weapons should be "as available for use as other munitions." Schelling argued that there's a good reason to fear nuclear weapons, just as babies fear crawling off a ledge. Fear can prevent catastrophes, large and small.

But fear is not all there is to stigma. Stigma combines fear with disgust, contempt, and lack of compassion, all of which flow from ignorance. It is not the fear of suicide that needs to be overcome; as much of this book has argued, suicide is very fearsome and intimidating, and it is right and natural that it should remain so. Making it less fearsome is dangerous. Current media guidelines on reporting suicides emphasize this point—no glorification, no romanticization, just acknowledgment. But the ignorance and its ugly bedfellows—disgust, contempt, hard hearts—have to go.

We need to get it in our heads that suicide is not easy, painless, cowardly, selfish, vengeful, self-masterful, or rash; that it is not caused by breast augmentation, medicines, "slow" methods like smoking or anorexia, or as some psychoanalysts thought, things like masturbation; that it is partly genetic and influenced by mental disorders, themselves often agonizing; and that it is preventable (e.g., through means restriction like bridge barriers) and treatable (talk about suicide is not cheap and should occasion treatment referral). And once we get all that in our heads at last, we need to let it lead our hearts.

References

Agargun, M. Y., Besiroglu, L., Cilli, A. S., et al. (2007). Nightmares, suicide attempts, and melancholic features in patients with unipolar major depression. *Journal of Affective Disorders, 98,* 267–270.

Agargun, M. Y., & Cartwright, R. (2003). REM sleep, dream variables and suicidality in depressed patients. *Psychiatry Research, 119,* 33–39.

Agargun, M. Y., Cilli, A. S., Kara, H., Tarhan, N., Kincir, F., & Oz, H. (1998). Repetitive and frightening dreams and suicidal behavior in patients with major depression. *Comprehensive Psychiatry, 39,* 198–202.

Alvarez, A. (1971). *The savage god: A study of suicide.* New York: Norton.

Ambrose, S. (1996). *Undaunted courage.* New York: Simon and Schuster.

American Psychiatric Association. (1994). *Diagnostic and statistical manual of mental disorders,* 4th ed. Washington, D.C.: Author.

Barak, Y. (2007). The aging of Holocaust survivors: Myth and reality. *Israeli Medical Association Journal, 9,* 196–198.

Baumeister, R. F. (1990). Suicide as escape from self. *Psychological Review, 97,* 90–113.

Bernert, R., & Joiner, T. (2007). Sleep disturbances and suicide risk: A review of the literature. *Neuropsychiatric Disease and Treatment, 3,* 735–743.

Bernert, R., Joiner, T., Cukrowicz, K., Schmidt, N. B., & Krakow, B. (2005). Suicidality and sleep disturbances. *Sleep, 28,* 1115–1121.

Blaine, B., & McElroy, J. (2002). Selling stereotypes: Weight loss infomercials, sexism, and weightism. *Sex Roles, 49,* 351–357.

Brown, R. (2001). *The art of suicide.* London: Reaktion Books.

Cacioppo, J., & Patrick, W. (2008). *Loneliness.* New York: Harper.

Camus, A. (1955). *The myth of Sisyphus and other essays.* New York: Knopf.

Cartwright, R., Young, M. A., Mercer, P., et al. (1998). Role of REM sleep and dream variables in the prediction of remission from depression. *Psychiatry Research, 80,* 249–255.

Cheney, T. (2008). *Manic.* New York: William Morrow.

Cleckley, H. (1941). *The mask of sanity.* St. Louis, MO: Mosby.

Coleman, L. (2004). *The copycat effect.* New York: Paraview.

Coyle, D. (2005). *Lance Armstrong's war.* New York: Harper Collins.

Dostoevsky, F. (1876/1949). *The diary of a writer.* New York: Charles Scribner's Sons.

——— (1862/2001). *Memoirs from the house of the dead.* Oxford: Oxford University Press.

Farley, T., & Colby, Z. (2008). *The Chris Farley Show.* New York: Viking.

Fawcett, J., Scheftner, W., Fogg, L., Clark, D. C., Young, M. A., Hedeker, D., & Gibbons, R. (1990). Time-related predictors of suicide in major affective disorder. *American Journal of Psychiatry, 147,* 1189–1194.

Fleischmann, A., Bertolote, J., Wasserman, D., De Leo, D., Bolhari, J., Botega, N., De Silva, D., Phillips, M., Vijayakumar, L., Värnik, A., Schlebusch, L., & Thanh, H. (2008). Effectiveness of brief intervention and contact for suicide attempters: A randomized controlled trial in five countries. *Bulletin of the World Health Organization, 86,* 703–709.

Freud, S. (1913). *Totem and taboo.* New York: Norton.

Gilbert, D. (2006). *Stumbling on happiness.* New York: Knopf.

Grossman, D. (1995). *On killing.* New York: Back Bay Books.

Harford, T. (2008). *The logic of life.* New York: Random House.

Hatzfeld, J. (2003). *A time for machetes.* New York: Farrar, Straus, and Giroux.

Hayek, F. A. (1988). *The fatal conceit.* Chicago: University of Chicago Press.

Hoffman, P. (2004). *Wings of madness.* New York: Hyperion.

Hoyer, G., & Lund, E. (1993). Suicide among women related to number of children in marriage. *Archives of General Psychiatry, 50,* 134–137.

Hunt, T. (2006). *Cliffs of despair.* New York: Random House.

Jenkins, C., & Frederick, J. (2008). *The reluctant communist.* Berkeley: University of California Press.

Joiner, T. (1999). The clustering and contagion of suicide. *Current Directions in Psychological Science, 8,* 89–92.

——— (2005). *Why people die by suicide.* Cambridge, MA: Harvard University Press.

Joiner, T., Pettit, J. W., Walker, R. L., Voelz, Z. R., Cruz, J., Rudd, M. D., & Lester, D. (2002). Perceived burdensomeness and suicidality: Two studies on the suicide notes of those attempting and those completing suicide. *Journal of Social and Clinical Psychology, 21,* 531–545.

Joiner, T., Petty, S., Perez, M., Sachs-Ericsson, N., & Rudd, M. D. (2008). Depressive symptoms induce paranoid symptoms in narcissistic personalities (but not narcissistic symptoms in paranoid personalities). *Psychiatry Research, 159,* 237–244.

Kershaw, A. (1997). *Jack London: A life.* New York: Thomas Dunne Books.

Keshavan, M. S., Reynolds, C. F., Montrose, D., Miewald, J., Downs, C., & Sabo, E. M. (1994). Sleep and suicidality in psychotic patients. *Acta Psychiatrica Scandinavica, 89,* 122–125.

Kitayama, S., Markus, H., & Kurokawa, M. (2000). Culture, emotion, and well-being: Good feelings in Japan and the United States. *Cognition and Emotion, 14,* 93–124.

Knyazev, G., Bocharov, A., Slobodskaya, H., & Ryabichenko, T. (2008). Personality-linked biases in perception of emotional facial expressions. *Personality and Individual Differences, 44,* 1093–1104.

Kraepelin, E. (1921). *Manic-depressive insanity and paranoia.* Edinburgh: Livingstone.

Krakauer, J. (1996). *Into the wild.* New York: Anchor Books.

——— (2003). *Under the banner of heaven.* New York: Random House.

Kushner, H. (1989). *American suicide.* New Brunswick, NJ: Rutgers University Press.

Liu, X. (2004). Sleep and adolescent suicidal behavior. *Sleep, 27,* 1351–1358.

Marinus, L. M., Chase, W. K., & Novak, M. A. (2000). Self-biting behavior in rhesus macaques (*Macaca mulatta*) is preferentially directed to body sites associated with acupuncture analgesia. *American Journal of Primatology, 51,* 71–72.

Menninger, K. (1938). *Man against himself.* New York: Harcourt, Brace, Jovanovich.

Minois, G. (1999). *A history of suicide.* Trans. L. Cochrane. Baltimore: Johns Hopkins University Press.

Motto, J. A., & Bostrom, A. (2001). A randomized controlled trial of postcrisis suicide prevention. *Psychiatric Services, 52,* 828–833.

Range, L. M., & Calhoun, L. G. (1990). Responses following suicide and other types of death: The perspective of the bereaved. *Omega, 21,* 311–320.

Ray, I. (1831–1878). *Treatise on the medical jurisprudence of insanity.* Boston: C. Little and J. Brown.

Reuter, C. (2004). *My life is a weapon.* Princeton, NJ: Princeton University Press.

Reynolds, D., & Farberow, N. (1976). *Suicide: Inside and out.* Berkeley: University of California Press.

Rosenhan, D. (1973). On being sane in insane places. *Science, 179,* 250–258.

Rosenthal, P. A., & Rosenthal, S. (1984). Suicidal behavior by preschool children. *American Journal of Psychiatry, 141,* 520–525.

Rudd, M. D., Rajab, M. H., Orman, D. T., Stulman, D. A., Joiner, Jr., T. E., & Dixon, W. (1996). Effectiveness of an outpatient problem-solving intervention targeting suicidal young adults:

Preliminary results. *Journal of Consulting and Clinical Psychology, 64,* 179–190.

Sabo, E., Reynolds, C. F., Kupfer, D. J., & Berman, S. R. (1991). Sleep, depression, and suicide. *Psychiatry Research, 36,* 265–277.

Seiden, R. (1978). Where are they now? A follow-up study of suicide attempters from the Golden Gate Bridge. *Suicide and Life-Threatening Behavior, 8,* 1–13.

Selby, E., Anestis, M., & Joiner, T. (2007). Daydreaming about death: Violent daydreaming as a form of emotion dysregulation in suicidality. *Behavior Modification, 31,* 867–879.

Shneidman, E. S. (2004). *Autopsy of a suicidal mind.* Oxford: Oxford University Press.

——— (1996). *The suicidal mind.* Oxford: Oxford University Press.

Silverman, M., Berman, A., Sandaal, N., O'Carroll, P., & Joiner, T. (2007a). Rebuilding the Tower of Babel: A revised nomenclature for the study of suicide and suicidal behaviors. Part I: Background, rationale, and methodology. *Suicide and Life-Threatening Behavior, 37,* 248–263.

——— (2007b). Rebuilding the Tower of Babel: A revised nomenclature for the study of suicide and suicidal behaviors. Part II: Suicide-related ideations, communications, and behaviors. *Suicide and Life-Threatening Behavior, 37,* 264–277.

Stevenson, R. L. (1878/2000). *The suicide club.* Mineola, NY: Dover.

Sullivan, H. S. (1953). *Conceptions of modern psychiatry: Collected works of Harry Stack Sullivan,* Vol. I. New York: Norton.

Tanskanen, A., Tuomilehto, J., Viinamaki, H., Vartiainen, E., Lehtonen, J., & Puska, P. (2001). Nightmares as predictors of suicide. *Sleep, 24,* 844–847.

Tautz, J. (2008). *The buzz about bees: Biology of a superorganism.* Berlin: Springer.

Timmermans, S. (2006). *Postmortem.* Chicago: University of Chicago Press.

Toolan, J. (1962). Suicide and suicidal attempts in children and adolescents. *American Journal of Psychiatry, 118,* 719–724.

Tschinkel, W. (2007). *The fire ants.* Cambridge, MA: Harvard University Press.

Turvey, C. L., Conwell, Y., Jones, M. P., Phillips, C., Simonsick, E.,

Pearson, J. L., & Wallace, R. (2002). Risk factors for late-life suicide. *American Journal of Geriatric Psychiatry, 10,* 398–406.

Van Orden, K., Witte, T., Gordon, K., Bender, T., & Joiner, T. (2008). Suicidal desire and the capability for suicide: Tests of the interpersonal-psychological theory of suicidal behavior in adults. *Journal of Consulting and Clinical Psychology, 76,* 72–83.

Verona, E., Patrick, C., & Joiner, T. (2001). Psychopathy, antisocial personality, and suicide risk. *Journal of Abnormal Psychology, 110,* 462–470.

Whittlesey, L. (1995). *Death in Yellowstone.* Lanham, MD: Roberts Rinehart.

Witte, T., Merrill, K., Stellrecht, N., Bernert, R., Hollar, D., Schatschneider, C., & Joiner, T. (2008). "Impulsive" youth suicide attempters are not necessarily all that impulsive. *Journal of Affective Disorders, 107,* 107–116.

Zahn, T. (2006). *Why I jumped.* Grand Rapids, MI: Revell.

Acknowledgments

I conceived of this book in Italy, at the Rockefeller Foundation's beautiful Bellagio facility (too few Americans understand that Bellagio is in Italy, not in Las Vegas; I had been one of those Americans). I owe the foundation my gratitude, and especially want to express my fondness for the "Bellagio Secret Society," which is not really secret, and is made up of the cohort of Bellagio fellows who happened to be placed there at the same time. We bonded like children at summer camp and I at least am the better for it.

I wrote this mostly at home, with Graciela, Malachi, Zekey, a dog, and a cat streaming in and out of the office. It is traditional to thank those at home for "patience and support," and I see why and don't want to buck tradition, but one thing that is uncontroversial is that the dog and cat were not very patient or supportive.

I wrote this at work too. Work is, fortunately for me, at the Department of Psychology at Florida State University, where it is notable that the department ranked fourth in the country (and thus I guess in the world) in research grants obtained by departments of psychology, whereas FSU's football team was not ranked in the top twenty-five following the 2007 season. I am not glad about the latter fact—I'm a season ticket holder—but the former fact, in the spirit of this book, might dispel a myth or two. Our department thrives for many reasons, but I'd highlight two: excellent graduate students (as of this writing, mine are Nadia Teale, Rebecca Bernert, Daniel Hollar, Kim Van Orden, Katie Timmons, Tracy Witte, Mike Anestis, Ted Bender, Scott Braithwaite, Eddie Selby, Erin Fink, April Smith, Jess Ribeiro, Lindsay Bodell, and Jen Hames, and this is to leave out the many alumni of my group who have completed their doctorates). Our department thrives also because of excellent leadership, both within the department (our chair is Janet Kistner) and outside it. FSU central administration is as capable as any I know of, and I'm not just saying that because of our new, spacious building or because we were awarded a coveted "cluster," several new faculty lines built around an intellectual theme, in our case the psychology and neurobiology of dysregulated behavior.

I wrote this on the road, too, and I am very grateful to be invited out on the road for consulting and speaking engagements. I thank David Covington, formerly of Behavioral Health Link in Atlanta, everyone associated with the National Suicide Prevention Lifeline (1-800-273-TALK), especially John Draper, Heather Stokes, and Richard McKeon, and the many people who asked me to speak at their meetings and conferences. I learned many new things because of this travel, and wound up writing parts of this book in places like the Old Faithful Inn in Yellowstone National Park in Wyoming, my mother's mountain house in North Carolina, NIH review meetings in San Francisco, the AAS meetings in New Orleans and Boston, a prevention meeting in Bar Harbor, Maine, and in Hollywood, where I appeared on the Dr. Phil show, just to name a few.

Thanks go to Harvard University Press, who I think handled my previous book *Why People Die by Suicide* adroitly, and especially to Elizabeth Knoll, who has the good editor's uncanny way of letting authors be until just the right moment.

I mean what I say in this book, that it's time to put a stop to the demeaning misunderstanding of those who die by suicide and who suffer from the mental disorders that underlie it. Suicide runs in my family and it is a point of honor for me to combat the thing that killed my relatives. Those who demean suicide decedents demean my dad, and in so doing, demean humanity and themselves.

Index

Learned fearlessness, 6, 22, 33, 62, 100, 101, 143, 179, 188, 193, 217
Lewis, Meriwether, 14, 28
Linehan, M., 138
London, Jack, 5

Major depressive disorder. *See* Depression
Manson, Marilyn, 14
Mass suicides, 146–147
McVeigh, Timothy, 132–133, 135, 139, 147
Media. *See* Publicizing suicide
Medications, 242–250
Meehl, P., 7, 208, 263
Menninger, K., 45, 61, 116, 202, 229–230, 231, 232
Mental disorders, 9, 89, 138, 187–190, 193, 236, 251; antisocial personality disorders, 48, 52; psychotic disorders, 87–90, 98, 99; substance use disorders, 90, 194, 197, 198, 201; borderline personality disorder, 177–178; partial syndrome mental disorders, 192, 193; schizophrenia, 206; bipolar disorder, 244, 251. *See also* Anorexia nervosa; Depression
Minois, G., 2, 204, 225, 257
Murder-suicide, 49, 65, 166, 180
Murray, H., 9

Nightmares. *See* Sleep disorders
Nonsuicidal self-injury, 6, 177–179, 206–207, 213–214

"Passive suicide," 200–201
Perceived burdensomeness, 6–7, 8, 9, 12, 33, 40–41, 44, 61, 100, 101, 188, 193, 213, 216, 217

Physician-assisted suicide, 191–193
Planning for suicidal behavior, 39
Plath, Sylvia, 115–116, 123
Psychoanalysis, 44–45, 220
Psychotic disorders. *See* Mental disorders, psychotic disorders
Publicizing suicide, 37, 71–72, 139

Race and ethnicity, 57, 238
Religious martyrdom, 7
Revenge, misunderstood role of in suicidal behavior, 31–38, 42, 54, 109
Rosellini, G., 20
Rosenhan, D., 30

Schizophrenia. *See* Mental disorders, schizophrenia
Seiden, R., Golden Gate Bridge study. *See* Golden Gate Bridge
Self-injury. *See* Nonsuicidal self-injury
Selfishness, misunderstood role of in suicidal behavior, 43–45, 46–50, 52–53, 54
Self-mastery, 58; suicide as a misunderstood form of, 53–62
Self-preservation instinct, 5, 6, 13, 22–23
Self-sacrifice: in insects/animals, 7, 204–214; in plants, 215–216
Serotonin system, 32, 214
Shakespeare, William, 3, 71, 83
Shneidman, E., 67, 204
Sleep disorders, 55, 250–256
"Slow" suicide, misunderstandings regarding, 196, 200
Stevenson, Robert Louis, 15
Substance use. *See* Mental disorders, substance use disorders